DISCOVERING GURDJIEFF

DOROTHY PHILLPOTTS

authorHOUSE®

AuthorHouse™ UK Ltd.
500 Avebury Boulevard
Central Milton Keynes, MK9 2BE
www.authorhouse.co.uk
Phone: 08001974150

First published by AuthorHouse 7/15/2008

ISBN: 978-1-4343-8871-1 (sc)
ISBN: 978-1-4343-8872-8 (hc)

Printed in the United States of America
Bloomington, Indiana

This book is printed on acid-free paper.

For George

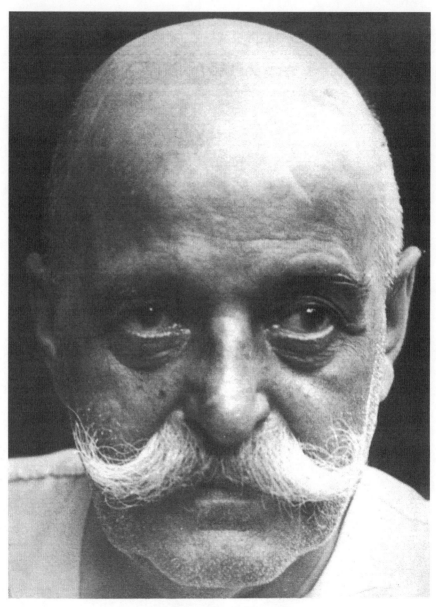

George Ivanovich Gurdjieff

ACKNOWLEDGEMENTS

Without the constant support and devotion of my late husband, George, this book would never have been written.

Much is owed, also, to past and present members of the Bristol and Cardiff Group that my husband and I started up so many years ago. In particular, I would like to thank Dolly Schwenk, whose patience and meticulous help ensured the present manuscript survived its many editions over the eighteen years it took to write.

And finally, I should thank my daughter-in-law, Judith, for her persistence in the last stages of getting 'Discovering Gurdjieff' published.

LIST OF PHOTOGRAPHS

CONTENTS

FOREWORD

A Pilgrim's Progress
by
Peter Brook

A way.

A vast word but one about which no two people can disagree. For there is always a 'here' and a 'there', and to pass from one to the other, a way is needed. But what way?

This book is the intimate chronicle of a specific traveller, a young woman in whom throbs a wish for understanding, a need to find her way. Dorothy Phillpotts' adventure starts through her lively enquiring mind: she is wide open to ideas and we can follow her excitement and fascination when she first hears a charismatic speaker unfolding a detailed analysis of the human condition in new and striking terms. In the first part of this book, she modestly keeps her own story in the background and reports verbatim what she heard. Then life begins to show her that the way of the thinking mind is an incomplete way, it can go just so far, before it turns back on itself. Gradually, she discovers that each way leads to its own impasse. She finds that unless mind, body and feeling are all mobilised together, a way is an illusion.

Now her story necessarily becomes more intimate. The ideas she hears, the teaching she enters need the soil of personal experience to become real. We follow the author into the thick of life where her most valued guides have to be questioned and her own convictions challenged. Gradually, this leads her to the source of her teaching, to her meetings with Gurdjieff. She is one of the few remaining pupils to speak of him from direct experience.

Today, Gurdjieff's teaching has become current currency. More and more books appear across the world which are mere explanations, rehashings of ideas that have already been fully presented by Gurdjieff himself, or by those who have lived beside him. Or else, the core of the author's narrative is talking about nothing but 'What happened to me'.

Dorothy Phillpotts' book brings the objective and the subjective together, showing that a way is not what we believe it to be. It is in fact neither 'here' nor 'there'. Through experience that evolves and changes, like life itself, through being at times guided by others and sometimes left on one's own, one's idea of what constitutes a way gradually vanishes. At that moment, a real way appears.

Peter Brook

PREFACE

Who was Gurdjieff?

The first time I saw him he was coming slowly into the room, an old man of 76, not tall, and of ponderous stature. He smiled in greeting to a friend and an extraordinary warmth radiated from him. One could see that although physical energy might be low, there was at the same time a tremendous inner strength and control over the bodily mechanism. His head, on which he usually wore a fez, attracted and held one's attention, as it was very finely proportioned, with a high domed forehead, and was clean-shaven. His dark eyes probed accurately, and at once, to the depth of any matter, while his long white moustache, worn Turkish fashion, adorned a face unusual in a man of his age, with its honey-coloured complexion surprisingly free of wrinkles.

It is only fair to say that it was often difficult to understand what Gurdjieff said. And this was not only because his mode of address was original - there was also the purely physical obstacle of language. Although he had a great feeling for words, and would converse, not grammatically, in many tongues, he nevertheless preferred to speak Russian, and unless one understood this language it was not always possible to grasp his meanings.

For a long time Gurdjieff's nationality was only known to his nearest friends; he was thought to be Russian, Armenian, Tartar, and even Indian. Actually his family came from the Ionian Greeks of Caesarea, whose history stretches back long before the Christian era, and he was born in Alexanderopol, a town of the Russian Caucasus, in 1872. Like true exiles these Greeks of Transcaucasia had preserved their culture throughout centuries of foreign domination. Certainly Gurdjieff himself typified a fair combination of the characteristics of Ancient Greece. Bertrand Russell in his 'History of Western Philosophy' talks of the two tendencies of Greece : one passionate, religious, mystical, other worldly; the other cheerful, empirical, rationalistic and interested in acquiring knowledge of a diversity of facts. In Gurdjieff's nature these two tendencies were welded together and conditioned by the rich environment of the Caucasus, with its legacy of many races, cultures and religions, while his home life made a very substantial contribution to his subsequent development, his father being one of the last of the Asiatic Bards, famed for his knowledge of the legends of Assyrian and Sumerian civilizations.

It was owing to the family misfortune of losing large herds of cattle from epidemics, that his father established himself as a carpenter at Kars, in the year 1877, a move which proved significant for Gurdjieff, as the subsequent friendship of both father and son with Father Borsch, Dean of the Military Cathedral in that town, resulted in the Dean's making himself responsible for Gurdjieff s education, his tutors being priests and doctors, in order to develop the boy's strongly marked religious interests and his scientific ability, and to fulfill his father's wish that he should undertake the dual profession of 'physician for the body and confessor for the soul'.

But his father could not have guessed in what unexpected ways his dreams would be fulfilled, and how Gurdjieff was to become a great religious teacher and healer - not in his own country, but in the countries of the West.

Chapter 1

EARLY LIFE

From the very beginning, Gurdjieff's ideas had been momentous. But I and the many others who had been invited to study 'The System as taught by P. D. Ouspensky', had never even heard his name. I was not at all sure that a 'system' was what I needed and, had I not been newly married to someone who was already a student, would probably not have seen it as the overwhelming answer to my perennial daily necessity of coming to terms with the life that was presented to me by my rational mind.

For me, the recognition that I was the plaything of quite random events and random thoughts was absolutely genuine, for I quite plainly needed to know how to think, and up to now had not discovered any way at all that this could be brought about. This need had been with me a long time, for it had gripped me in late adolescence, descending like a pall, on the day when I started to look for honest answers to practical questions which seemed inextricably mixed with religion.

During those years of approaching adulthood, when I suddenly found myself completely unable to think comfortably about life, to enjoy the present moment, or to picture any future that looked at all rewarding, I had felt that there must be something incomplete in me and that some other way of living must lie outside my experience. In a limited kind of way, appropriate to my age, I had tried to read about the Christian way in one or two evangelical books and had concluded that that kind of life which might exist somewhere, I had certainly never met. But how was one to live without some kind of religion?

With a newly awakened interest in what went on around me, it had seemed that the average life of most adults was unbelievable - an extraordinary farce - but that one could perhaps avoid being sucked in and swept along (particularly where sex and money were concerned) if, by appropriate mental effort, one could acquire a positive kind of judgment. By this, I simply meant a simple and reliable touchstone for recognising truth or falsehood and sensitive shades of meaning. Something that would, in fact, be a resting place which could be an appropriate echo of my childhood certainties. Naturally I hadn't realized then that this would involve not only considerable ability, but bravery far beyond anything I possessed.

I had enjoyed rather a happy childhood, always busy and interested and consoled in any difficulties I might meet by a natural kind of religion practised more or less in secret - though I attended church openly and regularly with one of my younger brothers.

As the middle of five children, very widely spaced, when I left childhood behind I would find myself rather too frequently caught between the passionate outbursts of a sister older and a brother younger than myself, and I sat in on the sidelines of many a heated discussion quite unconvinced by arguments and unattracted by solutions, always appearing unsatisfactorily as a lone contender for the 'don't knows'.

But I was sensitive about my repeated failure to take sides, and the taunts which this produced strengthened my powerful conviction that the things I felt most sincerely could never be honestly expressed. Yet as well as frequently experiencing this uncomfortable reaction, from time to time I would feel my awkward role completely reversed, having a sudden strong impulse to welcome new and strange areas of thought, and to say 'yes, yes, yes' as if I had temporarily slotted into a completely alien part of my brain.

These discussions were very rarely personal, but they almost always got quickly out of hand, starting with a kind of desperate sincerity to put the world to rights and ending with altercations so violent that often I would break off in the middle of a sentence to rush away by myself, retreating to a garden shed which I used as a darkroom where, among the cobwebs and developing trays, alone and forgotten, I could gradually calm myself by repeating old prayers which I had learned as a child in the parish church. This rarely failed, and was almost always enough to prepare me for the next onslaught for, even though part of me dreaded disagreements and had become physically jittery over the extraordinary violence of mere words, I nevertheless enjoyed belonging to our disputatious family. And although my mother complained of us, she was secretly proud that we had inherited the verve of my father's spirited family, this being the better side of a nature that on one hand could be apparently impartial, or brilliantly argumentative and witty, and on the other, withdrawn, remote and almost violently disdainful.

In fact, the five of us were the fruit of a rather successful marriage of opposites, and it was the somewhat rare harmony between our parents that encouraged us to be bold, both in our aims and in our actions. In families like ours at the time there was still a kind of consistent discipline, often rather unreasonable, and though the twenties were making their mark, expectations of a certain level of behaviour, though mild enough, were quite definitely there, with more than a reflection of the Victorian era in which both our parents had grown up. The welcome differences in our house almost certainly stemmed from the fact that my mother was one quarter French and her artistic Gallic temperament was of considerable use to us so that, whereas certain hard and fast mundane rules really had to be kept, and certain others acquired as we grew older, there was also a wide and distinctly un-English acceptance of foibles where human relations were concerned, and a quick readiness to forgive the kind of stupidities which in some environments would have been perpetually remembered. That this was often inconsistent had to be faced, but on the whole there was a very generous amount of amity and honesty, between both children and parents, that was by no means always observable in the homes of our friends.

It was not until I actually saw more of the world outside that I began to guess at the advantages of having a mother who, through thick and thin, so deeply admired her husband. For a long time before I reached adolescence, this generosity of spirit produced in me a great admiration and even adoration, and in my earliest years I learned to consult her and rely on her judgment; though it was clear, too, that as I grew older I was beginning to demonstrate that I had indeed inherited that sad streak of disdain which, being linked with an odd need for truth, was not always easy to handle, and from time to time would bring forth the well-earned rebuke that I was beginning to resemble just a little too closely my 'intellectual' aunt and my father's apparently eccentric family.

It was, of course, hard on my mother that at almost the age of fifteen, after a long spell of being an easily managed and contented child, I should suddenly sprout abstruse philosophical leanings (my father had been dead for five years). For her, there was always an inevitability about the thinking process and it was therefore quite useless to question or fight the thoughts that presented themselves unbidden, or to try and open one's mind to consider things from more sides than a mere 'yes' or 'no'.

'But how can you learn to think?' she would say, emphasizing her words with a toss of the head, 'Why upset yourself? Thoughts are there, this thought or that thought, as you need. Why must you be different from other people? Be content with yourself as you are. You would like to be sincere? But you are sincere, a good girl. What nonsense.' To me, of course, it wasn't nonsense. But I knew that most of all she did not like my growing distrust of popular ideas and accepted notions of the day. In fact I was actually beginning to be rather alarmed just then about the unpleasing world of adult double standards which now threatened to surround me. And at the opposite end of the spectrum, at school I had accidentally become connected with an evangelical religious circle of such excessive outward piety that my natural and relaxed religious beliefs were in danger of becoming severely strained.

The loneliness of this situation was of course intensified by what seemed to be the impossibility of talking about it to anyone else, for not one 'properly grown-up person' in our wide family circle seemed qualified in any real way to help me. They had somehow adjusted long ago to minds just as limited as mine and were clearly happy to have done so. Nor was this happiness entirely accidental. Their original dissatisfaction with life had simply been inverted and attached to some handy, unusual, and preferably dramatic enthusiasm. Here, firmly fixed, it could be safely transformed into an ornamental banner under which they could safely march to greater and greater heights.

In keeping with this way of solving the problem, although to myself I already seemed to be stretched to the absolute limit with school work and piano practice, as well as various artistic pursuits, I was generally recommended to find a new interest. Declining the more exotic and time-wasting suggestions was not too difficult, but the rest only intensified my confusion.

One thing which now struck me was that the professional helpers, doctors, lecturers, or schoolmistresses, actually seemed more helpless in their inability to proffer genuine practical advice based on sound judgment than their untrained down-to-earth competitors, the longstanding near relatives and friends, who if appealed to openly could only urge a policy of escapism. Quite the worst advice came from high intellectuals, friends of friends, well known for this or successful at that, who, smugly assuming that I was in need of Freudian tales from their early lives, regaled me with unsuitable stories designed to bring me down to earth.

Was it remarkable, I wonder, that the people who stood out from this varied hotchpotch of reasonably mature grown-ups consistently endeavoured to soothe me by pointing out that I was too intent on finding answers to questions which had actually baffled mankind for more than two thousand years? 'And shouldn't you spend more time away from books?'

Thrown back upon myself, temporarily, I now tried to re-examine some of my mother's favourite maxims. So far I had not been very successful in finding even partial answers to any of what seemed to be my real questions. Though I appeared to meet everyday life with normal intelligence, when put to an acid test my mind was strangely recalcitrant. To think 'positively', or what I had thought might be 'creatively' about any complex subject which closely concerned me was obviously impossible, and many new kinds of fear complicated my state.

For what, if it existed at all, was sincerity? And could there be a way to it?

Up until quite recently, I had supposed myself sincere about what I privately called 'my religion', and this had always been a source of dependable feeling (I found that I did not like the word 'comfort'). But had I been older just then, and maybe receiving a widely-based classical education (which would certainly have been rather unusual for any ordinary girl at the end of the nineteen twenties), by the time I began to have serious conversations with my mother I might perhaps have realised that she was a Sceptic, and that she had inherited this from the French part of her background and that however much we were bound by a truly deep affection, ultimately we were unlikely to agree.

As it was, at least externally, I endeavoured to fall in with her diagnoses, for I saw that I worried her dreadfully. In maintaining that my predilections depressed me, she was of course right, but had she for her part been only a trifle more perceptive, instead of trying to cheer me up by tuning the wireless to dance music and sending me off to the cinema or the theatre with my dependable elder brother, she would have given me the run of my father's widely ranging books. These volumes of philosophy, poetry, ancient history, religious commentary and drama had been a bone of contention for many years and were still rather a divisive factor, principally because they were exceptionally well bound and not one of us was to be allowed unlimited access to them until we were grown up. She also might have remembered that, as I had been an extremely early reader - something for which she herself was almost entirely responsible - from the point of view of valuing the written word and never leaving books of any kind on the floor, I must have been growing up an exceptionally long time.

* * *

6

Walking home with my brother one cold winter evening, however, I suddenly discovered a new kind of listener right under my nose. Latterly, we had not seen much of each other, and the heated discussions we had actually once enjoyed were now a thing of the past. Since he was some eight years older than me, he now inhabited another world.

'You know' he said, jumping right in 'you want things to be too black and white.' We were discussing our violent reactions to the handling of the film 'Man of Arran' - which we had just seen, 'It isn't really like that; you felt those people in the film were getting somewhere despite hardships and the bleak landscape and so on, but one needs to put more 'perhaps' into it. Assessing truth takes longer and there's no solution in premature conclusions; 'yes' and 'no' is always so tempting.'

At this point we agreed to disagree, but I arrived home distinctly comforted. The questions my mother brushed aside could now get a second airing where they would be turned this way and that before being put aside for a thorough questioning later.

Why was I comforted? I didn't know, but something had been right about the conversation; the subject was left open without being abandoned. But I surprised myself very much by still wishing to have discussions with my mother. This was partly because I did not enjoy arguing with her, but also because she was beginning to see that I was not in any danger of acquiring the kind of open mind of which she was so afraid. My position stemmed mainly from the oft repeated realisation that if in my silent inner debates I was obliged consistently to accept two equally inadmissible fixed positions, this always resulted in considerable unhappiness. Silent and perplexed, I could in fact be achingly unhappy, and my sense of being in a maze from which I should never be able to escape naturally increased.

It was a shock to me, years afterwards, when I too became a parent and all this had passed very far into the past, to remember that even as a very young child I had been in positive need of both sympathetic direction and dialogue, and as a basis for my simple, happy life I had received plenty of the first on a practical, mundane and very useful level. But dialogue, once initiated by my father, so satisfactory in my early years, and so much missed later, could never in any case have achieved more than to bring me to the precise cutting edge of real philosophical enquiry, and such an edge was much too sharp for a fifteen year old. Perhaps in a year or two I would have been able to reinterpret my warring limitations as the legitimate fruit of a paradoxical mischance originally designed for a happier outcome, but at the time I was faced with the need for repeated reassessments rather unsuitable for my circumstances.

*   *   *

My brother (who had remained remarkably unaffected by the lively controversial debates and furious arguments of our earliest years) was now becoming more and more interested in the youth work centred round a large and popular Nonconformist church not far from where we lived and, accepting a demanding position as Group Scoutmaster responsible for three distinct age groups, drew both my sister and myself into the brilliant comet's tail which at that time still fanned out in the wake of Lord Baden Powell.

Whatever one really felt about that (since as a family we had never before had any connection with Nonconformity), just at that precise juncture I was positively diverted by a delightful sense of newness, and even charmed with the haunting repetitive songs round campfires in the twilight as a kind of coda to the simplified but widely based, if rather shallow, nature study which suddenly became available, allied to a sharpening of all sorts of genuinely interesting rural skills which had not yet begun to die out from everyday country life.

All this, drawn together once a month in ornamental church parades, began quite naturally to take me into the chapel itself, a church full to the brim with a lively if rather informal congregation practising hearty extrovert religion.

Where this would eventually have led me was not yet questioned. For the moment I certainly needed people and occupation, apart from my school and my family, and by accidentally landing in this remarkably unsophisticated environment, where my preoccupation with still unanswered questions about sincere and honest thinking did not come anywhere near the surface, a kind of beneficial relaxation began to take root side by side with my unpredictable mental powers.

Would the boundary wall of a passive Wesleyanism eventually have enclosed me more or less completely, if one day an old friend had not taunted me with being well on the way to a very comfortable bigotry?

'You will become a teetotaller like your brother - that, of course is only a small thing, just a beginning, but there are other things... '. Here I expostulated. I was not at all prepared to criticize my brother, and drew away from the whole conversation rapidly just as my mind, hydra-like, began to creak into action with its diminishing, though still favourite, role.

While my difficult head, for the first time in years, had been more or less resting - almost completely fobbed off with the inescapable actualities of forthcoming examinations, and a real need in the uncomfortable world of the slump to begin to plan some kind of future career - it had somehow overlooked the new connection between ethics and over-simple theology which appeared to have taken me over, and I had not even begun to think about it.

Nor was it perturbed now. But it was definitely re-aroused and, after this long holiday, could call deliberately on a rather different quality. So far, I had only been absorbed by the externals of Wesleyanism. Quite clearly, I had not wanted and never would want to be a Nonconformist. I was definitely not in the mould. However, I would think about it later, not now. It was my sister, astonishingly, who finally tidied up this situation by announcing the compelling necessity of an early return to the parish church. We were becoming Wesleyans by accident, and it was really not for us.

'We are obviously not suited to Methodism. Can you honestly say you are a Methodist? I cannot. Is there anything in us that is even faintly Methodist . . . . . ?'

A little surprised at my sister's vehemence, I was in fact extremely happy to accompany her to Evensong on the coming Sunday, and the result of this rather sudden decision produced a most satisfactory outcome.

Arriving in the dusk of a golden autumn evening, we were greeted by a gentle organ voluntary, some good choral singing and a service that had not been tampered with. It was not an historic or beautiful church - there were neither stained glass windows, nor any kind of sculpture - but it actually had the special kind of dignity which had been bestowed on some of the best local houses at the turn of the century by the architect Norman Shaw. And one could go further that that, for whoever had completed the embellishment had thoroughly understood how to make the best use of shape and colour.

It was not surprising that we took to Evensong. It relaxed us very pleasantly and opened our eyes to a new kind of beauty, and when we were invited to join a confirmation class my sister didn't hesitate. But, wanting to find out exactly what this involved, I read and re-read my prayer book, telling myself that the Confirmation Service was only a formality and, in searching for something I didn't find, I gave in to my sister and decided to accompany her.

However, what was the deeply startling state which I experienced when waiting, with several girls of about my own age, to be received into the Church of England? Thankful for the ambience and aware that the formality was somehow beneficial, I eventually knelt to receive the blessing. But what I received was not formal - it was 'fire from heaven'. Had I been taught better or even a little more appropriately, perhaps I might have had some kind of understanding of the new and vibrant feeling which now inhabited me. As it was, in the years that followed, when the state ebbed and flowed and little by little dwindled into a mere echo of itself, I couldn't make the connection I hungered for.

And yet, when I was kneeling before the Bishop at the laying on of hands, and he prayed the ancient prayer:

'Defend, O Lord, this Thy child with Thy heavenly grace,
That she may continue there for ever;
And daily increase in Thy Holy Spirit, more and more,
Until she may come into Thy everlasting kingdom.'

I was suddenly conscious, as the Bishop's hands were placed upon my head, that the life I had lived so far was fundamentally different from what I was now experiencing. It was as if a light surrounded me: the thoughts which inhabited me had disappeared and a deep feeling was dwelling in me which gave me the very reason for existence.

*　*　*

During the more relaxed time when my brother was fitting me out according to his easy notions of a more or less desirable feminine role, much of the insecurity of adolescence had evaporated, and I was entertaining a new wish about my approaching adulthood, and a new approach to it.

Although for the moment I had no freedom at all in the world of ideas, I could now secretly assert that somehow or other this had to become a possibility and, in declining to align myself with automatic pessimism, I was almost indifferent to the blandishments of the modern world. There was no doctrine to help me with this, but it was as if my deepest religious feelings, long since dead, were now able to join with a steady desire for some kind of intellectual role which was apparently extraordinarily difficult to acquire.

I don't think that at the time I used the word integrity, although I was tremulously discovering the feeling. There was no question there for me. This was what I lacked most. And it was this lack that my persistent thoughts constantly displayed and even demanded, by demonstrating that a genuine adult should at least be capable of some kind of mental independence, however limited, and however inadequately this might be connected with the necessary actions and reactions of daily life. But how could I, just as I was, a completely inexperienced person, apparently locked up with paralysing opposing impulses and verbal conclusions, impinge even slightly differently on my own environment? And here again, something recognisable as a strong feeling swam deliberately into view. There was no desire to expand this in the direction of words, neither acceptance nor rejection were in question. It was as if a kind of invisible responsibility was very temporarily present which, while seeming to change constantly, also demanded a point of view that was more and more impossible to put into words at all, even to myself.

Inner responsibility. What could it be? Sometimes, in answer to a question, I would say I wanted to help people. But did I want to help people? What did it mean? What could I possibly do for anyone?

I could recall the first time I gave this answer to a slightly senior friend - the head girl of my school, no less, an apparently full fledged and very capable person, just about to disappear to a university. The words hung in the air and from some part of myself, very deeply hidden, I saw them as only partly true, mere usurpers trying to fabricate a public role for parts of myself that were deeply unsure of everything. But for all that, very strangely, these words were not to be rescinded; somewhere, in me, their truth rested.

* * *

When I finally had access to my father's books, it was a sudden source of wonder that so few of them were readily understandable; but, after the first surprise and something very like consternation, I saw them as a new and precise challenge. Up to now I had been too young to realise that I constantly used reading as an escape route. These books, so long idealised and so long desired could not in any case provide an ordinary sort of relaxation or ephemeral happiness; they were like a fuse laid by a beneficent, unknown hand. Newly careless of hopes or insufficiencies, I plunged in.

Philosophical books written long ago were even more difficult than I feared, but here and there a glimmer of light reached me - indirectly - like a reflection in a mirror. Philosophers of the seventeenth and eighteenth centuries, the rationalists and empiricists, I soon set aside for later study, their grinding style of reasoning seeming too like my own. I then settled down with the religious classics I had waited for.

Here I met a kind of confusion that troubled me and it was a very long time before I began to get a glimmer of the real situation. Again and again I would wrestle with 'Religio Medici', chosen at random because of the title, and then caught by one strong but fleeting idea in the opening paragraph. Here was an unreadable book if ever there was one (and I must say that subsequent editions openly deplored the very bad translation). My early edition presented archaic words, quite unacceptable grammar and capital letters completely out of place, which had all striven valiantly to capture the attention of readers born some three hundred years before my time.

This book, clearly intent on something I could not even begin to fathom, was like a thorn which helped to tear out some very comfortable illusions. Despising myself, but eventually unable to persevere, I would put it back on its shelf, planning a second attempt later, but it was not for a very long time that I was grateful for the unpalatable truths aroused by this special struggle with myself.

The Confessions of St Augustine was another work which fell more or less obviously into the same class for, despite its favourite passages, it had a very definite sting in its tail. How could I both approve and disapprove so strongly of a man like Augustine? Although I did not always understand the drift, I had thought that his poesy was something I could easily assent to, but here again some vital connection was missing. Some touchstone that Augustine had truly known about was entirely hidden from me. Finding a word for it didn't help. And without questioning in the same genuine, if baffled way, I certainly missed his real challenge.

Spurred on by all this reading and now rather ill at ease with the melange of ignorance and incapacity which seemed to typify the workings of my so-called independent mind, for more than a year I carried home large armfuls of books from the public library, utilizing all my family's non-fiction tickets and running up spectacular fines in a somewhat vain, if genuine, attempt to endow myself with a slightly deeper understanding of the human situation as a whole.

To begin with, like everyone else, I was disturbed by the increasingly noisy debate about the future of the League of Nations, as it was now becoming more and more difficult to find any objective commentaries on current European affairs.

My friends read Hansard and the weekly literary journals, seeking some kind of reasonable, intelligent comment which would somehow hold together, as everything that was uttered more or less publicly was always modified afterwards . . . . . . 'in an effort to be fair', or 'just a point of view' or - long suffering, over the so-called failings of the League of Nations - 'after all, there is a necessity for us to put things right'. These perpetual modifications, which never led anywhere, were at first more or less understandable, but quickly became baffling, and finally insupportable.

What was actually happening in Germany was still well out of sight, but in Italy Mussolini's *Blackshirts* had already aroused uncomfortable speculations. What exactly was Fascism and where was it leading? The claim that 'it was only intended as a cure for Bolshevism' seemed reasonable, but not entirely satisfactory for the onlooker. And although apparent indifference had long been one of England's strengths in international diplomacy, our current indifference had actually ceased overnight, when in 1934 the Austrian National Socialists had murdered Chancellor Dolfuss. In fact Hitler had already come halfway into the open before that in 1932 by beginning Germany's *Befreiungskampf* - 'the struggle for liberation' - by which he meant to set aside the Treaty of Versailles; although, despite this, he quite plainly continued his policy of throwing dust in his neighbour's eyes, declaring in 1933 after he had become Chancellor, that 'The German people had no thought of invading any country.'.

And his clever label of National Socialism still deceived us. Something called 'National Socialism' surely couldn't be bad? But once again we were blinded by recurring indifference. And it was astonishing that somehow or other Hitler had succeeded in masking the perfectly clear intentions published in '*Mein Kampf*'. After that, changes came thick and fast. A declaration that the German government had never questioned the Treaty of Locarne was actually followed by conscription, and the Locarne Pact being broken when troops were moved into the demilitarised zone of the Rhineland. The sequel to that was withdrawal from the Disarmament Conference and serving notice to quit the League of Nations.

*   *   *

Luckily throughout this time I still retained my early attachment to poetry and was just beginning to discover modern poets, who seemed to have something to say that was both objective and optimistic. But as the tensions mounted, poetry, however true, could not still the commentaries arriving from Europe, where Hitler's racial creed had now become a dire accompaniment to marching feet. Here was a religion that could have been countered earlier and would now give very much trouble in the near future, with its openly insane call for a belief embodied in 'the sublime knowledge that Nordic blood represents that mystery which has replaced and vanquished the ancient sacraments'. And this call was only a beginning. Soon it was possible to hear soldiers on the German radio openly singing 'National Socialism will break open the gates of eternity. You, our Fuehrer, will come among your people as a redeemer.'

It was not surprising that as long ago as 1930, the German bishops had condemned National Socialism, but somehow we had missed it.

If one follows more or less conscientiously the indistinct historical tracks of that time, the nervous political atmosphere begins to explain itself. Persistent popular enquiries into truth were non-existent; sophisticated non-party, internationally-minded literary magazines and newspapers, with large black and white supplements, had not yet been invented and independent news magazines without a party political bias were a thing of the future.

Then, towards the end of the nineteen thirties, the new Penguin and Pelican paperbacks began to throw some kind of light on current civilisation, but books like Edgar Mowrer's 'Germany Puts The Clock Back', or 'Mussolini's Roman Empire' by G.T.Garratt were few and far between.

Turning eagerly to the Penguin Specials, now arriving in ever increasing numbers, I discovered promising titles like 'The Mysterious Universe' by Sir James Jeans, offering old questions which went straight back to Plato, but which were now being rather disappointingly reinterpreted from the point of view of Kepler, with God reinstated as a pure mathematician. Surprises, good and bad, could be found in R.H.Tawney's 'Religion and the Rise of Capitalism' which had reappeared every few years in hard covers since the 1920's.

In the stultifying atmosphere towards the end of the nineteen thirties, it was in fact astonishing that I kept my direction. But it was as if, quite suddenly, I had seen a wider implication behind the struggles of my adolescent years. What I had then been engaged in was not the highly personal matter it had originally appeared to be, but went much deeper. To recall this faithfully is difficult.

And later on when I began to work behind Fleet Street among the *hoi polloi* of the literary world, I found little enough to trust.

Friends joined the Red Brigade and vanished forever in Spain. Others took in Basque refugees, whose continuing homelessness owed almost as much to British negligence as to the muddle and inefficiency of the Germans and Italians who had gone to Franco's rescue and bombed small towns and villages. I cudgelled my brains, disliked taking sides, but couldn't escape from the pendulum's swing which hit me every time.

Naturally, I tried one or two fashionable blind alleys. I took more than a glance at Roman Catholicism, spent an entire summer in the Oxford Group, but drew back completely from Occultism with its dramatic sideshoots of the Quabbalah, and from Theosophy with its rather concealed, but quite strong, devotion to Spiritualism. It is interesting to recall that Hinduism and Tibetan Buddhism - the root teaching of both these cults - were nowhere in evidence. And the Moslem sects emanating from Sufis and Dervishes who would later be arousing a cultivated interest in mysticism had not yet arrived. I resisted pure Buddhism - if one could call it that - rather reluctantly, in the face of some very attractive reading matter, with the odd conviction that I might meet it again; then, somewhat cautiously, but with very definite steps, retreated into the background where something had once been promised.

It is difficult to recapture the true wartime flavour of the early nineteen forties. Not to talk, not to think overmuch, could be serviceable temporarily. But the atmosphere of war produced strange opportunities, and one Saturday afternoon in the early autumn of 1941 found me seated in an obscure lecture hall somewhere north of Kingsway, waiting for the start of a series of special wartime lectures on the relationship between religion and psychology.

I had six weeks of marriage behind me.

Dorothy and her husband, George, on their wedding day, 1st August 1941

Chapter 2

AN INTRODUCTORY LECTURE

It had been a hard year for Londoners, with freak bombing attacks prolonging the Blitz, bad news abroad and much dispersal among families and friends. But it was a sunny afternoon and the mood was light.

Passing the time before we began, I ran over these events, and while somehow ignoring the dislocation of daily life, began to weigh up what I was now becoming involved in. These lectures had been introduced to me out of the blue, by my husband, as 'the first of a *new* series of lectures' and my grateful response was warm, if astonished, for in that beleaguered summer all escape from the war's embracing atmosphere was apt to arouse paradoxical questions.

He had thought 'it would help me' with some of the questions I always returned to and 'give me something quite new', and yes, he had attended similar lectures himself. He had known the lecturer some time. It was his employer J.G.Bennett. And it was stressed that I was fortunate. The lectures were by invitation only and it was not customary to be able to join this particular series in the middle, and at such short notice.

What the beginning had been couldn't be adequately explained now, and nor would it be actually helpful if he tried to give his own ideas about the course our studies would take. He agreed that the title of the whole series 'The System as taught by P.D.Ouspensky'[1] was not very helpful, but you couldn't really fault it. And, yes, I was right to comment. The lectures were wide ranging. There really was an original form of exposition that could be described as 'new', for the lectures ultimately aimed at practice rather than theory.

I did not at all know what to think of the word 'new', but I rather liked the mixture of diffidence and enthusiasm exhibited by my husband and, although his outline was limited, I asked no more questions.

How the introduction had first come about now appeared to be significant. One evening, while we were having a rather abstruse conversation, I suddenly burst out with 'Oh, but you *are* good!', seeing right round the corner of the argument and landing up on his side. This *non sequitur* had so pleased him that he too burst out 'But if I could only tell you . . .', and then stopped quite dead. And, after an extremely long pause, added 'Well, maybe I can, though not quite yet'.

But I had been distinctly unprepared when a slightly more detailed explanation was produced about 'these *psychological* lectures'. Up to now I had not openly admitted my extremely old-fashioned ignorance in this sphere, never choosing to talk of it and apparently never intending to take it any further.

I had looked into psychoanalysis. Like most of the people I knew, I had borrowed books, could use some of the more emotive terms and more or less separate the main conclusions about the basis of complexes arrived at by Freud, Jung and Adler. What I did not like to admit publicly was that I had found Freud's development of analysis worrying. And because of his very marked anti-religious prejudice, I was not at all convinced about the make-up of what he called the Super Ego.

But my husband, who certainly knew more about psychology than I did, was clearly very much at home with the idea of new lectures as an *approach* to psychology, and for the moment it therefore seemed

---

[1]See Notebooks - Origins

appropriate to leave completely aside my own inadequate knowledge of the subject.

*　*　*

I looked around rather covertly. Some twenty or thirty people, spanning a very wide age range, and with at least one man in khaki, were seated widely spaced in the large, well-cared for, classically-tiered lecture hall. There was a serious, but relaxed, atmosphere and no conversation at all.

But from the moment we started, I was completely absorbed, and moved very abruptly out of the artificial equanimity I had adopted as a newcomer sitting rather too near the front. Most of the terms that Bennett began to use were simple enough, even obvious, but his inferences and connections were like Chinese boxes, and my long unsatisfied mind slowly expanded.

Speaking of the very distant past, of the near future, and of an even farther future which one could hope for in time, Bennett outlined a sphere of study that was irresistible. Touching very briefly on illusions, questioning attitudes and throwing some light on our genuine possibilities, he then produced the *leitmotif* of the whole lecture: there was one thing that we all lacked, and this, of course, was fundamental self-knowledge.

In our present state we were all much too apt to think that self-knowledge meant a gathering together of the heterogeneous facts that could be gleaned about our relatively hidden traits. But this would only put us in a false position.

Really, to know himself a man must first become thoroughly acquainted with his complex physical structure. This meant that his urgent primary task was to acquire a reliable method of self-study. And such a study would enable him not only to observe his interrelated physical functions correctly, but also to gain insight into what physiologists called the reflex actions, which for the purposes of study nowadays we could perhaps refer to as the levers of the human machine.

This did involve the need for acceptance of a considerable change in viewpoint, though the start of our research was not actually as daunting as it might sound. In fact, if we could actually admit at once that we did not yet know what methods to use, or where we could begin, we would be correctly activated for a positive step forward.

So we could clear the ground almost at once if we could begin to look at ourselves deliberately from the point of view of our ordinary intellectual, emotional, moving and instinctive functions. In this way, we would be brought up rather sharply by our extraordinary ignorance about things we had hitherto taken for granted. But at this point also, we must be careful not to make the mistake of despising the state of affairs we were in the process of uncovering.

The human machine was powerfully and wonderfully made, a miracle of adaptation and possibility. Even a short period of really trying to observe ourselves impartially while an action was taking place would reveal our basic '*mechanicalness*' in a very unusual light. But we must also heed a word of warning about this.

It was perhaps more or less inevitable that this potent idea about man as a machine controlled by unseen inner and outer events, through his own reflexes and never by his own 'will', should have been taken up so enthusiastically by modern schools of psychology - and particularly the Behaviourists - whose search for a watertight hypothesis resulted ultimately in many limited and inaccurate conclusions. We would cover this interesting side issue later. Meanwhile, we must not get caught in the same trap for, if we accepted the idea of our own '*mechanicalness*' too intellectually or too readily in one vast philosophical sweep, this would later impose a limitation from which we should not find it easy to escape.

Our task was to go much deeper at once by committing ourselves to observe our *mechanicity* consistently, but, if possible, without comment. While resolutely refusing to accept immature conclusions, we must take the idea rather slowly and personally as a genuine basis for continual experimentation, though with a kind of innocence which could lead in a relaxed way to the difficult but essential understanding of our functional mechanism as a whole.

In short, we had to be absolutely clear that we were not being invited at any point to subscribe to a kind of loosely reasoned pessimistic philosophy of a materialistic nature. Since our aim was much more complex than we suspected, it was essential at the outset to understand for ourselves - from our very own personal experiments - the extent to which we were in fact entirely dependent on our own mechanical processes, as this would be our first vital step in the direction of real self-knowledge.

And it was also important to realise at the very beginning that we were absolutely not being recommended to engage in what most formal schools of psychology call 'introspection'. This word should only be applied to the process of looking *into* one's own thoughts or seeing *behind* one's feelings, neither of which we were concerned in.

'The basic act of self-observation   - what we might call '*looking on*' - was just that, a simple act of recognition. Comment and analysis of any kind must definitely not be engaged in, and although simple 'recognition' of our basic functions might at first glance seem rather elementary and scarcely connected with 'true self-knowledge', it would soon reveal itself as a safe and reliable groundwork for a thoroughgoing study of a rather scientific nature.

It should be sufficient at this stage to stress again and again that the act of 'looking on' which concerned us now, connected with our thinking, feeling, moving and instinctive processes, would actually involve the making of short mental notes or brief 'records' that we could register afresh, over and over again, day after day. Without these intentional 'notes', our approach would very soon deteriorate and lead nowhere. And, as for some time to come there might be difficulties in assigning many of our mannerisms and our commonest activities to the appropriate Centre, to start with we should probably find it very helpful to look at ourselves as if we were someone else, someone that we did not know at all well, and in this way we could arrive at one or two certainties which would be distinctly useful, even if our first attempts endowed us with complicated problems we had never considered before.

Few people were at all aware of how their everyday perceptions of common activities were arrived at. Some, of course, perceived chiefly through their thinking mind, others through a combination of thoughts and feelings, or again, through combined sensations and feelings, and so on, while with the help of the mind alone we saw only one aspect. Later, we would be studying each Centre separately, and the precise intricacies of the situation would only be fully available to us after further detailed researches taken in hand over a rather longer period. Then we should be able to understand that the aim of all this part of the work was the highlighting of our *exact* manner of thought and our *exact* manner of feeling, as well as the recognition of our underlying instinctual and moving mannerisms, which were frequently displayed in many bodily sensations and movements which we had never observed before.

In fact, this particular preliminary task of beginning to assign our quite commonplace activities to the 'Centre' or brain to which they belonged would not actually take us so very long if we persisted resolutely in our aim, and as our records began to mount we should easily be able to recognise for ourselves the quite undeniable basic '*mechanicalness*' of our human nature.

Although during our earliest researches we could only study the four main groups of functions which look after our everyday life, for which in fact it would be convenient from now on to adopt the term 'Lower Centres', eventually we would also take into account the Sex Centre, with its responsibility for the incredible richness of human relations, as well as its control of our sexual manifestations.

Later still we would give attention also to the Higher Emotional Centre and Higher Intellectual Centre, the two brains governing our possible experiencing of higher states of consciousness.

The existence of these states, sometimes referred to as cosmic or transcendental consciousness, having frequently been described throughout history in widespread philosophical and religious literature

24

from many cultures, could no longer be doubted, and it was easy to see that although they did not fall within the province of our everyday existence, in the complete study of man, which was our aim, they must indubitably take their proper place.

And, though, of course, it would be premature to discuss consciousness in very great detail, it was important to clear the ground by understanding at once, at the very start of our vast subject, that even our primary studies would reveal the necessity for becoming thoroughly acquainted with the continually shifting scale of awareness which was the natural element of each one of our Centres; there would also arise a need for a thoroughgoing re-examination of what some of us might have already culled from popular literature on this subject. So, turning back, just at this point, to the observations of our own perceptions, we should then be able to think philosophically and extend our ideas about consciousness a little further.

How exactly were we 'conscious'?

Modern philosophical debate had not as yet made room for different degrees of consciousness, and for the most part rejected the idea of '*higher* states of consciousness'.

In the West, physiologists still supposed that consciousness is related only to a very small part of the human organism - the head brain - while the majority of scientists believed that even this brain is not conscious in its entirety. And some still newer systems of psychology denied consciousness altogether. Thus modern scientific thought, which has insisted on the necessity for objective data about a category which, by its very nature, can never be systematically observed or measured, has done a remarkable disservice to mankind as a whole.

In contradistinction to this, in the East, the ancient science of Yoga, which is sometimes aptly called an applied psychology of religion, teaches a philosophical and practical system which clearly reveals different degrees and different levels of consciousness available to its pupils. And, much later on in our own studies, we should be using the terms 'Higher Emotional Centre' and 'Higher Intellectual Centre' for those parts of the organism which dealt with these phenomena.

It would be helpful for us to try to weigh up some of these conflicting ideas right away - at our very first acquaintance with the subject - and if we could then look at the question of awareness with very great care, we should be able to see that the taste of consciousness could only ever be understood personally, through our own sensation, so that, quite clearly, we could only actually *know* consciousness in ourselves. And if we succeeded in learning to observe ourselves appropriately, we should in time be able to register the experience of very short moments of heightened awareness, being separated by extremely long intervals of the completely unconscious mechanical working of our physical organism. From this it was a comparatively small step to inferring directly that for hours, or even days at a time, we do apparently think, feel and act without ever being actually conscious of it.

* * *

As I listened to Bennett repeating and re-stressing the need for understanding the connections between our mechanical mechanism and the different levels of consciousness responsible for the activity of our thoughts, feelings, movements and instinctive processes, it began to be wonderfully clear that although he was now actually speaking philosophically, in his call for a special study which would lead to self-knowledge, he was also indicating that it was essentially the recognition of one's own helplessness which could lead directly to the initiation of some kind of genuine practical training. And his theme, all the time enlarging more and more to bring in ever-changing aspects of man's whole being, at last turned full circle and went back to the beginning, but with a more personal flavour.

Because we were fundamentally mistaken about ourselves, had struggled for free will where it did not and could not exist, we had trusted in the wrong signposts and merely turned round and round in a narrow life presented to us by our reflexes.

But what if we began to see things differently, although still without changing anything?

What if we could catch a mere moment of a slightly higher consciousness? What then? Life might seem simple to analyse but it was not linear - there was a thickness which we could not as yet perceive.

While he was still speaking it was not possible to gauge my own reactions to many of his more unusual statements but, as I listened closely, a new expanding feeling began to inhabit me: 'So *that* is why my efforts at thinking and understanding could never in the end endow me with integrity.', ... And this was certainly the most enlightening perception that I had ever had.

As all of this, taken step by step, would lead us away from our recurring questions about the pattern of our own behaviour; little by little, having discovered a truly qualitative difference in our functioning, we would find it necessary to begin to think philosophically and add to our present research the study of consciousness.

Except for a parable that spoke of man's higher possibilities, which immediately enhanced my present state of newness, Bennett's pace scarcely varied. While speaking of dramatic things, he was not dramatic, as if he intentionally under-stressed and almost hid some revelation that needed a certain delicacy. And then, suddenly, it was over.

There were questions and more questions, seeming pale enough when compared with the new urgency inside me.

*   *   *

Before I went to the next lecture great things had passed through me and the force of the best that the Church had once tried to offer reared up again, though not in words or images - no phrases, no analyses and no conclusions. It was like happiness, but it was not happiness. It was deeply serious, silent but not solemn, like a dream but more substantial than a dream. Real, with a new reality, as if a feeling long dammed had at last burst its banks and begun to flow quite free, steady but strong.

From this silent vantage point, little by little, new questions about my life rose to the surface.

Chapter 3

INTELLECTUAL CENTRE

As the great scheme of the Intellectual Centre began to be laid down, I started to feel something I could never even have guessed. This land of thought where I had been defeated ever since I grew up was intrinsically different from anything I had discovered for myself. And whatever conclusions I should now have to meet would certainly provide a new and significant starting point.

Bennett began by setting man against a vast landscape using metaphors and analogies from an earlier metaphysical age. Our intellectual experience, poised as it was between concrete reality and imagination, was not nearly as simple as it first appeared to be, but ran more or less parallel to the complex psychological aspects of our nature: our intellects dealt in abstractions, and these would only be real when they referred to real events. So although the Intellectual Centre seemed relatively easy to study, in many ways it was the most difficult of our minds to understand. Many schools of philosophy had claimed that it actually depicted the essential being of man, and the rationalist school of today was even accepting concepts which were only rearrangements of our thoughts about ourselves based mostly upon the famous misleading statement of Descartes[2] 'I think, therefore

---

[2] cogito ergo sum

I am', although Pascal[3] with his '*toute notre dignité consiste, donc, en la pensée*', was equally misleading.

As a result of these severe comparisons, having always rather admired Pascal and even gone so far as to struggle with the 'Pensées' in an ancient but badly printed early French edition, I then managed to borrow Dr Bucke's[4] 'Cosmic Consciousness' in which there was a very sympathetic biography:

Pascal, though a somewhat delicate child had been very advanced mentally, and although also depicted as a normal and rather gregarious boy, had actually begun to propound advanced scientific views from the age of ten. However, by the time he was thirty-one all this was altered. On Monday the twenty third of November 1654, when looking back at the futility and ambition of the past few years, he had suddenly experienced an inner state which he regarded as changing his whole life '*feu, certitude, joie, sentiment, paix*'[5]. This great event was certainly difficult to reconcile with the claim that some philosophers liked to make about much that was in the 'Pensées', and particularly Pascal's opinion that 'although man could only be described as a reed, he was a *thinking* reed'. But I did find that Pascal became more and more difficult to unravel as I continued to delve into the French of the 'Pensées', where, for instance, in support of the existence of God, he had made one of the most famous quotations of all time '*Le coeur a ses raisons que la raison ne connaît point*' - (The heart has its reasons of which even reason is ignorant).[6]

So what about Descartes (1596 - 1650) and the bold assertions in support of his '*cogito ergo sum*', which finally earned him a place as the 'founder of modern philosophy'? However much I felt obliged to disagree with him, and particularly with his extreme claim that 'all things that we conceive very clearly and very distinctly are true', I nevertheless enjoyed his writings and comparisons and especially his

---

[3] Pascal (1623 - 1672)
[4] Dr Richard Bucke MD, 'Cosmic Consciousness', 1901
[5] see Notebooks
[6] History of the Pensées

explanations of Cartesian doubt where he had resolved to make himself doubt everything that he could manage to doubt, only regulating his conduct meanwhile by commonly received rules, thus leaving his mind unhampered by the possible consequences of doubts in relation to practice.

Beginning with scepticism in regard to his senses, 'Can I doubt' he says 'that I am sitting here by the fire in a dressing gown? Yes, for sometimes I have dreamed that I was here when in fact I was naked in bed - moreover, madmen sometimes have hallucinations, is it possible that I may be in like case?'. And it is odd, taking Descartes' thought as a whole, that he came out so very strongly in his support of the pre-eminence of the mind, even associating and submerging feeling with it.

Bennett's field of reference became wider and wider and more and more abstruse as the lecture proceeded and I began to be really thankful for what seemed to me to be a sudden and quite unexpected ability to hold in my mind much of what was being said. Before this series of lectures, I should have quailed at most of his long, learned quotations and his quasi-scientific information. Now, in direct contrast to my feelings of inability, I was astonished to discover how well it served me to oblige myself to listen with quite a different level of expectancy and determination.

That this was actually opening the gates to an entirely new way of acquiring knowledge I could not yet know; it interested me exceedingly to see that, as well as a necessity to have been exposed to facts in a completely innocent way, there was also a real and continuing need for on-going study. That this study also had to be handled very carefully, I had never before suspected, although I accepted the theory and began to take a look at the way I and my friends bought books which we read somewhat superficially and then left aside. The transcriptions could not be treated like that.

Study, 'real' study, was a much deeper occupation than the compulsive urge to read which had never left me since an unnaturally early age. Transcriptions, if issued, were read and re-read aloud over a limited period so that people could make observations and ask questions, and the basic facts that they conveyed were regarded as vital information which would assist our necessary self-study.

Acquiring the transcriptions of these lectures for oneself brought with it the responsibility of reading them to smaller and smaller groups of new people. At the time, I felt very keenly that it was necessary not to browse in a shallow sort of way or acquire a spurious familiarity that cancelled the extraordinary freshness that lingered still, from the very first hearing of these potent ideas.

As he went on to develop his central thesis about thinking, Bennett began to stress how our obsession with the intellectual function was one of the principal causes which have prevented man, especially in the West, from realising that we are immature beings, whose development has been arrested at the very point where it should really begin:

'It is very difficult to sacrifice our belief in the dignity of the human mind and accept its severe limitations. Nevertheless the importance of the Intellectual Centre must not be underestimated for it is the only instrument which, on our present level of being, we can directly control. Except in rare cases, the real work of self-creation does not begin with the Emotional, Instinctive or Moving functions, but with the attainment of self-knowledge through the work of the Intellectual Centre.

'We must come to look at our minds, not as the gateway to reality, but as the point of exit from illusion. Between the abandonment of illusion and the attainment of reality there is a long and arduous path which we can only traverse if all our functions can be made to contribute their quota of understanding.

'Our illusions as to the value of the intellectual mind arise from confusion of truth with reality. The Intellectual Centre has no immediate access to the external world, and it does not deal direct with facts, but with thoughts or ideas. Our ideas are for the most part, though not necessarily, expressed in words, so that words or symbols equivalent to words, are the currency of our intellectual commerce. This does not mean that ideas or thoughts have some kind of reality of their own, or that we think by means of fixed 'unit ideas' which are permanent and unchanging. Ideas and words are merely signs, which correspond more or less closely to groups of presentations from external experience, or to combinations produced by the intellectual process itself. They are abstractions which only gain substance by their relation to recurrent elements of experience.

'The work of the Intellectual Centre is essentially logical and it must be clearly understood that it is to this Centre, and to this Centre alone, that the laws of logic apply. The Intellectual Function consists in such processes as association and comparison, affirmation and negation. In its commonest and most usual form, the activity of the Intellectual Centre is dualistic, that is, the association and comparison of ideas - two at a time. A characteristic manifestation is seen in what are called 'trains of thought', or series of associations, in which each idea arises successively out of the one which precedes it.

'Typical work of the Intellectual Centre consists in dealing with numbers, which constitute the most abstract relation which we can have with the external world.

'The power of the Intellectual Centre is shown in such work and in all operations of classification and logical analysis, to which it brings precision and definiteness at the expense, however, of comparatively slow and limited work.

'Before we proceed to examine in detail the structure of the Centre, we must enquire about the unique position which it appears to occupy in our experience. How is it, if our Intellectual Centre is but one out of several minds, that it seems so much more intimately and closely *ourselves* than the rest of our psychic functions. We seem to live, as it were, in our own minds. To be 'out of one's mind' is to be lost to oneself. In spite of this, every normal man is bound to admit, if he interrogates his own memory, that his highest and most precious experiences have not been of an intellectual character at all, but have consisted in some kind of direct perception of reality which went far beyond words or thoughts.'

In fact, 'In higher states of consciousness, when the limitations of the immediate here-and-now are transcended, we can escape from bondage to the Intellectual Centre and perceive it as a very small part only, of our whole being.

'There are thus two facts about the Intellectual Centre which it behoves us to consider carefully and to verify by every means in our power. The first is that the Intellectual Centre is the necessary starting point of intentional Work on oneself. The second is that it is the starting point *only*, and cannot by itself take us very far upon the way.

'The assertion that the Intellectual Centre is the starting point of Work upon oneself does not preclude the possibility that there are 'Ways' which begin with work upon the Emotional, Instinctive, Moving, and even Sex Centres, but in every such case, the work requires a Teacher - a Spiritual Father or Guru, however he may be called, who, through the exercise of his own specialised knowledge, is able to compensate for the lack, or better to say, deferment - of intellectual work on the part of his pupil.

'The Intellectual Centre itself is an elaborate structure. Its connection with the cerebral cortex is sufficient to show that it utilises a very complex mechanism of excitation, registration, re-excitation of association and inhibition, to deal with the stream of sense impressions which pour continuously into the brain.

'The least observation of our mental processes also shows us that the brain is unceasingly initiating new trends of thought, using material stored up and registered in its cells, over and above this physiological structure which nevertheless enables it to perform operations of widely differing character.

'There is in the Intellectual Centre a primary division into three parts, each of which corresponds to a different quality of thought. The first division of the Intellectual Centre consists in the working of its mechanism without directed attention, and without will, that is without *intentional* doing. For this process, we shall use the term 'formation'. This is the rendering precise by limitation and classification of groups of sense impressions received from the outside world, as well as of those vague ideas which arise within the mind itself.

'By the 'formatory' process, we bring the concrete but undefined world structure as it is presented to our awareness into distinct forms which the Intellectual Centre can manipulate. Unfortunately, this Formatory Apparatus, which is a valuable and indeed, necessary, instrument within its own limited sphere of application, is inevitably employed for uses beyond its powers. This leads to artificiality of thought, and, worst of all, to the loss of ability to distinguish between concrete reality and mere abstractions. The defective working of the Formatory Apparatus, the part that it plays in our lives, and the work which is necessary to compensate for its disabilities form an important part of the practical work which will be studied in later lectures.

'The Formatory Apparatus, as we have said, constitutes of the purely mechanical aspects of the Intellectual Centre, that is, its work as a functional mechanism taken apart from consciousness and will. This means that the Formatory Apparatus can work even if consciousness and will only enter accidentally. When consciousness, in the form of intellectual attention is brought to bear on the thinking function, the result is a mental process of a higher order, which we call the Emotional Part of the Intellectual Centre. At this level consciousness is related to the object of thought, not by an act of will, but by the interest which the object itself arouses.

'The Emotional Part of the Intellectual Centre uses the same mechanism as the Formatory Apparatus, but differs from it by the fact that its work requires the co-ordinating influences of a wider consciousness. Consciousness is needed to maintain continuity and purposiveness when thinking of something new, or when thinking in a new way. The Formatory Apparatus is only capable of continuous thought in so far as it has specific training to a formed habit. The Emotional Part of the Intellectual Centre, on the other hand, can work towards a specified aim without any preformed habit or prior training. The effect of focusing consciousness upon the intellectual mechanism is to enhance its associative powers, producing results much richer than can be obtained from the linear or dualistic associations of the Formatory apparatus, so that a sense of novelty is always aroused. Mr. Gurdjieff used to say of this that 'in the work of the Emotional Part, you always have the sensation of *discovering America*'. These characteristics of vividness, excitement, novelty, and even unexpectedness, all helped us to recognise the work of the Emotional Part. It is also the seat of true intellectual emotion, the desire and the joy of knowing. And, for the great majority of people it represented the highest degree of intellectual functioning of which they were capable.

'The Intellectual Part of the Intellectual Centre is not mechanical at all, in the sense that this word can be applied to the other parts. This is because its working is at all times and by its very existence, *an act of Will*. Unfortunately, we are incapable of using the highest part of the Intellectual Centre except on rare occasions and then usually under emotional stimulus. Nearly all men pass the whole of their lives without ever using the Intellectual Part of the Intellectual Centre. It is reached when will, consciousness and function are all united in the mental process. This we can call voluntary attention.

'It must be clearly understood that the voluntary attention which belongs to the Intellectual Centre is an altogether higher order of function than anything we ordinarily experience. And we must not confuse the localised attention of the Formatory Apparatus with the unifying flood of light which illuminates the mind when the highest part of the Centre is awakened.

'This splendid instrument, when fully developed, endows man with those powers of creative thought to which all great advances in human knowledge are due. It possesses not merely that intensity to marshal and combine all its thoughts and ideas, but it has a power of directing thought which goes beyond mere combinations. In this way the mind can seize and translate into terms of ideas, expressible in words, the subtle perceptions of the Higher Centres. It can thus act as a bridge between higher levels of experience and the understanding of ordinary men.

'Examples of the work of the Intellectual Part of the Intellectual Centre can be found in some aphorisms which express in a few words an unlimited wealth of thought, and carry the mind to the very threshold of knowledge unknowable for men such as we are. The Intellectual Centre cannot itself partake in mystical levels of consciousness but it can, through its highest powers, record the authentic taste of such experience. The Intellectual Part of the Intellectual Centre thus plays a part which no other Centre could fulfil in transmitting, in terms which ordinary man can at least begin to apprehend, knowledge which has its origin in higher levels of being. Nevertheless, this transmission can go no further than the Emotional Part of the Intellectual Centre, for the Formatory Apparatus is quite powerless to apprehend truths which go beyond logic.

'And this is very difficult for us to understand as virtually the whole of our lives is passed on its level. The wrong use of the Formatory Apparatus is in no small degree responsible for the persistence of those laws which are the most formidable obstacle to be overcome in starting the work of self-creation. Long and persistent efforts are needed to verify for ourselves the great difference in quality which separate the different parts of the Intellectual Centre. It is at once man's great hope and his great danger.'

Now, nearly everything that Bennett was saying about the hidden limitations of what he had referred to as the Formatory Apparatus was familiar to me, but this familiarity was of a strange kind. It was the seat of my long questioning about my motives and what, up to now, I had called 'myself'; because I had been unable to observe any other clear mental connections, it had been so painful to taste truth and lies gathered together from my own observations. And since early discussions with my mother had failed so miserably I had found very few friends to follow my apparently limited reasoning. But if my experience, misunderstood as it was, was only one-third of my actual thinking possibilities, what then?

What then, indeed?

At question time, an elderly lady asked if she could refer to the first lecture. She saw how badly she needed to make more regular efforts at self-observation, but again and again found herself in the same trap. She wondered now whether it was in fact impossible for her to go any further. She would begin to observe a particular Centre and before she knew where she was her intellect had come in and taken over. It was absolutely impossible to observe differently. She felt that she had tried not to analyse, but something was missing in her understanding. She also felt she understood why Mr. Bennett didn't approve of Descartes, but the more she made consistent efforts the more she fell back on Descartes' point of view. For her now, 'I think therefore I am' was consistently true. Theoretically she agreed, and was moved by the lecture on the Intellectual Centre with its explanations of different levels of consciousness that were open to us. But practically, when she geared herself to observe more she was soon enmeshed in associations. As Mr. Bennett knew, this was not her first attempt at trying to come to grips with her own mechanical make-up, but she couldn't see where the actual obstacles were . . . . . . She paused as if not really finished, but Bennett made an involuntary movement that brought her to a dead stop.

He then corrected himself, sat up straighter and smoothed down his double breasted suit, preparing something but not yet ready to speak. In a minute or two he looked at the woman, almost fiercely, before dropping his eyes and remaining motionless. Nothing stirred until he arched his spine, threw back his head, released his arms and began to speak slowly in a very serious way. I retained this like a motion picture because in the succeeding months and years I noticed that Bennett frequently followed this routine when asked a contradictory question. And it also took me months and years to understand more or less completely why this happened.

'I'm very glad,' he said, 'that you have brought Descartes into it, because it is most important that we all understand each other when we talk about the intellect. We only need to look back to Europe in the 17th century to see how it was never even postulated that man could actually possess more than one mind. What is now known as Descartes' '*cogito*' (*cogito ergo sum*) had a much wider basis for him than it does for us and attaches to his general principle "All things that we conceive very clearly and very distinctly are true". What Descartes meant was not the simple rationalisation that people today mean by thinking. He meant this in the widest possible sense, and so that there should be no doubt about that he makes a list: when he 'affirms, denies, doubts, conceives, wills, imagines and even feels,' he submits that this is all 'thinking'. And, of course, in a way he is right, but he simply leaves the feeling background out of it, so that we cannot agree that his idea of '*being*' – 'the *I am*' which has come down to us through the centuries – actually relates, or perhaps we should really say *proves* its claim to reality merely because his mind is able to put it into words.'

After another pregnant pause Bennett then continued more quickly, 'You will recall how in the lecture you have referred to the point which was very strongly made: that to know oneself as a machine was our most appropriate aim at the beginning, and that in order to do this we must avoid analysis. You have very rightly observed that every glimpse of your true situation leads you into associations. And one has to confirm that this will happen for a very long time – but go on – don't be beaten. Self-study through self- observation is a sure path to self-knowledge. Try for yourself to find what is missing.'

After this I found I was holding my breath, and the silence in the room was slow in attracting more questions.

Chapter 4

EMOTIONAL CENTRE

Whereas I had felt both stimulated and enlightened at the very start of the lecture on the Intellectual Centre, I was unexpectedly disappointed with my efforts to come to grips with the novel information presented on the Emotional Centre.

In fact it was an unusual kind of shock to discover that I must begin by accepting that positive emotions such as joy, hope and love could not have even relative permanence in someone like myself. Joy simply evaporated, love too often became its own opposite, and hope was reduced to daydreaming. This meant that at the moment practical research or any kind of experimentation was not straightforward.

And as at this stage we could only make slow progress with a personal study of the emotions, it would help us if we were able to call to mind what we had already understood about the three primary divisions in the Intellectual Centre. These divisions represented a vast sweep of consciousness, and when we had discussed man it was clear that he lived almost entirely on a very low intellectual level, in the most mechanical part of the Centre, which partly because of its skill in the mere manipulation of words had been given the name of Formatory Apparatus. The middle or 'emotional' part, which actually approached ideas that were new to us, was also accessible and perfectly recognizable, though rather seldom experienced.

The third, or highest part, connected a man with 'truth', but was so rarely experienced even by the most remarkable men in any age, that we could not pretend to study it in any detail.

'The Emotional Centre differs in essential particulars from the Intellectual Centre as an instrument of cognition and response. In the first place, its tokens are not words or thoughts or ideas, but values. Its concern with external presentations was whether or not they mattered, and whether they were exciting and beautiful, or even ugly and dull. When the Centre works normally, it is able, with extreme delicacy, and at the same time with great power, to scrutinise any situation, whether arising within us or outside, and to appraise it in terns of like and dislike, or approval and disapproval.

'Then our emotions were never concerned with logical consistency. The Emotional Centre neither affirms nor denies. It does not even know that conflict of yes and no which in the Intellectual Centre takes the form of doubt. Everything for it is certain at the moment it is experienced. What the Emotional Centre likes at a given moment, it cannot doubt that it likes - it does not question the reality of its desires or aversions.

'As compared with the relative and localised knowledge of the Intellectual Centre the knowledge of the Emotional Centre dealt with situations as a whole. It was an assessment of value for the whole of a perception, the whole of an experience. The growth of knowledge in the Emotional Centre consisted in the building up of an orderly set of values which correspond to reality both inside and outside ourselves. This was the very foundation of self-development, since our values are the source of our intentional actions and intentional actions are the essence of Work.

'But we had been speaking of the normal and undistorted working of the Emotional Centre. The proviso that the work of the Centre should be normal was even more important than it was with the Intellectual Centre. Our Emotional Centre often worked wrongly and we were in consequence deprived almost entirely of the particular form of knowledge most essential for the work of self-development. There is no greater tragedy in the life of man as we know him than the fact that his Emotional Centre could not be relied upon as an instrument of cognition.

'As had already been pointed out, this abnormal working of the Emotional Centre was due almost entirely to self-love. The Centre was so powerful, and as we should see later, so little under the control of the intellectual mind that once bad habits had been formed, it was impossible without very long work of a very special kind to liberate ourselves and regain true emotional perception.

'We should consider the practical implications of this fact later - for the present it was sufficient not to lose sight of the true situation. And it was not really difficult to understand that natural emotions such as joy, wonder, excitement, awe, reverence, gaiety, and love of all that is good or beautiful, could only act positively if they were not vitiated by such states as fear, jealousy, anger, pride, worry, irritation, and all other varieties of violent and depressing emotions which enter into a man's life.

'But the power of the Emotional Centre is easy to establish. Its subtlety is often overlooked. There are two reasons for this. Firstly, in negative states all cognitive power disappears or is falsified, and, secondly, emotional distinctions cannot be fully expressed in words. This is one of the greatest difficulties in the transmission of knowledge. Far too little importance is attached in modem life to the possibilities of sharing true emotional experience. This again belongs to the practical study which will be dealt with in another lecture.

'The Emotional Centre is a machine which responds both to external stimuli and to influences from the other centres. Its work consists in a kind of orientation or polarisation somewhat analogous to an electric discharge. Just as an electric charge, so long as it persists, causes a body to orientate itself and move in an electric field, so does an emotional state create an attitude which leads to action. The operation of the Emotional Centre converts any presentation from something colourless and indifferent to something which *matters*. If an external stimulus reaches the Emotional Centre and causes a response there, by that very fact we either like it or dislike it, approve or disapprove, experience a movement of desire towards it or an aversion from it. The Emotional Centre can also respond to the work of other Centres. For example, some thought may arise in the Intellectual Centre. If it remains confined to the Formatory Apparatus a train of idle associations will be set up. But if, at any moment, the Emotional Centre is touched there will be a response of desire or aversion, or at least an incipient movement to satisfy the resultant emotional urge.

'It follows from what has been said that the Emotional Centre - like the Intellectual Centre - is divided into positive and negative parts corresponding respectively to desire and aversion. It is most important to distinguish between the natural play of like and dislike and the unnatural contrast of pleasant and unpleasant emotions, whether violent, such as anger, impatience, jealousy, envy; or depressing, such as grief, worry, doubt; these are all unnecessary and do not form part of the natural legitimate working of the Emotional Centre. It is thus necessary to look upon negative emotions as due to a diseased psychic condition. The distinction of 'pleasant' and 'unpleasant' between emotions does not apply in the same way as it does, for example, between pleasant and unpleasant sensations. Thus, there are no 'pleasant' counterparts to worry or jealousy or anger. The mechanism whereby they are manifested is an artificial construction in part borrowed from the negative side of the Instinctive Centre and in part formed by loss of balance in the Emotional Centre.

'It is an essential part of all systems which teach the doctrine of self-development that negative emotions are unnecessary and harmful, and can be eliminated. In Buddhism, the five hindrances of *Klesas*, which must be put aside at the very outset, are thus referred to in the *Samanna-phala Suttanta*[7]:

'Putting away the hankering after the world, he remains with a heart that hankers not, and purifies his mind of lusts. Putting away the corruption of the wish to injure, he remains with a heart free from ill-

---

[7] *Sammanna-phala Sutta: The Dialogues of Buddha,* Vol II, p.82, para.68

temper, and purifies his mind of malevolence. Putting away torpor of heart and mind, keeping his ideas alight, mindful and self-possessed, he purifies his mind of weakness and of sloth. Putting away flurry and worry, he remains free from fretfulness and with heart serene within, he purifies himself of irritability and vexation of spirit. Putting away wavering, he remains as one passed beyond perplexity; and no longer in suspense, as to what is good, he purifies his mind of doubt.'

'It should be unnecessary to say that in the Christian religion, negative emotions are condemned as hurtful and unnecessary. Unfortunately, this vitally important psychological fact has been so completely misunderstood and distorted that today nearly all the negative emotions are regarded as capable of justification, and some are even approved.

The Apostle Paul[8] says,

"Let all bitterness and wrath and anger and clamour

And evil speaking be put away from you with all malice."

'Cassian, commenting on this phrase, says that he "accepts none whatever as necessary or useful to us" making it clear that nothing will justify anger. Cassian says "From almost every cause the emotion of wrath boils over, and blinds the eyes of the soul, and, bringing the deadly beam of a worse disease over the keenness of our sight, prevents us from seeing the sun of righteousness. It makes no difference whether gold plates or lead, or what metal: it makes no difference to our blindness."[9]

'The value of this example lies in its psychological precision. It illustrates the facts that negative emotions (a) are unnecessary, (b) are due to our own inner states, and (c) destroy the cognitive power of the Emotional Centre.

'An example of a depressing emotion which was generally regarded as a misfortune for which the sufferer is to be pitied, is the heaviness or gloom described by Chaucer in the Canterbury Tales.

---

[8] St Paul's *Epistle to the Ephesians,* IV. 31
[9] *The Institutes of Jon Cassian,* Book VIII, 6. Nicene Fathers XI, p.59.

"After the sins of envy and or ire, now will I speak of the sin of accidie; for envy blinde the heart of a man and ire trouble a man, and accidie make him heavy, thoughtful and raw. Envy and ire make bitterness in heart which bitterness is mother of accidie, and benimet the love of all goodness. Then is accidie the anguish of a troubled heart."[10]

'This state is condemned by Cassian as an obstacle to the progress of the soul. He says, "All the inconveniences of this disease are admirably expressed by David in a single phrase, where he says *"My soul slept from weariness"* that is, from accidie. Quite rightly does he say, not that his body, but that his soul slept, *"for in truth the soul which is wounded by the shaft of this passion does sleep as regards all contemplation of the virtues and insight of the spiritual senses."*[11]

'It will he noted that for the Christian Fathers, the violent and the depressing negative emotions were substantially the same both in character and in effects. They were regarded as unnecessary and destructive of the cognitive powers. Thus, the Shepherd of Heremas says, 'Put on, therefore, joyfulness, which always has favour with God and is acceptable to him, and flourishes in it; for every joyful man does good deeds and has good thoughts, and despises grief, but the mournful man always does wickedly. First of all he does wickedly because he grieves the Holy Spirit, which is given to man in joyfulness, and secondly he grieves the Holy Spirit by doing wickedly, not praying nor confessing to the Lord. For the intercession of the mournful man has nowhere power to ascend to the Altar of God. Why, said I, does not the intercession of the mournful man ascend to the Altar? Because, said he, grief sits in his heart, therefore, the grief which is mixed with his intercession does not permit the intercession to ascend in purity to the Altar. For just as wine mixed with vinegar has not the same savour, so also, the Holy Spirit mixed with grief has not the same power of intercession. Therefore, purify yourself from this wicked grief and

---

[10] Chaucer, *Canterbury Tales,* The Parsones Tale, para. 53, p. 699, Ed, W.W.Skeat, Clarendon Press, *1920*

[11] op.cit.

you shall live to God, and all shall live to God who cast away from themselves grief, and put on all joyfulness.[12]

'A detailed discussion of negative emotions would occupy too much time and would not, in any case, be a substitute for the self-observation which alone can give a right understanding of their significance in man's life. It is, however, important to distinguish between a moral and a psychological attitude to negative emotions. Both the authors of the *Pali Pitikis* and the Early Christian Fathers looked upon negative emotions as a diseased state, the essential psychological character of which was to be an obstacle or impediment to cognition. The Buddhists explained that by struggling against the Five Hindrances, man gains access to the supranormal states known as the Four Ecstasies. The Christian Fathers, with a more precise psychology, show their immediate effect upon the cognitive powers.

'Confusion is inevitable if the study of negative emotions is approached from the standpoint of a system of morality. Any such system is essentially relative in space and time and has meaning only for a given race, country and epoch. The psychological conception of man remains unchanged through the ages and the consequences of its right and wrong working are always the same. The saying, 'As man soweth, so shall he also reap', is not a moral but a psychological truth.

'It is hardly possible to give a theoretical description of the Emotional Centre which will not be misleading and dangerous in practice on account of the 'denaturing' of all emotional processes by the presence or threat of negative emotions. Nevertheless, it is necessary, in order to understand the working of human functions and to assist in distinguishing between emotions and sensations to see how the Centre is divided in a manner analogous to the Intellectual Centre.'

Thus, 'The Mechanical Part of the Centre is that which works purely as a machine; that is, without self-consciousness or unified will. This means that it consists entirely of habitual reactions which have been acquired through imitation or repetition. Habitual likes

---

[12] *Shepherd of Hermas,* trans. Kirsopp Lake, London, 1930. Apostolic Fathers, Vol. II, Mandate X 3., p.115.

and dislikes and all stereotyped emotions, provoked by set stimuli, are manifested through it. This part of the Emotional Centre plays a very great part in our lives, for it operates all the ordinary judgments of value which determine our actions. Thus, love of praise, dislike of blame, pleasure of achievement, distress at failure, the excitement of a crowd, the boredom of solitude and a thousand other desires and aversions, attractions and repulsions, control a man's actions. These are acquired by the growing child through imitation of his elders and companions. They are accentuated by the conditions of his life and by the features of his Intellectual, Moving and other Centres. As we have already mentioned this positive and negative working of the Emotional Centre is so gravely distorted by the presence of negative emotions that only patient study of oneself and other people enables the natural working of the Centre to be discerned.

'The Emotional Part of the Emotional Centre is the seat of natural emotional judgment. That is to say, it is not dependent upon acquired habits, but upon the synthetic or constructive power of the Emotional Centre itself. Whereas the Intellectual Centre works only with tokens in the form of ideas or words, the Emotional Centre constructs a complete attitude or judgment which is unique and appropriate to the situation presented.

'This working of the Emotional Part of the Emotional Centre may sometimes be recognized in our judgment of other people. Many people have the power – some to a marked degree – of forming a total judgment of the 'character' of a person at the first meeting, almost at the very first contact. Such judgments may be mistaken, indeed they almost always require correction after fuller acquaintance, but their outstanding character is their 'organic completeness and simplicity'. Thus the whole of our reaction may be expressed by the simple feeling 'I like that man.', but at the same time, we know that this liking is based on a combination of a very large number of factors. If we pay careful attention to our emotional reactions, we can see that features and gestures remind us of similar traits in people whom from experience we have learned to like and trust. Fine shades in the tone of voice have conveyed to us very much of the quality of the man himself. With some people this power of emotional judgment is so great, and can be developed so that they can predict with considerable accuracy the tastes and inclinations of a person, with their views on many subjects, their behaviour in a variety of circumstances, with no speech or other intellectual exchange and after the very shortest acquaintance - measured perhaps in seconds.

'The working of the Emotional Part of the Emotional Centre should conform to the foregoing examples in all emotional judgments, but here again we are unfortunately obstructed and obscured by the effect of negative emotions. Even so this instrument is one of man's most precious possessions, for it bestows on him the power of *discrimination*. Unlike the Intellectual Centre, which makes abstract judgments divorced from being, the judgments of the Emotional Centre are always judgments of being and therefore judgments of consciousness. The Emotional Part of the Emotional Centre can distinguish between two influences presented to it, that which is more and that which is less conscious.

'So much for the right working of the second part of the Emotional Centre. It is necessary here to refer briefly also to its wrong working, for even when tainted by negative emotions, it can give rise to acute and powerful judgments and decisions which endow some men with a great, though limited, power.

'Nevertheless, it is possible to see after a certain amount of self-observation that what we call negative emotions did not originate in the Emotional Centre in the same way as negative thoughts play a part in the Intellectual Centre. There, the need to say 'no' did not indicate any wrong working of the Centre as a whole. But when we discuss negative emotions, we are of course referring to feelings which actually denature our emotional existence, and we can safely conclude that states such as anger, fear, hatred, suspicion and so on are clearly instinctive aberrations - physical shocks - which actually utilises energy stored for another purpose.

'It also must be emphasised that the Emotional Part of the Emotional Centre is a machine in the sense that it is set in motion by external influences or by processes arising in other Centres, and that it can only make judgments within the limits of this own structure and powers. At the same time, it cannot work without consciousness, though here again consciousness is not united with will, but aroused by the stimulus that sets the Centre in motion.

'Finally, it must be understood that the Emotional Part of the Emotional Centre is very rarely used. In most people's lives, it occupies no significant part at all, and among the few in whom it is effectively operative, its effect is rather to create a general sense of direction and system of values than to determine their actions.

'The Intellectual Part of the Emotional Centre is an instrument of a very high order. Its principal distinction from the Emotional Part is that it is capable of initiating emotional judgments and is not dependent on external presentations. From this it follows that it can only work in a state of voluntary attention. It is, in fact, the seat of emotional will, and its highest function in man is to furnish a bridge between his lower and higher centres. When self-consciousness is fully present in it, that is when it works with the energy of Hydrogen 12, the Intellectual Part of the Emotional Centre has access to the Higher Emotional Centre.

'The Intellectual Part of the Emotional Centre is also the instrument through which freedom can work in man to produce what is sometimes called 'artistic inspiration'. This is a very rare gift, not only by reason of the small number of people in every age to whom it is vouchsafed, but also by the infrequency of its appearance even among the most favoured. When it does operate, it produces results which are unmistakably different from all ordinary intellectual, physical or emotional processes. At the moment of the artist's vision, *his Will is free.*

'The moment is characterised by completeness, by certainty and by timelessness, even though it may only last for an instant. The external greatness of the artist will depend, of course, not only upon his moment of vision, but also upon his ability to retain it and upon his intellectual and bodily powers of interpretation and execution. These are necessary elements in the complete work of art, but they are nothing without the divine spark which can only be struck upon the Intellectual Part of the Emotional Centre.

'In the work of self-development, the higher parts of the Emotional Centre have an all-important role, first in the attainment of self-knowledge, and afterwards in gaining mastery over the warring legions which constitute the mechanical parts of all the Centres.

'Sleeping man is a discord. There is no unity in his thoughts, and what is far more serious, there is no unity in his values. Different voices speak in him, each demanding action to satisfy the desire of the moment.

'The way in which it is possible to bring harmony into man's being and to raise his life above the level of the mechanical parts of his Centres, was illustrated by Mr. Gurdjieff in a parable 'The House With Many Servants'.

"Try to conceive", he says, "a great estate with many servants; indoor servants, gardeners, farm workers and the like, but no Master, no Steward or overseer. Suppose that each of these servants imagines himself to be the master and owner of the estate. Each will disregard his fellow servants and, if he gets the opportunity of giving orders will do so as if he alone were concerned in all the welfare of the house.

"There being no overseer, each servant will do whatever work his caprice may dictate. The groom will go into the house and do the cooking; the cook will go into the stables and wash the horses. In time the whole house will be in disorder and yet each servant will continue to think that he and his activities are the sole and only interest of the whole place.

"This state of chaos may continue indefinitely or it may happen that one of the servants, wiser than the others or perhaps taught by some bitter experience, will realise that something is wrong and discover that things can be otherwise; that there are possibilities of quite a different existence for the house and for its inhabitants if only order and discipline could be introduced. Others among the servants may come to similar conclusions. One may have heard, for example, that there should be a Master of the house and that the real aim and purpose of their existence is to serve a Master, and that the Master might come to the house if it were made ready to receive him.

"If these wiser servants really understand the position, they will know that none of them is fit or able to receive the Master and that before his advent the house must be brought under the control of a Steward who knows the Master and his wishes. They will, therefore, set themselves, in the first instance, the task of preparing for the Steward. They will begin by agreeing to recognise one amongst themselves as Deputy Steward and entrust to him the task of getting the cook back into the kitchen and the groom to the stables; they will try to support his authority with the others, and will expect him to answer for them all in dealing with people outside the house.

"At this stage the estate still presents a picture of multiplicity and there is no person in it who can claim any *rights* either as against the other servants or in respect of the house as a whole.

"If the Deputy Steward so succeeds in his work, that he imbues the majority of the servants with desire to know and serve the Master, and deals with the remainder either by bringing them under strict discipline or, if they are utterly recalcitrant, by expelling them; then comes the moment at which the Steward comes to the house.

"The Steward knows the Master and he acts in the master's name. From him the servants learn - not those simple duties which the deputy-steward taught them - but the Will of the Master and their true and highest welfare. They forget their separate interests as they come to understand what the Master can bring them. Finally the Master himself comes to the house.

"At first perhaps for a few moments only for they cannot support the glory of his presence, but ultimately, when all are purged forever from the illusions of self-hood and separateness, he will make his permanent dwelling with them and they will find infinite happiness and eternal security."

'The main point of the allegory is to emphasise the differences of *level*. The servants and Deputy Steward are all on the same level. They belong to the parts of the Centres in which we usually live. The Steward is different, he is not the Master; but he comes from the Master and knows the Master.

'It is through the Emotional Centre that the Steward appears. The Intellectual Part of the Emotional Centre is the seat of *conscience*. Without conscience we should never be able to work by ourselves without help. Until conscience comes, help is needed. This means that, until the Intellectual Part of the Emotional Centre wakes up, we have no infallible sense of values by which to judge ourselves *as a whole*. Conscience has been called by Mr. Gurdjieff the voice of the Steward. The Steward speaks to us in a quiet voice, which we cannot hear amid the vociferous clamour of the many I's, each proclaiming some petty interest or desire, or even some idle fancy. The Steward, above all, speaks the *truth*, and, such as we are, the truth is the one thing we cannot bear, and therefore we do not even attempt to still the lying voices which drown his voice. But some calamitous experience, or a real effort towards sincerity, may for a moment silence the voices and the clear judgment of the Emotional Part of the Emotional Centre will be passed, not on someone else or some outward presentation, but on ourselves. This is the work of conscience to see ourselves as we really are, to feel all our contradictions and meannesses, and, worst of all, to know that besides these things, we are *nothing*. We are not strong enough to bear the seat of conscience, for until we begin to move on the path of self-creation, the vision which it reveals is too appalling to be endured. This explains why in the allegory, the Deputy Steward must first undertake his task of setting the house in order.

'Conscience is to the Emotional Centre what self-consciousness is to the Intellectual. It is the working of the second part of the Centre - that is, the union of Function and Consciousness - turned upon oneself. This leads to emotional self-knowledge, which means knowledge and *judgment* combined. Through conscience, one not merely knows oneself, but assesses one's own value and level of being objectively.

'Conscience, in the highest part of the Emotional Centre, has power over all the Centres. This is the Steward in the full exercise of his authority, preparing the whole of the house for the Master's advent. Then conscience is no longer terrifying, but on the contrary gives the first taste of the positive emotions which belong to the Higher Emotional Centre, emotions which in our present state we should not presume even to name.'

It was perhaps to be expected that allegory of 'The House With Many Servants' would become the focal point of question time, though it was started hesitantly. This time I couldn't see the questioner but it was a young voice which asked "May I go back to what you have just told us about the parable of the master and the servants, and could you tell me from whom the original impetus comes - whether from the master or from the servants? Or perhaps I could put it another way? Is the first rumour originated by the Master towards this unruly house? Or is it by sheer chance that they happen to hear?"

Mr. Bennett lost no time with this question with a very definite 'No' - he answered briskly - 'it does not come directly from the Master - we can accept the idea that the Master is actually still a child and the house is being prepared for him . . . . . The Steward does not go away, he must remain to serve the Master. The Master is He whom we serve. He whom we exist to serve.

'There must arise in us the desire to serve. We have to ask ourselves whether this desire is even born in us. We speak now of such very big things. But even of such things as this, we have no reality. We must have an *attitude* towards them. I cannot know the Master. He can only be known by the Steward. But I can have an attitude towards this relationship. That means I can ask myself: *whom* do I wish to serve? And I must even oblige myself to answer the question as to whether I wish to serve my own egoism, or whether I wish to serve the Master.'

Perhaps it was to be expected that there would be more questions than usual after the lecture on Emotional Centre, centred on religion, all of which could be brought together in the one demand to know 'How could one become a Christian?'.

In order to answer this, Bennett had referred to a lecture Ouspensky had once attended in St Petersburg. There were no half measures in this. We were machines and 'a machine cannot be a Christian'. A Christian must live in accordance with Christ's precepts. He must be able to 'do'. But we could not do - with us everything 'happens'. Christ says 'Love your enemies.' But how can we love our enemies when we cannot even love our friends? Sometimes 'it loves' and sometimes 'it does not love'. Such as we are, we cannot even really desire to be Christians because one and the same thing cannot be desired for long. In order to be a good Christian, one must *be*. 'To be' means to be master of oneself.

To be master of oneself was the basic desire, and without this nothing else was possible . . . . . and we could look upon our teaching as esoteric Christianity.

One answer about the differences between emotions and instincts was particularly interesting. Having stressed the fact that the theory, which claimed that emotions were based upon the development of instincts, was actually faulty, Bennett then went on to explain that the pleasure-pain reactions in instinctive processes had a direct biological significance since they could ward off actions which might in fact be harmful to the body. The emotional function belonged to a different world, always tending to stimulate activity, implying like or dislike, interest and excitement and so on.

After a particularly long and complex answer about negative emotions and the possibility, or otherwise, of observing them, it occurred to me that I had something I simply must ask about which had arisen from the previous lecture. But before I had fully decided on how I was going to put this I had suddenly found myself immersed in an extraordinary inner dialogue about why I wrote poetry - in fact I hadn't written any for a long time. What produced a poem? Clearly the existence of the Emotional Part of the Intellectual Centre explained many things and the allegory of The House With Many Servants had somehow re-activated this question.

Very tentatively, in a voice that didn't seem to be mine, I put about one quarter of my question into words.

This time Bennett's answering routine seemed slightly different. Looking at me with his eyes a little more wide open than usual, then glancing down and moving his hand sideways, vertically and horizontally, he started to speak very slowly,

"I would have to see the poem" he said, "What sort of poem?".

I looked at him, he looked at me.

"Just a poem", ever so slightly I shrugged my shoulders. He then smiled rather kindly and shook his head very slowly. There was a long silence.

Somehow the lack of a possible answer ceased to matter. What I had been given by the past two lectures was a present of the Emotional Part of the Intellectual Centre . . . . .

Chapter 5

DIAGNOSIS

With much of this in mind I was now able to approach that welcome wartime rarity, a new book, written by Dr Kenneth Walker, a pupil of P.D.Ouspensky. Walker was a surgeon who also seemed to practise as a psychologist, making the claim that biology, psychology, philosophy and religion needed to throw their separate findings into a pool if they were to succeed in gaining insight into the nature of man. He went on to say that he had tried to give an indication of the atmosphere in which the book was written, because a start had been made almost simultaneously with the bursting of the blitzkrieg in London, and war was a great destroyer, not only of lives and property but also of illusions. Thoughts that nowhere touched reality but were merely creatures of fancy were swept aside leaving us with little that was our own. And even those opinions and beliefs that were genuinely ours were re-submitted to careful scrutiny, war having become a great clarifier of values.

With his cool medical mind Walker could efficiently pick holes in what he called 'Medical Psychology' and especially in generalisations which gave rise to dogmatic theories. Thus, at the end of the last century, the main concern of Sigmund Freud at the Medical School of Vienna was to cure sick human beings, and in the beginning, his theories about 'Analysis' were simply working hypotheses which he and his followers found to be useful. But as time went on, what was merely a method of treatment grew into something like a system of psychology, and when the nature of the self obtruded itself Freud felt constrained to furnish an answer to it. In fact it is for having stressed the importance of understanding how conflicts produce neurotic symptoms, and having initiated a method of believing them, that he will be regarded as a pioneer in medical psychology.

In a lightning sketch, Walker demonstrated how Freud's most famous pupils, Adler and Jung, were destined to leave behind this system which concentrated so strongly on sexuality as the main driving force in Man. Alfred Adler, with his emphasis on a patient's need to recognise that a 'struggle for power' lay at the heart of his style of living, founded the school of Individual Psychology, while Carl Jung with his strong religious bias concentrated on the answer to one fundamental question - "What is the essential task in the patient's life that he will not fulfil and from which he recoils?".

Into this uncomfortable arena - which reminded me somewhat painfully of psychological lectures I had attended in my last year as a schoolgirl - there erupted, in the twenties, Dr. J. B. Watson, an American. Watson was frankly sceptical about all the Viennese clinicians and particularly opposed to the analysis of consciousness by introspection as a suitable aim for psychology, saying that the fault was in the method. He believed that psychology must be accepted as the Science of Behaviour and that psychologists could not go back to the concepts of consciousness or mind. Thus his new school of Behaviourism approached the problem of human nature from the standpoint of the physiologist, and had as one of its stated aims the explanation of life in terms of mechanics.

By using Pavlov's work on reflexes and setting up his own experiments on conditioning Watson simplified everything to such a degree that he could solve overnight the age-long dilemma of the relationship between mind and body by simply disposing of mind altogether. Absolutely everything was be explained by reflexes, with man the puppet pulled hither and thither by numerous strings, being unable at any time to move, think or speak of his own accord.[13]

Although Dr Walker's conclusions seemed at first to be almost as stark as Watson's - because it was obvious that man's mechanicalness had to be accepted - his genuine quest for truth could make room for philosophy and religion as well as for science, and he had much more to offer than the bleak scientific method. By use of the scientific method, resorted to in a sphere where the real results must always be largely invisible, the Behaviourist school had claimed a much greater degree of determinism in man's behaviour than could possibly exist. And by banning consciousness completely on the grounds that it could neither be observed, weighed nor measured, they produced a paradoxical hypothesis which was basically absurd, for in place of every lifetime striving one was now to be offered only the blanket conclusion that nothing whatsoever could be attained.

And Dr. Walker explained further, 'with the reflex as its fundamental unit, the Behaviourists had built up a school of psychology in which everything is explained by such means. Reflexes of a lower order were conceived to have been shaped mainly by heredity, and those of a higher order by environment. An instinct, according to this view, was a 'hereditary pattern reaction', the separate elements of which were principally movements principally of unstriped muscles'. This conception of instinct was formerly held by William James who wrote:

'The actions we call instinctive all conform to the general reflex type; they are called forth by determinate sensory stimuli in contact with the animate body, or at a distance, in its environment.'

Not only were the more obviously automatic reactions explained by such means, but all forms of psychic activity. According to the Behaviourists, all mental growth and all education were accompanied by linking together of more and more reflex arcs, and by a greater

---

[13] Nearer our day. See NOTEBOOKS - Behaviourism for Skinner interpreted by Koestler

and greater elaboration of an already vastly complicated network of neuroses.

Nor could we overlook that the idea of different levels of thought was far more prominent in Eastern than in Western system of psychology. This being stated clearly by Patanjali, who divides mental activities and states of consciousness into five categories: clear thinking, confused thinking, fancies, sleep and memory. Because the mind, the instrument of thought, was usually caught up and controlled by the external world (*prakriti*) it was rarely capable of clear thinking. Only when it was detached from that could it reveal the truth. What explanation would the Behaviourist offer of these higher levels of thought? He would offer none, for the simple reason that he denied their existence. The Behaviourist entirely ignored the subject of consciousness and also holds the view that because states of consciousness are not objectively verifiable, for that reason they could never become data for science. Walker[14], of course, in this extended comment, was laying bare Ouspensky's account of Gurdjieff's teaching, though in a very anonymous form. In short, it could be proved by very different kinds of experiment, that should man come to observe the extent of his dependence on external influences by accepting emotionally his deeply seated mechanicalness, he could begin to know his machine, not in a spirit of either fatalism or rejection, but as the first real move towards understanding completely different levels of consciousness.

After reading and re-reading Dr Walker's chapters on 'The Brain and Central Nervous System', 'Medical Psychology' and 'Different Paths to Truth' it was extremely helpful in his chapters on consciousness to have an introduction to the second edition of Ouspensky's 'New Model of the Universe', for here he touched briefly on the Upanishads and the Mahabharata before devoting two long chapters to the Vedanta and Yoga. This was a welcome coincidence, as in answering many questions Bennett had already announced that he would be including these two subjects near the beginning of his forthcoming lectures on the Law of Three.

---

[14] See Notebooks - Behaviourism

I was becoming more and more curious about Ouspensky. It had taken me a few weeks to discover that he was not the founder of 'his' System, but it was very difficult to understand the air of mystery that surrounded any mention of its origins. Little by little I got to the official account. A nearly fatal 'accident' had happened to the teacher whose pupil Ouspensky had once been, and somehow this was responsible for a change in the teacher as well as a change in the teaching. It was not known now whether this man, Gurdjieff, was alive or dead. In any case, a long time ago, Ouspensky had separated from him.

There was an odd kind of parochialism that did not quite match the objectivity and majesty of the ideas that I had heard so far, but after a number of rather one-sided conversations in which I amassed basic information, I discovered that Ouspensky had actually only been with Gurdjieff for a very few years before he parted from him, though this was never spoken of.

At length, someone gave me Rom Landau's book - 'God Is My Adventure' - to read. This painted Gurdjieff in a definitely uncomplimentary light, while praising Ouspensky, and stimulated, I studied it several times. Trying to set aside the unreliability of popular journalism in book form, and the complete impossibility of second-hand judgments, I endeavoured to read between the lines. For some reason difficult to assess Gurdjieff had thoroughly offended Landau, but the unusual thing was that he appeared to have done this intentionally, not caring at all about the outcome. Obviously he was not looking for the kind of publicity that Landau's book could bestow – absolutely did not want it – and therefore refused to co-operate. This seemed in some way significant, but was it? Everything that Ouspensky had to say had been liberal and pleasing. He had tried to 'help' Gurdjieff, had tried to resume work 'in common'.

Read for a third time, this began to be a little disturbing, for despite the parsimony of the accounts which had been handed out to me, Ouspensky had always been a pupil, and Gurdjieff had always insisted that the great work on which he was engaged could never be hurried. So although one might be better or worse prepared, to become a fully equipped teacher rather than a student-instructor must be a work of a great many years. Nor, when I was urged to look again at the photographs, did that assist me much. Ouspensky, rather severe, like a good headmaster, did not really make the appropriate impression. What lingered after seeing the photograph of Gurdjieff, despite my professional opinion that there had been too much retouching to the admittedly magnetic eyes, was the really extraordinary spherical head . . . .

More lectures on Saturday afternoons gave me fresh insights into this odd situation, but I soon realised that I would be unable to get to the bottom of it. To all intents and purposes Gurdjieff had indeed disappeared. Apart from the fact that the possibility of his continued existence seemed to be rather an embarrassment to some of Ouspensky's pupils, it was clear that their ignorance about his present whereabouts was absolutely genuine. Neither they, nor the handful of people who had actually made contact with Gurdjieff in the nineteen twenties, knew anything at all about his present existence. And if there were pupils somewhere who actually were in contact with him, they kept themselves to themselves.

People who had only been a short while with Ouspensky felt that it didn't and couldn't matter. We had a whole body of teaching to assimilate and this had to be enough for the present. Should the future bring about any kind of *rapprochement*, that would have to look after itself.

As soon as Ouspensky had left England for America at the end of January 1941 Bennett believed that it was his duty to write what he could remember of the System. Ouspensky was increasingly convinced that Germany would win the war and that this would lead to revolution spreading across Europe. Though most of the evidence was in his favour, few would have shared his views. But it was a strange time, for the cataclysm that washed around us in London seemed to strengthen our spirits and inject a light-hearted resolve.

The rule about not writing or commenting on his teaching was still in force, and Ouspensky had announced that he had not as yet any intention of publishing, although he might change his mind later. Bennett questioned him about this when he went to say goodbye, and asked quite openly if the occasion had arrived at last when he might write out the System as far as he could remember it. But although Ouspensky had originally encouraged him, he now maintained that a systematic written presentation was in fact impossible, and if Bennett attempted one he would soon find that out for himself.

With this somewhat qualified assent Bennett had been obliged to be satisfied, and although disheartened by Ouspensky's defeatism he looked upon his efforts as something necessary that must be done for posterity. And there was one theme that he particularly wished to work on, feeling that it would lend coherence to some of the apparently unrelated ideas. This was the 'Law of Three' which had interested him very deeply since the early nineteen thirties when he had worked on tracing its roots in Indian sacred literature.

So from that time on he worked out the hypothesis that the interaction of six fundamental laws must govern all eventualities in the Universe, having themselves been derived from different combinations of what Mr Gurdjieff had called the basic principles of all existence: the affirming, denying and neutralizing forces. When Bennett had actually worked with these before, his exposition had not been completed and eventually he had set it aside believing that he was just marking time.

So month by month, as we picked our way through devastated thoroughfares to Saturday afternoon meetings, Bennett went on with his great task of bringing the philosophical ideas of the System before us, allowing us a recapitulation period in small groups where questions and observations could clear our minds and also help him to work towards some kind of final draft. As well as looking at everything from the point of view of the interaction of three forces, he was pursuing a scheme which separated the philosophical and cosmic ideas from the theoretical and practical, in a way which seemed to highlight the teaching.

I remember that I had one woman friend of my own generation who had come from the days of Ouspensky's reign and who every week consistently asked for more practical work and more psychological ideas, and was as consistently told that we actually needed a sound philosophical basis before we could profitably absorb any more psychological ideas. We used to discuss this, and it was absorbingly interesting to find that our common discoveries about day-to-day life stemmed from widely different starting points. My needs corresponded with the lectures at that time because my thoughts and aims of the past had been frustrated, and it was as if all my life possibilities had been set aside before any new strands of meaning began to be forged. And above all, now I needed truth.

In his endless quest for descriptions of the Laws which might appeal to those who had no talent for philosophical thinking, and no scientific training, Bennett had discussed the scientific principles that had been laid down in the Vedas thousands of years ago, explaining that in India, philosophy, science and religion made up an harmonious whole, although modern technology was beginning to disturb this desirable state of affairs. The great Vedic age was said to have emerged about 2000 B.C. and it was extraordinary to reflect that scientific concepts like the interchangeable roles of 'matter' and 'energy' and the theories about conservation of energy were all to be found in the oral tradition. The word *Veda* meant 'superior knowledge'. It was 'superior' because it was revealed – beyond the reaches of the ordinary thinking mind, and it was supposed to have come from the original *rishis* – the 'teachers' of the ancient Indian world.

The original texts and summaries had for centuries been passed down by word of mouth, between teacher and pupil, until finally they were transcribed onto parchment. The *Rig-Veda*, which was the oldest, was one of the most ancient of all religious documents, and the *Upanishads*, with which many of us were now becoming familiar, were a kind of philosophical summary of the truth in the *Vedas*. This term was derived from the Sanskrit and meant 'sitting down near', referring to the necessary phase of discipleship.

The *Upanishads* teach that the 'Divine Ground', or 'That One Being' referred to in the Vedic hymns, is not just an idea but may be experienced directly, for the 'Greater Self' or 'Atman' dwells within all people. And through efforts to transcend the egoistic everyday self, and the practice of inner discipline, inner union with Brahman could ultimately be attained.

It was pointed out that *Vedanta* – or the ending, i.e. the 'summing up' of the Vedas – was entirely practical. The Vedantist philosopher started from the obvious existence of self, and how in the early stages of life a man saw himself and the world as independent entities which had meaning in themselves, and where every event occurring was the effect of some recognisable antecedent cause. Therefore, when examined closely, all events appeared to occur in time, and all objects occupy space. But a further stage of man's development might arise where he began to question his existence, and this could result in the recognition that both cause and effect and space and time were mere concepts created by the mind, and thus could only be looked upon as 'dependent realities'. If these mental constructions could be seen for what they were, then a man could begin to be less enslaved by a wide range of happenings, both inside and outside himself.

But *Vedanta* also drew attention to the other side of the coin, in that it taught unwaveringly that until a higher state of spiritual perfection was attained, and the sense of 'I' and 'Thou' and 'Mine' and 'Thine' had completely disappeared, there was no profit in denying the reality of the Universe. For ordinary man the world was not illusory, and this stage could not be abandoned in a false way. When the personal ego ceased to be the driving force, the true character of the Supreme Self would be realisable, and the illusory nature of the world as a self-subsisting entity would be obvious.

This introduction we were given to the idea of the three qualities or '*gunas*' making up the creative force of Nature was, in fact, very brief, though quite concise and to the point, as my husband and I discovered when later we were able to take the opportunity to attend a special lecture on *Vedanta* given by a visitor from India, one of a series, which loosed us upon the whole dizzy, rich and complex world of the Hindu religion. But the outstanding merit of all this was that we were

65

introduced to the *Yoga Sutras* of Patanjali, which though unobtainable then, were of enormous help to us later. We took to Patanjali – he had previously been just a name to me – but, as he had also been recommended by Dr Walker, we were extremely fortunate in eventually finding a second hand copy of his 'Way of Transformation' in one of the Oriental bookshops near the British Museum.

Who Patanjali was, and when he actually worked, is not known. It is thought that his version of the *Sutras* dates from between 400 B.C. and 400 A.D. On first acquaintance, their simplicity is daunting, but with a good commentary they open the door to a living, searching look at the inner state. The best translation of the word 'sutra' is 'thread'. A *sutra* is, as it were, the thread of an exposition – the absolute minimum to hold it together. These threads were meant to be memorised, and were actually intended as the basis for further exposition and expansion. Swami Vivekananda of the Advaita Ashrama, Calcutta, wrote what has been described as a 'wonderful commentary' in his small volume entitled 'Raja Yoga' (already in its eighteenth edition ten years ago).

But these threads, for us, could not in fact have led to the practice of Raja Yoga, for which an appropriate teacher would have been necessary. What they did do was to open our eyes further to a basically different way of thinking about our own minds, and with the idea of the three *gunas* I even found it easy to begin to think more concretely about the Law of Three and Triads, which seemed so very far divorced from the questions which arose from my acute feeling of lack, that I always carried with me. That I had, quite by myself, found this to be some kind of defeat in the realm of the mind I recognised as an absolute fluke. In modern style I might so easily have looked for a different religion, love affairs, or a more satisfying profession, but I had turned round and round – not in a vicious circle, but as if I were inspecting the circumference of a wheel and then continually returning to the hub, and in this way had seen the mind as the vital key.

So what, for me, had an understanding of the *gunas* to add?

It was necessary in the first instance to understand something of their distinctive qualities. *Rajas* was the restless, urgent principle, *Tamas* was heavy, inert and enveloping, and *Sattva* light and illuminating. These three, like a twisted root, ran through the whole of Nature. When the creative force was dormant the three were in equilibrium. When *Purusha* - spirit - acted on them, *Prakriti* - the diversity of nature - was the result. Difference in the creation resulted from one quality predominating over another.

Samkhya philosophy, transmitted from the far distant past, explained the essential distinctions thus: 'If the only operating quality were *Rajas*, the universe would be an increasing round of activity. So Nature provides against this by the restraining influence of *Tamas*. Again, if there were no enlightening agency in the shape of *Sattva*, Nature would be nothing better than a mass of blind forces acting haphazardly.'

Since mind itself is the result of the action of the three *gunas*, having described the hindrances to thought in an untrained mind, Patanjali then concluded: 'Mind stuff has three aspects (*gunas*), as appears from the fact that it has a disposition to vividness, to activity and to inertia. The *Sattva* of the mind – vividness – when commingled with *Rajas* and *Tamas*, acquired a fondness for supremacy and for objects of sense; while the very same *Sattva*, when pervaded with *Tamas*, tends toward demerit, non-perception and passion, and toward failure of its own rightful supremacy.

In fact it was to Dr Walker's chapter on Yoga that I often turned, long after Bennett's special lectures on the Law of Three were finished - and Patanjali's conclusions have stayed with me.

67

Chapter 6

MOVING CENTRE

I approached the Moving and Instinctive Centres rather cautiously. I had already accepted the idea that these were separate minds, but had I been asked to explain my acceptance fully, I should have been rather embarrassed. I could see how blindly I often moved from place to place, a little too fast and breathlessly. And what should I have been learning about my occasional physical laziness, and the frequent need to straighten my back in a slightly exaggerated way?

I did not have long to wait. Apparently one of the difficulties that everyone encountered on passing from a consideration of the Emotional Centre to the Moving Centre was the fact that to begin with we could only produce observations about the lowest, mechanical parts of our centres and this was naturally an anticlimax. Nevertheless it would help us to understand that man was neither a mere automaton nor a conscious being. Wrong working of the Moving Centre frequently interfered with the right working of other centres, and in some cases could even inhibit their work completely . . . . . so what we had to be content with at the moment was a theoretical study, and then little by little we could liberate ourselves from the dualistic distinction which we were apt to make between mental and non-mental processes. And it would actually be a great help to us for the time being if we could be patient enough to accept explanations which might seem over-emphatic and even unduly repetitive.

Having given this unusual introduction to our study of the Moving Centre, Bennett then proceeded at a fast-ish pace with all the essential background.

'The functions which we ascribe to the Moving Centre are usually regarded as reflex in character and therefore independent of consciousness. We are supposed to learn new movements by a mere extension of the process whereby reflexes are conditioned by repetition, assisted by a greater or lesser degree of intellectual co-ordination. Quite apart from the gap between the reflex arcs which depend only upon the chord and frontal lobes on the one hand, and the 'so-called' conscious work of the cerebral hemispheres on the other, this description fails to account for the acquisition of skills. It gives, indeed, quite a false picture of our moving functions. It fails to explain adequately the elaborate system of movements which are in constant use, and it breaks down completely in dealing with those rarer cases of a high degree of adaptability in movement where there is no trace whatsoever of intellectual co-operation.

"The existence of a separate 'mind', which controls movements, has been suggested by experimental psychology, but never very clearly formulated. Evidence of the existence of a separate Moving Centre is to be found in the learning of skilled movements. For example Vanderveldte[15] described a variety of experiments involving the acquisition of skill in co-ordinated movements and concluded that, 'The typical process of learning a complex motor act proceeds from whole to part and back to whole again.' All Vanderveldte's work gains an immediate simplicity and clarity lacking in his own descriptions if it is interpreted in terms of a separate Moving Centre which learns with the aid of the Intellectual Centre or by imitation of other people.

'Convincing though Vanderveldte's examples must be for anyone who studies them carefully, they are not by any means the most

---

[15] Vanderveldte "L'Apprentissage du Mouvement et de l'Automatisme"

conclusive evidence for the existence of a moving mind. Conclusive evidence can be derived from the study of trained movements. For instance, in the far more exacting requirements of training in the use of a musical instrument it can be seen that we are concerned with a process that cannot be explained as a mere set of automatic reflexes. It has now been generally recognised that two entirely different methods can be followed in teaching a musical instrument such as a violin or pianoforte. In one type of method, the body is treated as an automaton and the required movements are taught by insistent repetition, without demand for attention. These are the methods which call for five, six, or up to eight hours of practice every day, and which confer high technique only at the expense of unremitting work. Other methods, which have been largely responsible for the astonishing progress of instrumental technique in the last two generations, bring into play - though without full understanding of what is being done - the cognitive power of the Moving Centre itself. The Moving Centre is trained not merely to imitate fixed movements learned through the Intellectual Centre, but to perceive directly what it should do, first slowly, and then more rapidly. All who are familiar with the difference between the two methods will readily understand that, in the one case, the moving mind is made to work intelligently, and in the other, it is used as a mere machine as in the former example.

'Passing from the consideration of training and the acquisition of skill, we may now examine the evidence based on the study of 'ability' and 'mental tests'. Although the authors themselves do not fully realise its implications, the work of Spearman and his school on the so-called 'mental factors' leads to inexplicable anomalies unless mental and 'moving' processes are separated and referred to as different centres. The whole development of the various tests used by industrial psychologists has shown that it is necessary to distinguish between tests to determine the aptitude of candidates for work involving bodily skill and those for candidates whose work will be requiring both intellectual and emotional aptitudes.

'The transfer of skill in carrying out a movement from one hand to another was observed by Weber in 1844. In 1894, Scripture showed that steadiness in tracing could even be transferred from the hands to the feet and *vice versa*, and a large variety of more complicated transfer experiments have been made during the past fifteen or twenty years. Woodworth, in discussing these[16], makes the significant statement that 'Each of these bits of knowledge and skill depends on some high level cerebral mechanism - to be conceived as widespread rather than confined to a small area of the cortex - and transfer shows that the same mechanism is available to feet as well as to hands when they both execute the movement. A better statement is that either hand is available for the use of the same cerebral mechanism; for the core of the act corresponds to the cerebral mechanism and not to the muscles or receptors employed.' This is in full agreement with the view that moving processes are controlled by a separate moving mind which is distinct from the intellectual mind, for it is easy to show that the transfer is not helped, but on the contrary, often greatly impeded by intellectual attention. For example, in transferring from the right to the left hand, intellectual interference leads to a confusion between the direct movement and its mirror image which is absent when the Moving Centre is left to do the work alone.

'Notwithstanding the considerable body of evidence, of which the foregoing are only examples, it must be said that modern experimental psychology has so largely restricted its study of movement to artificial cases that it has failed to establish the full significance of a separate Moving Centre. We must therefore consider in detail, by means of a specific example, the nature of complex motor activities. Speech is a function which involves a very high degree of co-ordination, and can by no means be regarded as a mere system of conditioned reflexes. At the same time, speech as a motor act is unmistakably distinct from any purely intellectual process. It has been suggested that speech is itself controlled by a separate centre which, though differing from the

---

[16] R.S.Woodsworth 'Experimental Psychology', p.189.

intellectual mind, is not allied to the motor functions in general. This view is supported by the localisation of an elaborate nervous system controlling speech in the fore part of the brain. It is, however, not difficult to show by conclusive experiments that speech and the other motor functions belong to one and the same mind. For example, a poem may be learned by heart and continually repeated. It is then found that the repetition of the poem can continue without interference while quite unconnected intellectual processes take place. Certain classes of habitual movements, e.g. walking, can also be performed without interfering with the repetition. As soon, however, as an attempt is made to perform movements which require attention, the repetition comes to a stop. If an effort is made to keep it going, there is an unmistakable conflict of attention between two parts of the same mechanism which is quite different from the division of attention between repetition and thoughts.

'When it becomes clear that a function so complex and so highly co-ordinated as speech has to be ascribed to a mind distinct from the Intellectual Centre, it becomes much easier to understand how and why man should be looked upon as a machine. A very large proportion of our actions, including many of those which are apparently intentional, are in fact controlled by the Moving Centre, with no intervention of the Intellectual Centre at all.

"A man returning home from his work in the evening may perform an elaborate series of accurately timed and closely co-ordinated movements over a period of an hour or more, and never, as the saying is, 'give them a moment's thought.' He may go to a station, ask and pay for a ticket, find the right platform and the right train, and take his usual seat in it. He then reads his usual evening paper, recognises and gets out of the train at the right station, and finds his way home, entirely through the stored-up memories and experiences of his Moving Centre, without once calling his Intellectual Centre into play. All the time, the latter may be occupied with thoughts quite unconnected with his journey, so that, in effect, he will be living two lives simultaneously; one life - that of his Moving Centre - will be concerned with getting home as quickly and with as little trouble as possible, and another life - that of his Intellectual Centre — will be occupied with the activities of the day and with a thousand and one thoughts and dreams localised far away from the present whereabouts of his body.

'It will be seen from this description that the Moving Centre is to be regarded as a mind which controls not merely simple movements, but complete and sometimes very elaborate processes involving adaptation as well as co-ordination. In other words, it has all the characteristics of a mind and is entitled to an equal status in this respect with the Intellectual Centre with which we are accustomed to identify our existence."

Bennett now paused as if to take stock and then continued more slowly:

"The distinction we have already made between the Intellectual and Emotional Centres means, in effect, that we have to recognise in ourselves two different persons - an *intellectual* person whose life is passed in terms of thoughts - and an *emotional* person whose whole existence is in feelings. Even while recognising this distinction, we are probably left with our sense of psychic unity unimpaired, for we are able to regard ourselves as somehow a composite being in whom thoughts and feelings, though distinct, nevertheless interpenetrate and are usually combined in a single system of experience which gives us our 'I' feeling. But now we have come into contact with a new *mind*, of whose life we are not directly aware and which cannot by any means be assimilated by our usual 'I-feeling'. We have just said that this mind must be accorded a status equal to that of the intellectual mind. In other words, we have admitted that there is in us a 'moving person' just as real as the 'thinking person' or the 'feeling person'.

"But the uniting of our Moving Centre - with its wonderful powers - with the Intellectual, Emotional and other centres, cannot come about by a mere fusion which would destroy their particular attributes, but only through a higher *Self*, in which all will be united and yet preserved. It is necessary, moreover, to understand that the mechanical parts of our centres are isolated from each other as regards

74

consciousness, but interlocked mechanically, so that they nearly always interfere and seldom help one another. The Emotional Parts of the Centres, although separate, are not isolated, nor do they interfere with one another except in negative states. The Intellectual Parts of all the Centres are in direct contact and, if we can be free from identification and imagination, they can unite and work as a single harmonious organ of perception and response.

'Let us now turn to the actual inner structure and working of the Moving Centre itself. In the first place, like the other centres, it has a positive and negative side. Sherrington[17] has shown that all movements can ultimately be reduced to processes of excitation and inhibition. A state of rest is not really absence of movement, but involves a definite message from the centre to the periphery as does an actual movement. Thus, the Moving Centre works by an exceedingly rapid and highly complex succession of excitatory and inhibitory impulses which it has the power to combine into the smooth and harmonious working of the normal healthy body. The extent and wonder of this miracle can only be appreciated when the working of the Moving Centre is disturbed by nervous diseases, for then it becomes clear how the Intellectual Centre is powerless to assume the essential functions of the Moving Centre.

'Although the division into positive and negative parts is inherent in even the simplest movements, this has not the same psychological importance that we see in the corresponding divisions of the Intellectual and Emotional Centres. And the reason for this is that we observe the operations of the Moving Centre in terms of the net result, that is, externally, while the division of excitation and inhibition is internal to the centre, and for reasons connected with the difference in rates of perception (to which we shall come later), cannot actually be perceived at all by the intellectual mind.

'The Mechanical Part of the Moving Centre comprises the whole range of acquired and learnt movements which are not dependent on consciousness. All the examples given above to illustrate the autonomy

---

[17] Sir Charles Sherrington 'The Mind and its Mechanicalness' 1933, p.16

of the Moving Centre refer to the Mechanical Part, and therefore at this present stage we need not elaborate its working. It is, however, necessary to give some explanation of the manner in which the content of the Moving Centre is built up. Earlier, in distinguishing between Moving and Instinctive functions, we said that the latter are innate and the former acquired.

'In the new-born child, the Moving Centre is in a state corresponding to an undifferentiated organ in the foetus. At first, all movements are instinctive. There is, however, a form of perception and response for which the Moving Centre has a peculiar and special aptitude exceeding that of all other centres, namely the *power of imitation*. The young child imitates other people and even imitates itself. For example, it soon begins to imitate through the Moving Centre its own instinctive cries. And its purely reflex clutching is imitated by the Moving Centre in the grasping of discerned objects. The reflex extension of arms and legs is imitated in thrusting and pushing against any resistance. From this self-imitation, the child passes by degrees to the imitation of other people. In his cries, he begins to imitate the sounds they make and he grasps the objects which they give him to play with.

'In this way, by the end of his first year, the Moving Mind is already well on its way to independent existence separate from the Instinctive Centre, although his intellectual mind is still void of content. (It should be noted that the Emotional Mind follows entirely different laws of growth and that emotional understanding is possible almost from the moment of birth.) The continued development of the Moving Centre goes at an accelerated pace, and as the Intellectual Centre comes into play, a new method of learning becomes available. The Intellectual Centre is able to control some of the most important groups of muscles which usually work through the Moving Centre and so teach them without an external model. The Moving Centre then imitates the Intellectual Centre and gradually takes over control of the movement. As it does so, there is an unmistakable gain in fluency, because the Intellectual Centre is quite incapable of that intimate co-ordination which is required by complex movements.

'The ability of the Moving Centre to learn by imitation is retained long after childhood by people whose conditions of life require this power, but under the conditions of so-called civilisation, the development of the Moving Centre either stops at an early age, or is directed into restricted channels by such activities as athletics and the tending of specialised machines.

"The Emotional Part of the Moving Centre is required for movements which involve purposive adaptation, but all the work of the Moving Centre implies some degree of adaptation - for example, even in walking there is a constant adjustment of the height and length of step to irregularities of the terrain, and such adaptation does not require attention, for it is learnt together with the movement itself. By *purposive adaptation* is meant the adjustment of a movement to obtain results over and above the immediate necessity of the moment. This takes place with the help of attention and carries with it a feeling of interest and excitement.

'The work of the Emotional Part of the Moving Centre is well exemplified in dancing, where movements are adapted to external rhythms which the Centre can easily interpret. In dancing, the Moving Centre not only co-ordinates the muscles in a smooth series of movements, but, in addition, regulates them at every moment and the distinction between rhythmic movements performed with the Emotional Part of the Moving Centre as compared with the same movements produced by the Mechanical Part is quite unmistakable.

'In modern civilised man, the Emotional Part of the Moving Centre is woefully neglected. (This has many unfortunate consequences, including the decline of harmony and mutual understanding in small communities.) Sport untainted with professionalism and almost free from the competitive element; ceremonial and festival dances; occupational rhythms and village crafts; all helped in the past to develop the working of the Emotional Part of the Moving Centre. Owing to the imitativeness of the Moving Centre, these common activities created a form of understanding, the importance of which is really quite impossible to overrate. We can understand therefore that the Moving Centre is not only an instrument of action but also one of cognition, and it is moreover a very valuable instrument of cognition, the work of which cannot be adequately replaced by any of the other centres.

'The Intellectual Part of the Moving Centre is an instrument the use of which is less rare than that of the corresponding parts of the Intellectual and Emotional Centres. Even so, it only works freely in a few gifted people who have a high capacity for invention. The man in whom this part of the Centre can work has a feeling for the working of nature which completely baffles the Intellectual Centre. And scientists who have this gift appear to their contemporaries to have an unfair power of guessing at the working of natural laws, and of devising experiments. All inventors who find new and better ways of carrying out a process must, to a greater or lesser extent, make use of the Intellectual Part of the Moving Centre. And although the power of invention usually requires the combination of other centres, and must be looked on as comparatively rare, a really skilful worker will constantly find ways to overcome difficulties and *improvise*.

'While the work of the Intellectual Part of the Moving Centre in direct connection with motor acts is not uncommon, its use as an instrument of cognition is really very rare. This, of course, is due to differences in the rate of perception of the Intellectual Centre. We have already discussed the insights which some scientists appear to have into the working of nature. This example of the cognitive use of the Moving Centre, when fully developed, gives man access to a world of which he scarcely dreams, enmeshed as he is in the artificial constructions of the Formatory Apparatus.'

Chapter 7

INSTINCTIVE CENTRE

Having come to the end of the Moving Centre while I was still marvelling at all the new facts I had acquired, I was not quite ready to switch over to the consideration of a separate instinctive 'brain'. One thing I had retained as we went along was that in distinguishing between moving and instinctive functions we could see that the latter are innate and the former acquired, and that in the new-born babe the Moving Centre was in a state that differed very little from that of a foetus, in which all the movements were instinctive.

However, in infants we could already see the presence of a very special aptitude for imitation. And the availability to learn by imitation could be retained long after childhood, though this had been somewhat diminished by the doubtful advantages of western civilization.

So what about myself?

I noticed that in answering questions, Bennett had frequently linked the Moving and Instinctive Centres together and I more or less understood that this was because they had an identical level of consciousness although in action they were essentially different. Trying to find a genuine question was not easy but when I considered observations I had make about other people I knew well I was inevitably reminded of my mother.

On the death of my father and our unfortunate plunge into penury, she had very soon acquired an extraordinarily practical repertoire (most of which was not in keeping with our family background), and this she had achieved by simply watching my elder brother at work on necessary tasks about the house. He in turn, having attended a small public school until about the age of seventeen or eighteen, had fortunately been endowed with a keenness for meticulous woodwork which he liked to practice in a small attic on the second floor of our house (we are speaking, of course of the mid-nineteen twenties, the era of charwomen, 'odd men' with pails and ladders, and afternoon gardeners - all gone from us for ever).

Nevertheless, fate was much kinder to us that it might have seemed at the beginning of that period; for the extraordinary collaboration of my mother and brother prised open unsuspected doors and out of our unused attics a commodious flat was made that nearly doubled my mother's income . . . . .

But even more impressive to me than my mother's extraordinary versatility were her rare short interludes of musical inspiration. Seated on a heavy piano stool, she would lean a little forward over the ivory keyboard, as if listening, and quite suddenly break into a sonata, something very well known by Chopin, Mozart or Schumann (probably revived recently on our elementary wireless set). From time to time, after the opening bars, she would stop dead, and adopting her listening pose say 'No', then making two or three attempts to change the key, start off again. She would never go very far with whatever she attempted but would repeat and improve time and time again, and for me it was spell-binding.

During my father's lifetime we had often enjoyed musical evenings and afterwards she would recount to me that because she had been trained as a singer she 'really couldn't' play the piano. Singing lessons with one master after another had been so very expensive in the 1890's that in the end she was only left with the 'sol-fa'. Well! I who had enjoyed years of music lessons and yet was still very musically backward was so fascinated by my mother's extraordinary performances that I would leave almost anything I was doing to watch her.

Picture me standing more or less in the centre of the drawing room at an angle of forty five degrees to the piano where I could see her hands without obscuring her vision - a gangling girl not quite in her teens, much too tall for her age and outgrowing all her clothes - receiving a wonderful lesson on how to appreciate music . . . . . what was music? Where did it fit in? And could I really appreciate it? . . . . .

It would not be true to say that I was daydreaming in the middle of a Bennett lecture on the Centres, but I certainly recognized the Intellectual Centre joining in to 'discover America'. And my head left the need to battle on with its attractive questioning, and accepted instead a completely new possibility in a genuine effort really to understand the physiology of my instincts.

'An elementary acquaintance with physiology is enough to inspire us with wonder at the power possessed by the body to control and co-ordinate the most complicated chemical and physical processes necessary for the maintenance of life. Every advance in physiological science, so far from destroying the halo of the miraculous which surrounds the phenomena of life, only serves to strengthen the conviction that we are in the presence of a mechanism, which as greatly transcends the construction of the human mind as the most delicate of human mechanisms outstrips the intelligence of an earthworm. The ingenuity of a thousand chemists with all the resources of modern science could not maintain the complicated system of superimposed equilibria present in the blood against the manifold disturbing influences which play on it varying from moment to moment, each of which have secondary, tertiary and even more indirect repercussions upon the remainder.

'Taken separately, many physiological processes are tolerably easy to explain, but when, with our minds, we attempt to grasp as a whole the system of regulating devices, we are driven to the conclusion that without consciousness the mechanism could not possibly operate as harmoniously as it does day and night from birth to death.

'If the working of the other Centres has been grasped, the conclusion is irresistible that these physiological processes are controlled by an analogous mechanism or mind, and it is therefore actually simple to accept the view that we have an Instinctive Centre or instinctive mind which is responsible for the regulation and co-ordination of all physiological processes. An obvious objection to this of course is that we are not conscious of having such a mind and that if it were unconscious it could not perform the very duties on account of which its existence is postulated. This objection is based on   the assumption that consciousness must necessarily take the same form as intellectual awareness, and that there cannot actually be conscious processes of which our Intellectual Centre knows nothing. The difficulty is much the same as that which prevents us from recognizing that we have a separate mind to direct our movements.

'However, the problem of the Instinctive Centre is rather different from that of the Moving Centre by reason of the common ground of awareness which the Instinctive and Intellectual Centres share in respect of external perceptions.

'But consciousness in the Instinctive Centre makes itself known to us in our awareness of internal and external sensations. It is easy to verify that *consciousness* of a sensation is quite different from *thinking* about it. In fact it is as different as the phrase 'Heat is a form of motion' is from the actual touch of a red-hot poker!

'The Instinctive Centre has two sides, positive and negative, corresponding to what is beneficial and what is harmful to the body. It is through this direct sense of good and bad, with reference to the body's needs, that the Instinctive Centre performs its regulative function. Its office also includes the task of watching over external influences, avoiding those which are dangerous and harmful, and seeking to augment those that are beneficial.

'This it does by distinguishing between pleasant and unpleasant sensations. When the Instinctive Centre is working normally, it takes pleasure in tastes, smells, sounds and sights which correspond to conditions favourable to life and it is ill at ease when exposed to sensations which indicate conditions that are dangerous or detrimental to our physical welfare.

'It is important to observe that the discrimination of the Instinctive Centre is quite unlike that of the Emotional Centre. The former distinguishes between what is good or bad for the life of the body, and the latter differentiates between what is more conscious and what is less conscious, and its true nature is to strive towards consciousness even though the body die. Once this distinction is grasped, the absurdity of regarding emotions as a by-product of instinct becomes perfectly obvious.

'The Mechanical Part of the Instinctive Centre is the regulating mechanism for all physiological processes. It is able to deal with all the vicissitudes of daily life, constantly adjusting the various chemical systems required to give man that high degree of independence of his environment which distinguishes him from all other animals. Unlike the mechanical parts of the other Centres, the first part of the Instinctive Centre works in normal healthy people very well indeed, and has relatively few 'habits' which require correction. This is due, no doubt, to the intrinsic character of the Instinctive Centre itself, whereby it strives continually for the body's welfare.

'The Emotional Part of the Instinctive Centre is responsible for regulation of a higher order. It is largely concerned with the external relations of the body, with protection against danger and disease, the reception of sense impressions and their transformation into sensations, and the adjustment of life to the rhythms and processes of nature. The Emotional Part of the Instinctive Centre is, however, far more than a mere transmitting station. It is the primary and the most direct instrument of cognition that we possess. It constructs for us a representation of the external world and incessantly relates our bodies to that world.

'We shall see when we come to study the means whereby man is provided with the energy required for both his lower and higher functions that actually we depend on three kinds of food – the animal and vegetable tissue that we eat, the air that we breathe, and the impressions which we receive through our senses. The Emotional Part of the Instinctive Centre ensures that adequate attention is paid to all these vital needs.

'When necessary it takes control of the whole organism, thrusting aside every vestige of other activity, as when a drowning man struggles for air. When all goes well with the body, there is a sense of inward balance, as of a sensitively poised seismograph ready at every moment to give warning of any impending disturbance. The sense of well-being which accompanies this state is unmistakable and when it is fully established, transition to the third part of the Instinctive Centre can open up new forms of cognition, the very possibility of which we do not suspect.

'Our virtual exclusion from the Intellectual Part of the Instinctive Centre is one of the penalties which modern man has to incur for the benefits of civilization. Many powers which are commonly regarded as supra-normal and either denied as unscientific or attributed to pathological conditions, have their seat in the conscious regions of the Instinctive Centre.

'In reply to a question, Mr. Gurdjieff once said: 'If you were conscious in Instinctive Centre you could talk with animals, even with worms.' This expresses the close connection between Instinctive Centre and Organic Life on the Earth. In Western man, the Will is never exercised in Instinctive Centre, except in quite trivial cases such as temporary acceleration of the rate of breathing, or the overcoming of aversion caused by an unpleasant sensation.

'The true working of Will in the Instinctive Centre is in the Intellectual Part, where the almost miraculous power which the body possesses of cognition and regulation can be exercised consciously. This is the true 'Communion with Nature' of which the poets dream. It has also the power of discerning and curing disease, and for this purpose is able to control sources of energy in the body immensely greater than those usually available to the Centres. These powers, external manifestations of which have often been described, are acquired by means of special exercises, the knowledge of which is confined to hidden schools.   Unfortunately, however, so much charlatanism surrounds these manifestations that it is almost impossible to distinguish between real and false descriptions.   While these powers require special training, they are not in any sense supernatural, nor, taken alone, does their possession necessarily imply a higher level of being.

'Finally, it must be said that the highest parts of all four Centres – the Intellectual, Emotional, Moving and Instinctive are capable of co-ordinated working which can give results entirely beyond any ordinary human understanding – and living as we do almost entirely in the mechanical parts of our Centres we can in fact have no conception of the wealth of effective action which actually are our birthright.'

*   *   *

There was an exceptionally long pause at the end of this lecture, as if we had been given so much material that we now had to be allowed to get it into focus, but eventually a man who sounded like a scientist asked a long and very complicated question about physiology.   And Bennett went back to his original explanation about Will and the 'Communion with Nature', enlarging on what he had said, and being much more abstruse that he had sounded the first time.   Knowing that I should have the opportunity of hearing this lecture again at our small meeting for recapitulation only three days away, instead of listening to Bennett I turned my attention to an intriguing invitation I had only just been given, and endeavoured to understand what kind of opportunity I was now being offered.

In fact it was a very simple proposition - the lectures in London would be continuing on Saturday afternoons but in future we should also be meeting on Sundays for 'Organised Work' at the house where Mr Bennett lived and this would be from eleven in the morning until 5.30 in the afternoon, at first fortnightly and then at weekly intervals. This work was designed to give us suitable opportunities on a fortnightly basis to extend our understanding of attention.

Asking my husband what exactly was meant by Organised Work he thought a little and then said,

"I think the alternative name which I've sometimes heard used probably describes it better - 'Practical Work in suitable conditions'. The idea behind this is that it helps us to learn to do tasks in an environment which is different from every day life so that we can observe ourselves more easily. Mr Ouspensky had a house where people could go for days at a time and Bennett is just beginning to expand in the same way. It will be interesting to see how this develops on a fortnightly basis."

Chapter 8

VALUES

By accident, apparently, after all my recent questions and pondering, and before the lectures on the Centres were finished, I became involved in the preparation of what was to become the first of Bennett's published works - a small book called 'Values' - printed for private circulation. Except for a translation of the 'Katha Upanishads', Bennett contributed only the preface to this volume, stressing that his intention was to bring together both ancient and modern religious texts in Eastern and Western literature in an effort to formulate a common doctrines of values. And to complete the picture he had also included passages from standard works like Plato's 'Republic', and Hume's 'Treatise Of Human Nature', which were now both impossible to procure from wartime bookshops.

Up until the time that I joined the people working on these texts they were mostly passed round in the form of typescript, and I cannot remember now the exact occasion when I suggested that perhaps we could afford, as a co-operative effort, to have them printed. Realising that as I was employed in publishing I might well have strings to pull, and even find a publisher, Bennett was only too glad to turn over to me the practical side of the undertaking. But this was not nearly as easy as it might have been before the war, and all I could do was to produce a good printer with paper to spare, and even that apparently ordinary feat was an achievement. Publishing just then was at a very low ebb. All paper was rationed and it would be a very bold printer or publisher who would be able to handle an anthology, however rare, as a business proposition.

While the plans were going ahead I was only allowed limited access to the typescript, but the short preface by Bennett was very helpful in setting the scene for our study together.

"The sacred literature of all ages and the speculative writings of all philosophers abound in passages which endeavour to express the ultimate values which form the goal of human striving. Some of these passages are well known - the most perfect are to be found in the Gospels - some are hidden away in obscure and ancient texts. In the present compilation no attempt is being made to embrace either the best known or, necessarily, the most valuable attempts to formulate a doctrine of values. A few are included that will be known to all, and some that will be new to the majority of readers. The object has been to give ready access to a few of the more precise and also the more pregnant statements in Eastern and Western literature. Passages from the Bible have been deliberately excluded as belonging to a different order of truth.

"Jalal'u din Rumi is the author from whom the largest number of quotations have been drawn. The 'Mathnavi' must be regarded as the flower of Persian mysticism as showing in some ways a closer insight into the practical tales of self-creation than any other book. Its defects are obvious, but its virtues go far beyond any ordinary understanding . . . . .

"An extract remote from any mystical content has been drawn from Hume, on account of the importance of realising that it is not the Buddhists only who emphasise the difficulties of any doctrine of the existence in man of any self or soul. Until we recognise our present limitations, we can neither formulate our aim nor hope to find our way."

After his preface Bennett mentions by name only a few of the extracts, and it is with a real sense of surprise that we lead off with a John Keats' commentary on 'The Vale Of Soul-Making'.

Trained as a doctor and obtaining his licentiate in July 1819 he had then decided to devote his whole life to poetry. When he died at the age of twenty four, barely five years later, it was said of his odes that they were too well known for description and too perfect for criticism - "standing alone in literature, new in form and spirit, and owing nothing to any predecessor".

'The Vale Of Soulmaking' was actually a letter quoted by R.C.Bradley in an Oxford lecture, "The whole appears to resolve into this - that man is originally a poor forked creature, subject to the same mischances as the beasts of the forest, destined to hardships and disquietude of some kind or other. If he improves by degrees his bodily accommodations and comforts, at each stage, at each ascent, there are waiting for him a fresh set of annoyances - he is mortal, and there is still a heaven with its stars above his head. The most interesting question that can come before us is, how far by the persevering endeavours of a seldom-appearing Socrates mankind may be made happy? I can imagine such happiness carried to an extreme, but what must it end in? Death - and who could in such case bear with death? The whole troubles with life, which are now frittered away in a series of years, would then be accumulated for the last days of a being who, instead of hailing its approach, would leave this world as Eve left Paradise. But in truth I do not at all believe in this sort of perfectibility. The nature of the world will not admit of it - the inhabitants of the world will correspond to itself. Let the fish philosophise the ice away from the rivers in winter-time, they shall be at continual play in the tepid delight of summer. Look at the Poles, and at the sands of Africa - whirlpools and volcanoes. Let man exterminate them, and I will say that they may arrive at earthly happiness. The point at which man may arrive is as far as the parallel state in inanimate nature, and no further. For instance, suppose a rose to have sensation; it blooms one beautiful morning; it enjoys itself; but then comes a cold wind, a hot sun. It cannot escape it, it cannot destroy its annoyances - they are as native to the world as itself. No more can man be happy in spite of the worldly elements which will prey upon his nature.

"The common cognomen of this world among the misguided and superstitious is 'a vale of tears' from which we are to be redeemed by a certain arbitrary interposition of God and taken to Heaven. What a little circumscribed straitened notion! Call the world if you please the Vale of Soul-making. Then you will find out the use of the world (I am now speaking in the highest terms for human nature, admitting it to be immortal, which I will here take for granted for the purpose of showing a thought which has struck me concerning it). I say 'soul-making' - Soul as distinguished from an Intelligence. There may be intelligences or sparks of the divinity in millions, but they are not Souls till they acquire identities, till each one is personally itself. Intelligences are atoms of perception - they know and they see and they are pure; in short, they are God. How then are Souls to be made? How then are these sparks which are God to have identity given them - so as even to possess a bliss peculiar to each one by individual existence?   How but by the medium of a world like this? This point I sincerely wish to consider, because I think it a grander system of salvation than the Christian religion - or rather it is a system of Spirit-creation. This is effected by three grand materials acting thus one upon the other for a series of years. These three materials are the *Intelligence*, the *human heart* (as distinguished from intelligence or mind), and the World or elemental space suited for the proper action of *Mind* and *Heart* on each other for the purpose of forming the *Soul* or *Intelligence destined to possess the sense of Identity*. I can scarcely express what I but dimly perceive - and yet I think I perceive it. That you may judge the more clearly I will put it in the most homely form possible. I will call the world a School instituted for the purpose of teaching little children to read. I will call the *human heart* the horn-book read in that school, and I will call the *Child able to read* the *Soul* made from that School and its horn-book. Do you not see how necessary a world of pains and troubles is to school an Intelligence and make it a Soul? A pace where the heart must feel and suffer in a thousand diverse ways. Not merely is the Heart a horn-book, but it is the Mind's Bible, it is the Mind's experience, it is the text from which the Mind or Intelligence sucks its identity. As various as the lives of men are, so various become their Souls; and thus does God make individual beings, Souls, identical Souls, of the sparks of his own essence. This appears to me a faint sketch of a system of salvation which does not offend our reason and humanity."

* * *

In fact thirty eight excerpts were finally chosen. Side by side with Keats we are offered Islam, the Desert Fathers, a Yoga Sutra, and Plato's tale of the Underground Cave. Bennett's 'Three Vallis' of the 'Katha Upanishad' are long by comparison but they need our attention. We can also read David Hume's 'Personal Identity'. The philosophy of David Hume (1711-76) had been mentioned once or twice in the lectures and very much later on I was fortunate enough to discover him in Bertrand Russell's 'History Of Western Philosophy'. Russell obviously looked upon him as a friend first and a philosopher afterwards - telling us that he was a very young man, not yet in his thirties; and he was not well known, his conclusions being those which almost all schools would find unwelcome. Nevertheless 'he hoped for vehement attacks, which he would meet with brilliant retorts'. But no-one noticed the book; and though he lamented that 'it fell dead born from the press', he also said that as he was 'naturally of a cheerful and sanguine temper, he very soon recovered from the blow'.

In 1744 having failed to obtain a professorship in Edinburgh he became 'at first a tutor to a lunatic and then a secretary to a general', and 'fortified by these credentials, he returned again to philosophy.'

'Personal Identity'[18]

"There are some philosophers who imagine we are every moment intimately conscious of what we call our *self*, that we feel its existence

---

[18] David Hume A Treatise of Human Nature

and its continuance in existence; and are certain, beyond the evidence of a demonstration, both of its perfect identity and simplicity. The strongest sensation, the most violent passion, say they, instead of distracting us from this view, only fix it the more intensely, and make us consider their influence on *self* either by their pain or pleasure. To attempt a further proof of this were to weaken its evidence; since no proof can be derived, from any fact of which we are so intimately conscious; nor is there any thing, of which we can be certain, if we doubt of this.

"Unluckily all these positive assertions are contrary to that very experience which is pleaded for them; nor have we any idea of *self*, after the manner it is here explained. For, from what impression could this idea be derived? This question it is impossible to answer without a manifest contradiction and absurdity; and yet it is a question which must necessarily be answered, if we would have the idea of self pass for clear and intelligible. It must be some one impression that gives rise to every real ideal. But self or person is not any one impression, but that to which our several impressions and ideas are supposed to have a reference. If any impression gives rise to the idea of self, that impression must continue invariably the same, throughout the whole course of our lives; since self is supposed to exist after that manner. But there is no impression constant and invariable. Pain and pleasure, grief and joy, passions and sensations succeed each other, and never all exist at the same time. It cannot therefore be from any of these impressions, or from any other, that the idea of self is derived; and consequently there is no such idea.

"But further, what must become of all our particular perceptions upon this hypothesis? All these are different, and distinguishable, and separable from each other, and may be separately considered, and may exist separately, and have no need of anything to support their existence. After what manner, therefore, do they belong to self, and how are they connected with it? For my part, when I enter most intimately into what I call *myself*, I always stumble on some particular perception or other, of heat or cold, light or shade, love or hatred, pain or pleasure.

I never can catch *myself* at any time without a perception, and never can observe anything but the perception. When my perceptions are removed for any time, as by sound sleep, so long am I insensible to *myself*, and may truly be said not to exist. And were all my perceptions removed by death, and could I neither think, nor feel, nor see, nor love, nor hate, after the dissolution of my body, I should be entirely annihilated, nor do I conceive what is further requisite to make me a perfect nonentity. If any one, upon serious and unprejudiced reflection, thinks he had a different notion of *himself*, I must confess I can reason no longer with him. All I can allow him is, that he may be in the right as well as I, and that we are essentially different in this particular. He may, perhaps, perceive something simple and continued, which he calls *himself*; though I am certain there is no such principle in me.

"But setting aside some metaphysicians of this kind, I may venture to affirm of the rest of mankind, that they are nothing but a bundle or collection of different perceptions, which succeed each other with an inconceivable rapidity, and are in a perpetual flux and movement. Our eyes cannot turn in their sockets without varying our perceptions. Our thought is still more variable that our sight; and all our other senses and faculties contribute to this change; nor is there any single power of the soul, which remains unalterably the same, perhaps for one moment. The mind is a kind of theatre, where several perceptions successively make their appearance; pass, re-pass, glide away, and mingle in an infinite variety of posture and situations. There is properly no *simplicity* in it at one time, nor *identity* in difference, whatever natural propension we may have to imagine that simplicity and identity. The comparison of the theatre must not mislead us. They are successive perceptions only, that constitute the mind; nor have we the most distant notion of the place where these scenes are represented, or of the materials of which it is composed.

"What, then, gives us so great a propension to ascribe an identity to these successive perceptions, and to suppose ourselves possessed of an invariable and uninterrupted existence through the whole course of our lives? In order to answer this question we must distinguish between personal identity, as it regards our thought and imagination, and as it regards our passions or the concern we take in ourselves. The first is our present subject; and to explain it perfectly we must take the matter pretty deep, and account for that identity, which we attribute to plants and animals; there being a great analogy betwixt it and the identity of self or person.

"We have a distinct idea of an object that remains invariable and uninterrupted through a supposed variation of time; and this idea we call that of *identity* or sameness. We also have a distinct idea of several different objects existing in succession, and connected together by a close relation; and this to an accurate view affords as perfect a notion of *diversity* as if there was no manner of relation among the objects. But though these two ideas of identity, and a succession of related objects, be in themselves perfectly distinct, and even contrary, yet it is certain that, in our common way of thinking, they are generally confounded with each other.

"That action of the imagination, by which we consider the uninterrupted and invariable object, and that by which we reflect on the succession of related objects, are almost the same to the feelings; nor is there much more effort of thought required in the latter case than in the former. The relation facilitates the transition of the mind from one object to another, and renders its passage as smooth as if it contemplated one continued object. This resemblance is the cause of the confusion and mistake, and makes us substitute the notion of identity, instead of that of related objects.

"However, at one instant we may consider the related succession as variable or interrupted, we are sure the next to ascribe to it a perfect identity, and regard it as invariable and uninterrupted. Our propensity to this mistake is so great from the resemblance above mentioned, that we fall into it before we are aware; and though we incessantly correct ourselves by reflection, and return to a more accurate method of thinking, yet we cannot long sustain our philosophy, or take off this bias from the imagination.

"Our last resource is to yield to it, and boldly assert that these different related objects are in effect the same, however interrupted and variable. In order to justify to ourselves this absurdity, we often feign some new and unintelligible principle, that connects the objects together, and prevents their interruption or variation. Thus we feign continued existence of the perceptions of our senses, to remove the interruption; and run into the notion of a *soul* or *self*, and *substance*, to disguise the variation. But, we may further observe, that where we do not give rise to such a fiction, our propension to confound identity with relation is so great, that we are apt to imagine something unknown and mysterious, connecting these parts, beside their relation; and this I take to be the case with regard to the identity we ascribe to plants and vegetables. And even when this does not take place, we still feel a propensity to confound these ideas, though we are not able to fully satisfy ourselves in that particular, nor find anything invariable and interrupted to justify our notion of identity."

It was an introduction to Rumi through 'Moses & The Shepherd' that brought about my change of attitude to Islam. This was simple enough after all, but was a big thing, and opened the flood gates. The Shepherd can speak for me better than I can,

'The Story Of Moses & The Shepherd

Moses saw a shepherd on the way, who was saying, 'O God who choosest whom Thou will,
'Where art Thou, that I may become servant and sew Thy shoes and comb Thy head?
'That I may wash Thy clothes and kill Thy lice and bring milk to Thee, O worshipful One;
'That I may kiss Thy little head and rub Thy little foot, and when bedtime comes I may sweep Thy little room,
'O Thou to whom all my goats be a sacrifice, O Thou in remembrance of whom are my cries of ay and ah!'

The shepherd was speaking foolish words in this wise.
Moses said, 'Man, to whom is this addressed?'

He answered, 'To the One who created us; by whom this earth and sky were brought to sight.'

'Hark!' said Moses, 'you have become very backsliding - indeed you have not become a Moslem, you have become an infidel.

'What babble is this? What blasphemy and raving? Stuff some cotton in your mouth!

'The stench of your blasphemy has turned the silk robe of religion into rags.

'Shoes and socks are fitting for you, but how are such things right for One who is a Sun?

'If you do not stop your throat from uttering these words, a fire will come and burn up the people.

'If a fire has not come, then what is this smoke? Why had your soul become black and your spirit reflected by God?

'If you know that God is the Judge, how is it right for you to indulge in this doting talk and familiarity?

'Truly, the friendship of a witless man in enmity: the high God is not in want of suchlike service.

'To whom are you saying this? To your paternal and maternal uncles? 'Are the body and its needs among the attributes of the Lord of glory?

'Only he that is waxing and growing drinks milk; in relation to the holiness of God they are pollution.

'The world He begat not, He was not begotten, are appropriate to him: He is the Creator of begetter and begotten.

'Birth is the attribute of everything that is a body: whatever is born on this side of the river.

'Because it is of the world of becoming and decay and is contemptible: it is originated and certainly requires an Originator.'

The Shepherd said, 'O Moses, thou hast closed my mouth and thou hast burned my soul with repentance.'
He rent his garment and heaved a sigh, and hastily turned his head towards the desert and went his way.

"How The High God Rebuked Moses, On Whom Be Peace, On Account Of The Shepherd.

A revelation came to Moses from God - 'Thou has parted My servant from Me.
'Didst thou come as a prophet to unite, or didst thou come to sever?
'So far as thou canst, do not set foot in separation: of all things the most hateful to Me is divorce.
'I have bestowed on every one a special way of acting: I have given to every one a peculiar form of expression.
'In regard to him it is worth of praise, and in regard to thee it is worthy of blame: in regard to him honey, and in regard to thee poison.
'I am independent of all purity and impurity, of all slothfulness and alacrity in worshipping Me.
'I did not ordain Divine worship that I might make any profit; nay, but that I might do a kindness to My servants.
'In the Hindoos the idiom of Hind is praiseworthy; in the Sindians the idiom of Sind is praiseworthy.
'I am not sanctified by their glorification of Me; 'tis they that become sanctified and pearl-scattering, pure and radiant.
'I look not at the tongue and speech; I look at the inward spirit and the state of feeling.
'I gaze into the heart to see whether it be lowly, though the words uttered be not lowly.
'Because the heart is the substance, speech only the accident; so accident is subservient, the substance is the real object.

'How much more of these phrases and conceptions and metaphors? I want burning, burning: become friendly with that burning!

'Light up a fire of love in thy soul, burn thought and expression entirely away!

'O Moses, they that know the conventions are of one sort, they whose souls and spirits burn are of another sort.

'To lovers there is a burning which consumes them at every moment: tax and tithe are not imposed on a ruined village.

'If he the lover speak faultily, do not call him faulty; and if he be bathed in blood, do not wash those who are martyrs.

'For martyrs, blood is better than water: this fault committed by him is better than an hundred right actions of another.

'Within the Ka'ba the rule of the qibla does not exist: what matter if the diver has no snow-shoes?

'Do not seek guidance from the drunken: why dost thou order those whose garments are rent in pieces to mend them?

'The religion of Love is apart from all religions: for lover the only religion and creed is - God.

'If the ruby have not a seal graven on it, 'tis no harm: Love in the sea of sorrows is not sorrowful.'

"How The Divine Revelation Came To Moses, On Whom Be Peace, Excusing That Shepherd.

After that God hid in the inmost heart of Moses, mysteries which cannot be spoken.

Words were poured upon his heart: vision and speech were mingled together.

How oft did he become beside himself and how oft return to himself! How oft did he fly from eternity to everlastingness!

If I should unfold his tale after this, 'tis foolishness in me because the explanation of this is beyond our understanding;

And if I should speak thereof, 'twould root up men's minds; and if I should write thereof, 'twould shatter many pens.

When Moses heard these reproaches from God, he ran into the desert in quest of the shepherd.

He pushed on over the footprints of the bewildered man, he scattered dust from the skirt of the desert.

The footstep of a man distraught is, in truth, distance from the footsteps of others:

At one step, he moves like the rook straight from top to bottom of the chessboard; at one step he goes crossways, like the bishop;

Now lifting his crest like a wave; now going on his belly like a fish;

Now writing a description of his state on some dust, like a geomancer who takes an omen by drawing lines on earth or sand.

At last Moses overtook and beheld him; the giver of glad news said, 'Permission has come from God.

'Do not seek any rules or method of worship; say whatsoever your distressful heart desires.

'Your blasphemy is the true religion, and your religion is the light of the spirit: you are saved, and through you a whole world is in salvation.

'O you who are made secure by 'God doeth whatsoever He willeth', go loose your tongue without regard for what you say.'

He said, 'O Moses, I have passed beyond that: I am now bathed in my heart's blood.

'I have passed beyond the Lot-tree of the farthest bourn, I have gone a hundred thousand year journey on the other side.

'Thou didst ply the lash, and my horse shied, made a bound, and passed beyond the sky.

'May the divine nature be intimate with my human nature - blessings be on thy hand and on thine are!

'Now my state is beyond telling: this which I am telling is not my real state.'

You behold the image which is in a mirror: it is your own image, it is not the image of the mirror.

The breath which the flute-player puts into the flute - does it belong to the flute? No, it belongs to the man.

Take good heed! Whether you speak praise of God or thanksgiving, know that it is even as the unseemly words of that shepherd.

Though your praise is better in comparison with that, yet in relation to God it too is maimed and feeble.

How often will you say, when the lid has been raised, 'This was not what I expected.' "

And it was in this frame of mind that I could turn to the long conversation of the boy Nachiketas in the 'Katha Upanishad'. I found the poetry of Bennett's translation exceptionally moving, or perhaps I was simply ready for it. I didn't analyse, but read like a person released from a spell. Deep feelings that I barely touched in the most significant experiences of my everyday life moved in me, and the simplicity that I tasted when I first handled the typescript unobtrusively deepened.

"Vajashravas, moved by desire for heaven, gave away all his possessions. Now he had a son whose name was Nachiketas.

As the gifts were being led away, though but a boy, faith entered into him and he thought:

'Wretched indeed must be the place to which that man goes who sacrifices naught save cows which will no more eat grass nor drink water, no more give milk nor bear calves.'

So he said to his father, 'To whom will thou give me?'. Twice he asked and thrice his father said, 'To Death do I give thee'.

Nachiketas thought within himself, 'I go to what for many is the first state. I go to what for many is the middle state. What, I wonder, does Death need done, that he will do with me to-day.

'Look back into the past, as it was with men then, so will it be in the future. Like corn a mortal ripens, like corn he is born again!'

Nachiketas went into the house of Death. It is like fire when a Brahmin visits a house, 'Bring water, O Death'.

'Hope and expectations, friendship and joy, sacrifices and works, sons, cattle, all are lost to him in whose house a Brahmin remains unfed.'

Therefore when Death returned, he said, 'Brahmin, thou hast passed three nights in my house unfed, a guest to whom reverence was due. Homage therefore, to thee, oh Brahmin, and for the sake of my welfare, I offer thee the choice of three gifts'.

Nachiketas said: 'As first gift of the three, O Death, I choose that thou shouldst restore me to my father, that with grief allayed and danger gone he may recognize and welcome me'.

Death answered, 'I will indeed restore thee and thy father shall know thee and be as he was before. Tranquil shall he sleep at night, his anger gone, when he sees thee delivered from the jaws of Death'.

Then Nachiketas continued: 'In that place of light there is no fear whatever. Thou, Death, are not there, nor is there a growing old. Passing beyond hunger and thirst, passing beyond sorrow, a man rejoices in that place of light.

'The fire that lead to that state thou knowest, O Death! By him who enter that place of light immortality is gained. 'Tis this I choose as second of my gifts.'

Death answered, 'To thee I will declare it. Learn from me. To understand the heavenly fire, Nachiketas, thou must know that the way to the infinite world and its foundations is hidden in the secret place of the heart'.

He told him of that fire, source of the world, what bricks are needed, how many and how best arranged. Nachiketas in his turn repeated it exactly and Death, delighted, spoke yet once again.

Well disposed, thus spoke the Great One: 'I give thee here to-day another boon. By thy name shall this fire be called. Take thou this way endowed with many forms.

'Having three times kindled the threefold Nachiketas fire, having known the Three, and accomplished the Threefold work man passes beyond birth and death. Knowing that beloved God who is born of Brahma and cleaving to him, he attains everlasting peace.

'Having established the threefold fire and having known this Three, he who thus knowing, constantly tends the fire, passes beyond sorrow and rejoices in the Heavenly place.

'This, Nachiketas, is the life which leads to the place of bliss which thou hast chosen for they second gift. By thy name henceforth shall this fire be called. Choose now, O Nachiketas, thy third gift.'

Nachiketas replied: 'This doubt there is about a man departed. Some say, 'He is!' and some say 'He is not!'. This would I know, and fain would have thee teach me. Of the three gifts this shall be the third'.

Death said, 'Even the Great Ones of old were harassed with doubt as to this, for the truth it is subtle and very hard to know. Choose then another gift, oh Nachiketas. Do not entreat me, give up this demand'.

Then Nachiketas, 'True it is that even the Great Ones of old were filled with doubt about this, which even thou, O Death, declarest hard to know. No other teacher of this knowledge can be found like thee, nor is there any other gift equal to this'.

Death said, 'Choose sons and grandsons who shall live a hundred years, rich herds of cattle, elephants, gold and horses. Choose far flung dominion on the earth, O Nachiketas, be thou king; of they desires I make thee free enjoyer.

'Whatever desires in mortal world are hard to gain - choose what thou wilst. Damsels most fair with chariots and lutes, such as men cannot win, will I bestow and they shall wait on thee. Only, O Nachiketas, seek not to know the secret of death.'

Nachiketas said, 'Ephemeral things, O Death! They wear away whatever force and power a man may have. all life, moreover, at the best is brief. Keep thou the chariots, keep the dance and song.

'Never with wealth can man be satisfied. What wealth can help us when we see thy face? Do we live, O Death, so long as thou dost reign? That gift then must I choose and that alone.

'What ageing mortal here below, that understands the agelessness of immortality, can prize the joys of beauty and of love, can find delight in length of days?

'Tell me this thing whereon they doubt, O Death. Reveal to me the secret of our passing. This gift which penetrates the mystery; none but this will Nachiketas choose.'

Death answered, 'The best is one thing - the most pleasant is another: both draw man on to action, but to different ends. Choosing the best, he gains the highest; grasping the pleasant, he gains not even that.

'The good and the pleasant present themselves to man; comparing the two, the resolute man discriminates; he chooses the good and not the pleasant. The fool chooses the pleasant and dreams he can keep it . . .'

Know the Self as master of the chariot - the body the chariot alone. Know mind as chariot driver and thoughts as bridles and reins.

Feelings and sensations are called the horses. The external world is called the road. When the Self controls thoughts and feelings, then wise men say 'He is the master.'

He who is unawakened, who does not restrain his thoughts, has feelings uncontrolled, like vicious horses of a charioteer.

He who is awakened and restrains his thoughts, controls his feelings, like good horses of a charioteer.

He who is unawakened, ever careless and without ardour, never reaches the goal and returns again and again to the wheel of existence.

He who is awakened, ever attentive and aflame, attains that state from whence he is not born again.

He whose mind awakened is the charioteer, whose thoughts are well reined, reaches the end of the journey, the highest Vishnu state.

Higher than sensations and feelings are intentions, higher than intentions are thoughts, higher than thoughts is mind, higher than mind is the Great Self.

Higher than the Great Self is the Unmanifested, higher than the Unmanifested, the One. Than the one there is nothing higher, that is the end, that is the final goal.

That Self is not manifest, which is hidden in all beings. Yet he is seen by the Highest Awakened Ones, with subtle, piercing vision.

The wise man should bring his speech and thoughts under control. They should obey the knowing self. The knowing self should obey the Great Self and the Great Self should obey the Self of Peace.

Arise! Awake! Receive your gifts, and understand! Narrow as a razor's edge the path and hard to follow: those who have known it well declare.

That soundless, touchless, formless One, unknowable through the senses, unchanging, eternal, endless, without beginning, abiding beyond the Infinite - he who has known that One is freed forever from the jaws of death.

Those wise men who learn and teach to others this Nachiketas story - Death's immemorial teaching - grow great and increase within the Brahman world.

Whosoever shall recite this highest mystery, when Brahmins meet in session, or at the holy funeral rites prepareth for eternity. He prepareth for eternity indeed."

* * *

It didn't occur to me at first that my putting together of 'Values' was actually the 'Organised Work' I had been asking about, and when it was over I worked in the garden or in the kitchen. The house where Mr & Mrs Bennett now lived - called Coombe Springs - was a decayed Edwardian mansion with excellent opportunities for 'Practical Work in suitable conditions'. And at the weekends we had access to the garden of several acres which provided work for us all. On weekdays it was the headquarters of a scientific organisation, the British Coal Utilisation Research Association, which Bennett had started before the war (and was where my husband worked as a scientific officer). This association had recently moved out of London so that new laboratories could be built in a safe area away from the increasing number of air raids.

For lunch we sat in a large room known as the Library and when we had finished eating, after a brief question time, the tables and chairs were cleared away to make room for a practice of Mr Gurdjieff's 'Movements'. Very little was explained to me and since I had never heard of the Movements before I didn't know what to do, so I decided that for the time being I would stand at the back and imitate the people in front of me. And when Bennett came to take the class he explained very briefly that these Movements were known as Rhythmic Exercises, and one of the objectives of doing them was to improve our overall consciousness by helping us to give attention to our bodies.

He then gave a short description of the First Obligatories, which were the simplest Movements of all.

Chapter 9

SEX CENTRE

Bennett gave a short preamble to the Sex Centre. Like the Centres we had already discussed it was 'ceaselessly at work' in our everyday life, but its construction and typical level of consciousness was different from theirs:

'The four Centres studied in the last lecture all have a similar construction in that they are divided into positive and negative parts and comprise three distinct levels of experience which we have called mechanical, emotional, and intellectual. These four Centres constitute the entire mechanism of our daily life and, with one important exception, embrace the whole of usual human experience. This important exception consists in our relations with other people in so far as these transcend our own personal interest and desires, or our self-centred thoughts and feelings.

'The Sex Centre occupies an intermediate position, differentiating from the lower Centres by the fact that it had no independent organ of perception and response in the way that the brain is the organ of the Intellectual Centre and the musculature that of the Moving Centre. And since its impulses are transmitted through the other Centres it can not be understood through our usual processes of ratiocination.

'Art and Religion both teach us that our truest and most permanent values are not those which are centred in ourselves, but those which reach out to our fellow men and upward to whatever vision we may have of the beautiful, the true and the good. Love has always been accepted as one of the highest - sometimes the very highest - of human functions. And yet everyone must feel a profound disappointment and sadness when they survey the manifestations of this function in themselves and their fellow men. Who has not turned his critical gaze upon his own thoughts and feelings and admitted with shame the predominance, if not the monopoly, held by self-centred motives? As we search for sincerity, our best and apparently most disinterested actions seem to turn before our very eyes into expressions of vanity, self-indulgence or even mere habit. 'My only motive' cries Rousseau, 'is desire for my own happiness'. The Utilitarians of the nineteenth century erected the doctrine of selfishness into a system and attempted to base all social and religious values on the principle of 'the greatest good of the greatest number'.

'The inherent absurdity of crude utilitarianism was exposed by Bradley in his 'Ethical Studies' and only more discreet forms survive today; and yet neither Bradley nor the whole succession of philosophers from Plato to Hegel, who tried to demonstrate some absolute principle of self-transcendence, could remove the terrible fact of introspection, for when we look into ourselves, we cannot find any driving power save desire for our own good and our own happiness. From such introspection there tends to arise an attitude of pure pessimism when we say with Bradley 'Where all is rotten, it is a man's business to cry 'stinking fish'. But even in the midst of this self-castigation we feel something that is false, and as we remind ourselves of the self-sacrifice of a mother or the devotion of a saint, we say to ourselves again, 'Away with all this despisery. Love and unselfishness are real, even if we cannot catch specimens to stick on a pin'.

'The key to this riddle is to be found in the doctrine of the seven Centres. In the four lower Centres, there is no love, and their motives are purely selfish, even at their highest level. The Sex Centre and the two Higher Centres are very different, for their motives are so far beyond our own limited individuality, and they work so differently and so much faster than the Intellectual Mind that their processes elude us altogether. Though the Higher Centres do not affect our behaviour except on the rarest and most extraordinary occasions, the Sex Centre is fully active in normal man and without it we should be sorry creatures indeed.

'The four lower Centres can only give us knowledge of ourselves, and it is through the Sex Centre and the Higher Centres that we can participate directly in the experience of others as well as having direct communication with other worlds. As with perceptions, so also with motives, for these are similarly distinguished between those originating in ourselves and those which have their mainspring outside us. This does not mean, of course, that our Intellectual Centre is unable to conceive good reasons for unselfish action, or that our Emotional Centre is incapable of a movement of genuine sympathy and approval. It does mean, however, that all our thoughts and emotions, sensations and movements start from us, are centred in ourselves, and cannot be separated from ourselves. 'I think this person is good. I like him. I want to be good to him'. Any such process is without defence against the accusation 'Yes but you want it - it makes you happy. You are only doing it for your own sake'.

'Let us now interrogate someone who has just performed some unpremeditated, obviously unselfish action, for example, a mother who has sacrificed pleasure or comfort for the sake of her child. She will probably answer 'I don't know why I did it. I simply acted without so much as thinking of any alternative'. Therein lies the secret. The Sex Centre working far faster than the Intellectual Centre, felt the child's need and set the whole machine in motion to satisfy that need long before the Intellectual Centre could ask why or how.

'At this point, we evidently must face the objection that this description could just as well apply to the Instinctive Centre and that it is unusual to class the 'maternal instincts' among the natural instincts common to us and to the animals. This would further imply that there is no essential difference between the instinct of self-preservation and the instinct of maternity. To meet this objection fully, we shall have to examine the cognitive powers of the Sex Centre, when we shall see that they are different, in their very essence, from the cognitions of the Instinctive Centre. Even without the conclusive evidence derived from this examination, we should recognise that there is a radical distinction between the self-centred processes whereby the Instinctive Centre works for the welfare of our bodily organism and the self-transcending impulses which can lead to actions which imperil the body's very existence. Careful thought will show how impossible it is to explain, as two functions of one and the same mind, the impulse to flee from the danger of fire and the impulse to plunge into the flames to save a child.

'We are now almost ready to attempt a description of the Sex Centre and its functions, but before doing so, we have to sound the now familiar warning that our observational data is rendered unreliable in us by the presence of negative emotions which quite obscure the working of the Sex Centre. Indeed, the study of the Sex Centre is peculiarly difficult, for it is an organ of cognition and motivation but not of action. The Sex Centre, as we have already noted, does not control any of the bodily mechanisms. Its impulses are transmitted through the other Centres. This means that we can actually only observe the indirect operation of the Sex Centre, and we are therefore obliged to content ourselves with a very general description of the Centre and its functions.

'In the first place, the Sex Centre, like the Higher Centres, is not divided into positive and negative sides. It is exempt from 'yes' and 'no', like and dislike, pleasure and pain. Its cognitions are direct like those of the Emotional Centre, but they are free from any element of judgement. The Emotional Centre judges all its cognitions, likes or dislikes, approves or disapproves them. The Sex Centre knows by direct participation. The same applies to its motives. It has no attraction or aversion, but simply one single movement outwards from ourselves. We are so accustomed to dualistic processes that we find it hard to grasp the simplicity of the Sex Centre. This difficulty will become still greater when we come to the Higher Centres, and our understanding of them will be much easier if we can observe how the Sex Centre works in this respect. Reverting to the example of the mother who sacrifices herself for her child, we can see that in this action there is no distinction of desire and aversion, but simply a positive impulse which sets all the other Centres in motion.

'The denial of any division of the Sex Centre may seem to contradict the most typical manifestation of the sex function, namely, the marital relation, in which there seems to be acceptance of one mate and rejection of others. The high selectivity of sexual attraction is not based on any dualistic process such as like and dislike. Sexual choice if it occurs at all is essentially affirmative. Owing to the power of the Sex Centre and the high order of the energy with which it works, it often seems to require the complete exclusion of all other interests and affections. We must, however, separate the unifying influence which the Sex Centre can exercise over the other functions, and the 'singleness of heart' which it produces, from any suggestion of exclusion or negation. The poets have always recognised that the successful choice of a mate is accompanied in normal men and women by an enhanced sympathy towards the whole world. If there ever appears to be any dualism in the sex function, this can always be traced, by careful observation, to other Centres, which act as agents for its external manifestations.

'Now we must try and examine the nature of the Sex Centre's cognitions. We shall soon see that they are far more important, and play a far greater part in our lives than we suppose. The problem can be formulated thus: 'Since we can only know what is presented to our consciousness, how can we be sure that any centre of consciousness exists except our own'. Intellectually we cannot be sure. Emotionally we do not care, for we take it for granted. But through our Sex Centre, we do know. Everyone who has studied philosophical discussions on this subject is bound to have stopped and said to himself 'This, no doubt, is all very fine, but I do know. I really have no more doubt about A or B's consciousness than about my own'. This is right, because the Sex Centre actually has the power to go outside our own consciousness, and apprehend that of others. We fail to see the steps through which we pass, because the time scale of the Sex Centre is so different from that of our Thinking Centre. Nevertheless the result is not open to question. We do know other minds. We could know them much better and more distinctly if we were not so enslaved by the Formatory Apparatus and could free ourselves from the tendency to regard it as the centre of our being.

'Direct observation of the work of the Sex Centre is possible in those rare moments when we know that a direct communication has been established with another person, quite different from ordinary exchanges. It is possible in one glance to reach a degree of mutual understanding which beggars description. Such experiences establish clearly for us both the speed of the Sex Centre and its power of projecting our consciousness out of ourselves.

'Of the power of the Sex Centre, it is unnecessary to speak. Neither intellectual difficulties, emotional judgments, physical pain, nor bodily fatigue can withstand the impulses of the Sex Centre. It commands energy to which none of the lower Centres has access, but we cannot follow its processes or hear its voice unless our consciousness is actually awakened within it. This accounts on the one hand for the 'unconscious acts of unselfishness' to which we have already referred, and on the other, for the low degree of mutual understanding which exists between people generally.

'The differences between the sexes, and their role in the life of humanity, and of organic life generally, fall outside the scope of the present lecture. We shall return to them when we pass from the study of individual man to that of mankind and its inner structure.

'Having seen the crucial importance in the life of man of the Sex Centre with its power of transferring our consciousness beyond the limitations of our own bodies, and its even greater significance as the source of unselfish motives, we are now bound to ask ourselves why the manifestations of sex have been so harshly treated in most religious systems, and why in fact they accord so seldom with the lofty status we have ascribed to them. Although the Sex Centre has no negative part, its manifestations can be poisoned by Imagination and Identification. These do not touch the Centre directly, but they intercept the impulses which come from it and turn them, as they reach the Intellectual, Emotional and even the Instinctive and Moving Centres, into negative and sometimes even horrible caricatures. It is this denaturing of the Sex Centre, which is to be condemned by both religion and practical psychology, not its true and natural work. At every step, our study of human nature has shown us how deep and wide is the gulf which separates what we are from what we might be. The four lower Centres contain latent possibilities beside which our usual life is mere beggary. But all the wealth hidden in the lower Centres is trifling compared with the treasures which we lose through the enslavement of the Sex Centre.

'We are captives in the most wretched of prisons: our own egoism. But having studied both the nature of the egoistic illusion and also the true character of our ordinary functions and their multiplicity we can understand that in the Sex Centre we have seen the first of the three gates through which we can escape into a freer and richer world. We already know that we can only reach and make our abode in the two Higher Centres through long preparation and after deep-seated changes in our very being, but in the Sex Centre we possess a fully developed and operative means of liberation from some of the chains that bind us. Life hemmed in by perceptions and motives centred in our own petty selves is narrow and futile. The clamour of these selves drowns the voices of the Higher Centres. One of these voices, if we but choose to hear it, speaks within us but from our fellow men.

'There is a Sufi story of a man who knocked at a friend's door and in reply to his question, 'Who comes?' answered 'It is I,' 'Begone' said the friend 'this is no place for the raw'. For a year he wandered sorrowful, burned in the fire of separation, until love drove him back to the friend's door. This time in answer to 'Who comes?' he replied 'Thou, thou only, there is no other', 'Now' said the friend 'since thou art I, come in. For myself, there is not room in this house for two I's'.'

I was not the only questioner who seemed rather unsatisfied at the lack of explanations about the everyday processes of wooing, mating and procreation. It had been noticeable that in the whole series up to now, Bennett had always sidestepped questions about love and responsibility, responsibility and sacrifice, religion and relationships and so on, even when the questioner explained that he supposed this was connected with 'different parts of Centres' and different levels of understanding that could be brought to this whole subject.

But recognising my need for more information and trying to be honest about what I could and could not grasp did not do very much to remove my disappointment. However, after another long pause, and after looking round in a questioning way, Bennett had a little more to offer - whereas full-scale lectures on both the Higher Emotional and the Higher Intellectual Centres had originally been planned for our next two meetings, he now felt that it would probably be more profitable if we deferred these until later and transferred our attention to the implications inherent in the existence of a scale of consciousness which we now needed to take into consideration.

Chapter 10

SELF REMEMBERING

The golden autumn lingered a long time before being swallowed up by the darkness and uncertainty of our third wartime winter. Although the acute raids of the summer had suddenly diminished, the intensification of the Atlantic blockade and the vicious war at sea were now arousing painful speculations. Each lull in the bombing made us question afresh; it was still unthinkable that we could ever find ourselves in the position of a Hitlerite state. With the change of season we remembered too acutely the nightly fires over London when even the sky glowed red, a giant torch which could be seen far away in the Surrey hills, and could not easily be extinguished. My brother, before he went into the Air Force, had helped to fight these fires. But little could be done about the high explosive raids which followed and claimed hundreds of lives night after night.

By now, most of us who continued to live and work in London had gone beyond the first pains of fearing death for ourselves. Often without water, light or gas for days on end and, during the summer, disorganised by tight rationing and the actual disappearance of our necessary food shops, it was as if we barely noticed our own inconvenience and egoistic preoccupations. An oft-repeated experience in respectable South Kensington was the practical necessity of carefully stepping over pile upon pile of jagged window glass on our way to the morning bus, raising our eyes involuntarily to the latest evidence of another direct hit of the night before. Whose death, last night, was there? High above, on the top of a substantial looking terrace house a cavernous hole displayed dangling clothing, underwear, an evening dress, or a doll suspended by one arm against a backdrop of crooked pictures, a bed-head, a fireplace and a slowly swinging door.

And what of the deaths which would be brought about by our own bombers going east in the same night?

This double pain must at all times be kept well hidden. As the desperate need to win was linked inevitably with the need to defeat our enemy by killing and reducing him to an abject stance, a good deal of emotional juggling came into play. Nor could this essentially uncomfortable flight of the imagination be practised once and for all. There were constant flashbacks. 'Prophecy prophecy, who smote thee?' cried the soldiers, over and over again fulfilling their ancient role, recalling this antique theme many times. And when the tide of the war little by little changed and it was our own bombers that rolled across the late afternoon sky, a new poignancy lit up my own quest for freedom and for truth.

When Bennett had introduced the idea of Consciousness in the first lecture he had explained that before we could proceed with the acquisition of full self-knowledge it was important for us to observe for ourselves the most simple activity of our different brains. Consciousness always denoted awareness of a function. One could be conscious of thinking, conscious of feeling or conscious of moving. It was not difficult to see that this consciousness was variable.

For the purpose of our studies we must now bear in mind that someone we would regard as a fully developed man would actually possess four recognisable states of consciousness,

'But man as we know him, whom we shall now be describing as 'sleeping man' is only aware of two clearly defined states. The passive state of sleep in bed at night, in which at least a third, or maybe even half his life is passed, and the so-called active 'waking state' of the daytime which although generally regarded as clear consciousness is actually nothing of the kind, but simply another state of sleep. For an ordinary man everything 'happens'. He cannot stop his thoughts; he cannot control anything in his subjective world, although to him it does appear to be made up of what he believes he wants and what he feels he does not want. He does not see real events.

'In fact it is necessary to understand more about these first two levels of consciousness before we can consider in detail the entire scale, including the third and fourth states to which we can aspire but which we will only describe briefly now as the *self* consciousness which is connected with *self- remembering*, and the state of objective consciousness in which we can truly see things as they are.

'The first state of night-time sleep is of course entirely subjective. In this state, although we may not remember them, a man is occupied with dreams. When he wakes up his first impression is that this is entirely different. He can talk, make complicated plans, go to work, travel round the world, think ahead and so on. But if we take a longer look at his actual level of consciousness, where lie the hidden causes of his actions and thoughts, we can see that he is living in much the same world as when he was in bed at night. In fact as we have seen his new state is not as dependable as it appears and it is by no means a state of 'clear consciousness'. He cannot control his daydreams, he cannot control his feelings or his thoughts. And because he does not remember himself at the very moment of outward action or inner reflection, the real world, observed by his own imagination, is hidden from him, and the two further states of self consciousness and objective consciousness which should be available to every normal man and woman mean nothing to him at all.

'In fact it is customary to suppose that we do all enjoy the third state of consciousness daily, or at least can have it at will, but actually we cannot create it by our own desire or decision. And this fact can be easily established by various experiments set up artificially to give us a brief but unmistakable taste of remembering ourselves. The fourth state, which is called the objective state of consciousness, and has been described in the literature of all major religions, we shall leave aside for the time being.'

It so happened that on the day when the idea of a possible scale of consciousness was presented to us I was in a peculiarly emotional frame of mind.

It had been suggested, in quite simple terms, that when we tried to observe ourselves we should also 'remember ourselves', for this lack of self remembering lay at the root of our problem. While engaged in any activity, whether large or small, we were simply not conscious of ourselves at the time. Something that could most appropriately be labelled 'it', thought or observed, spoke or laughed. There was no feeling of 'I' at all, of 'I, here, now'. We were urged to try particularly for this special feeling of ourselves. It was especially important in moments of activity. And we must come to see that we could not see ourselves accurately at all unless we could also achieve the state of 'I – here'.

Going away to translate some of this into practice produced entirely new questions, for it was not to be put into practice just like that. When the moment seemed most propitious it eluded one's grasp. As this was a simple and direct confirmation of everything I had confronted in my earliest juvenile struggles with thinking, I was not really surprised. Thinking went on, irrespective of me and in defiance of me, and it was of course this double lack of assent that had made me so dissatisfied when I had persevered with the practices of religion, although I certainly couldn't have put it that way at the time. Something always obeyed the outer form, something went on - on and on - but to call it 'I' was laughable.

When I returned with my puny results I was comforted with explanations. I had made an important realisation, something unknown to the majority of western people, who would almost certainly reject the idea that they did not remember themselves if this was put to them. And yet, with the small results that all of us had to show, there was one incontrovertible fact. Self remembering was possible. And each one of us could clearly recall a time in the past when life had completely sprung into focus. We could even produce one or two observations of an unusual moment in the preceding week. Suddenly time stood still. We were in the moment but there was much more of us than usual. We looked, we heard, we smelled, we touched, then, all at once it was gone. For me, in these efforts, was the first uncomfortable, genuine acceptance that my ordinary everyday life lived out in thoughts, without any real feeling of 'I' was actually linked to lies, or at best, to half truths.

Sometimes, when the observation left an aftertaste, the shamelessness of this situation would leave me literally gasping. I had done it again, using energy, gusto and valuable time and trouble to nail to my mast some palpable phantom, obviously false. But why, had I never known this before? It was noticeable that the conversations which were taking place when this kind of observation sprang into focus had always a certain kind of vehemence, though quite often this was entirely hidden and only ricocheted inside me. This vehemence completely collapsed if I suddenly experienced one long moment of recognisable existence, as if some self I rather rarely met was serenely looking out of my eyes. And the relief of this was always accompanied by the added realisation that my tenacious and everlastingly troublesome thoughts had suddenly stopped.

So alongside my apparently wholehearted desire and willingness to involve myself in this apparently unrewarding effort, I now had to turn back rather carefully to my memories of the first lecture. On the one hand I seemed to be doomed to continue with the odd experience of failing to remember myself for more than a few seconds at a time, and on the other I was being led to the conclusion that I obviously had no centrally established and recognised self of any kind.

At first, when I had heard about self remembering, a great relief had spread through me. Now I was being forced to question this, but with the odd conviction that although my seconds of remembering myself would never be expanded, I still regarded these intrinsically unsuccessful experiments as a considerable gain.

Each day I decided in advance that I would remember myself on the way to work as I rounded the pavement in Bedford Square, under the lingering golden leaves of the giant plane trees. Mounting the black and white steps of the little Georgian house where I managed and sub-edited an inconsequential politico-philosophical news sheet, I could re-face what seemed to be a genuine wish. I was there on the steps experiencing my existence until I pushed open the black door and it then closed resolutely behind me, drowning me as completely as if waters had closed over my head.

During the morning I completed a wide range of tasks, all more or less requiring intelligence. I dictated letters, re-wrote articles, corrected proofs, sent galleys to the printer, discussed conferences, settled queries and 'handled' elderly émigré Council Members who had been eminent statesmen in their defeated Central European countries. But from the point of view of my newly learned teaching, 'I' was not there at all. 'I' dealt with everything. Wore my clothes, laughed my laugh, curried favour with the famous, wheedled the printer and even corrected obscure grammatical errors from its apparently inexhaustible knowledge of how to set forth someone else's writing in a more attractive form. 'I' was perfectly satisfied with this entire performance, and from a practical point of view there was not really so very much to find fault with. Even the quid pro quo mind behaved perfectly adequately under these conditions so long as it was not pushed too far out of its limited sphere.

That its sphere was indeed limited, I was only just beginning to grasp. I might be called upon to choose between two equally untrue statements or to pronounce upon an interesting idea that actually floated on no foundation at all. Then the perfect mechanicality of 'it' faltered, sensing defeat, and this could herald a whole range of temporarily puzzling happenings. 'Somebody' heavily influenced by 'it', a kind of drugged prisoner, made a supreme effort to struggle to the surface.

After such a statement, things would happen so fast that the drugged prisoner would quickly repent of its intervention, disappearing very rapidly from sight, and enormous efforts would be made by 'it' to carry on more or less as if nothing unusual had happened. That this was my opportunity to try another sort of self remembering did not occur to me for several years. For although something which seemed to have the same density as self remembering could somehow take place, this was very quickly swallowed up by the efficient 'it', and happily forgotten over the next cup of tea.

Then, all at once, it was time for lunch, so down the stairs, along the corridor out of the front door, and hey presto, there I was in my body. I stopped in my tracks, appreciative but surprised, and then, finally, remorseful, lingering on the black and white tiled steps.

Where had I been? What had been happening? Already the prisoner was awake and felt its plight, walking slowly and carefully away under the trees, wanting to stay so much looking at the sunlight and the sky - freedom. But the freedom was soon engulfed and rarely returned until some three-quarters of an hour later I mysteriously awakened a second time in a crowded wartime restaurant . . . . .

Why couldn't I do it?

Bennett explained at length, in answer to many questions and observations on one's extraordinary inner paralysis, that at present our power to remember ourselves *was* limited, and the experience momentary. What was important was not to be deterred by a sense of failure. The power to remember ourselves frequently must be cultivated. Our sleep and mechanicalness were not mere metaphors for lack of balance. We were literally asleep unless we made this vital connection. Nor was thinking about a recognisable scale of consciousness, a mere poetic convention, something that people might refer to as a mystical experience. The taste of self remembering achieved in our earliest efforts was the first recognisable step away from the slavery to dreams and associative thoughts which typified the whole of daily life.

And what else could prove to us that a scale of consciousness existed? People liked to think that Science was an arbiter for this kind of question. But Science had jettisoned consciousness and its arguments were more or less ludicrous. Going step by step, at first a little tortuously, we must find a beginning for ourselves.

And this beginning was true. One could achieve a sudden extraordinary moment, but only one moment, like a flower bursting open in sunshine, an acknowledgment that this was life with an entirely new face, an undreamed of possibility. But an effort to prolong the moment, to gather some fruit as it were, always failed. Nor, mysteriously, was it ever possible to track down the exact second when this new state disappeared. What happened varied.

Chapter 11

THE HIGHER CENTRES

'The Higher Centres are beyond either sensible perception or intellectual apprehension. We have reached the threshold of the unknowable. Innumerable descriptions of supranormal experience have been left to us by saints and monks, Yogis and Bhikkus, Sufis and dervishes, philosophers and mystics from every country and from every age. They can give us little help in our search for the meaning and aim of life beyond the assurance that we are not setting foot upon an untrodden path. There is too much confusion due, in general, to failure to distinguish between function and consciousness and in particular to ignorance of the different levels of consciousness and the structure of the seven Centres. The rhetoric seeks to disguise the fact that only the merest vestige of an experience of the Higher Centres can be transferred to the Intellectual Centre. And we must regard as suspect all the imagery, sometimes circumstantial, which is drawn from some particular philosophical theory or religious creed. There are only two positive conclusions which we can draw from this. The first is that the reality of supranormal experiences cannot be doubted, and the second that this is so different from ordinary experience as to be inexpressible in our usual linguistic forms.

'But before we study the actual work of the Higher Centres and their work, let us examine more closely the observation made in the preceding section that there is a great difference in the speed of working of the Sex Centre as compared with the working of the lower Centres. This raises the more general question of how it is that seven different minds can be related to a single body and make use to a great extent of the same functional mechanism and yet not enter fully into one another's experience.

'We must not be misled by the descriptions which we have given of the higher parts of the Centres, and the glimpses which they disclose of our latent possibilities, into thinking that they play an important part in the life of man. On the contrary, they are seldom operative in us, for consciousness and will are both accidental, or, at best, focused by some specific interest or disposition. We and all other men and women live almost entirely in the mechanical parts of our Centres; that is, as machines, and nothing more. On pain of losing the very possibilities to which we aspire, we must never be deceived into thinking that we have already realized them.

'Bearing this warning in mind, we shall do well to break off our study of the structure of the Centres; and, before embarking on the very difficult task of attempting to express in words the character of the Higher Centres, which essentially transcends all language, ask ourselves how much the four lower Centres can give us - even when working fully in all three parts - and how much they cannot give. This can be expressed very simply – they can give us nothing but ourselves and our relations to the outside world. If we wish to pass beyond the limitations of our personal existence, it is to the Sex Centre and to the Higher Centres that we must turn.

'Each of the four lower Centres can, in its own way, bring us into communication with the outside world and with other living beings, but this communication is always mediated and never attains to direct participation in the experience and consciousness of another.

'Philosophers have always debated the question whether we can have knowledge of other minds. No satisfactory answer can be given without understanding of the seven Centres, for we are faced with this very same question within our own selves; in the form, that is to say, of asking whether our different minds can have knowledge of each other. Before we can hope to understand how, and to what extent, we can know the minds of beings other than ourselves, we must clear away the analogous difficulty which is bound to occur to anyone who reflects on the implications of the assertion that we have not one, but seven psychic Centres.

'If we accept the evidence for the existence of separate Centres, we have still to explain how it is that seven different minds can be related to a single body and yet not enter fully into one another's experience. We know that, to a restricted extent, they can enjoy a common awareness, as, for instance, when our thoughts and feelings are directed to the same object, or a sensation or a movement is presented to our awareness together with a thought. The existence of these common frontiers makes it all the more surprising that our several minds should not merge into a common mechanism which, however subdivided, would still be *one single mind.*

'The solution of this enigma, and at the same time the key to much that is mysterious about man's nature and his latent powers, comes from the realization that each Centre has its own time. This means that, measured on a common time scale, the Centres appear to work at different speeds. We have compared the Centres to a number of machines working in a room. To complete the analogy, we now have to add that the machines work at different speeds. Since we know that they often take part in the same general response to a given situation, we should expect hopeless confusion from a number of machines which are not kept in time with one another and yet have to do the same work. In practice, however, no such confusion occurs, for the times of the different Centres are incommensurable. This is why, on the one hand, they are able to work together without causing a more blurred confusion in our consciousness, and why, on the other hand, one Centre does not enter into the experience of another.

'The slowest of all the seven Centres is the Intellectual. Its time is that of our usual experience. The time of the Intellectual Centre can be measured by the rate at which distinct thoughts can arise successively, and also by the duration of the present moment, the sense of 'now'. All these things for the Instinctive and Moving Centres are very much more rapid.

'That a great difference in speed exists between the Instinctive and the Intellectual Centres can be verified directly if we examine our perceptions. For example, I hear a sound and think 'aeroplane'. Or my eyes, wandering idly about the room, may focus on an object, and I may think 'that picture is crooked'. In each case, I am presented with a complete structure of impressions, in which immense numbers of separate nerve messages are classified and related to the memory of past experience.

'To my Intellectual Centre, this work is presented as a complete whole, and it ponderously produces from it one single thought. A consideration of such examples as these helps to explain the necessity that the times of Centres should be incommensurable. Unless the work of the Instinctive Centre were, for all practical purposes, infinitely faster than that of the Intellectual, it would be still continuing while we were evolving the corresponding thought, and then the latter could never be clear and well-defined, for it would be continually endeavouring to adjust itself to the slowly forming sense impression. These considerations are so obvious, if we but reflect on them, and if we stop to observe in what manner our thoughts and impressions are related, that it is very strange that the existence in us of incommensurable time scales has never been recognized by psychologists.

'Exactly similar considerations apply to the relation of the Intellectual and Moving Centres. As I am driving a car, I make an exceedingly complicated series of muscular adjustments to avoid a collision, and when it is all over, find myself thinking, 'That was a narrow escape!' The Instinctive and Moving Centres worked at the same speed; perception and response were co-ordinated and the necessary movements completed 'before I had time to think'. Had my Intellectual Centre worked quicker, it would have done harm rather than good, for it would have attempted to assist the Moving Centre without being able to keep pace with it, and the result would have been an accident. Instances can be multiplied which establish quite unmistakably the qualitative differences which exist between the time scale of the Instinctive and Moving Centres and that of the Intellectual Centre; but it is much more difficult to give a quantitative value to these differences. First of all, we have to decide whether we are in the presence of a genuine difference in *time scales*, or merely in speeds of action. If the former, we should expect to find a definite fixed ratio, the same for all manifestations of the respective Centres; if the latter, any ratio might occur, for Centres might sometimes work quicker and sometimes slower, always by reference to a single time scale common to all.

'There are weighty reasons for adopting the view that each Centre has its own distinctive time scale, bearing a definite ratio of duration to that of the time scales of the other Centres. These reasons are in part experimental, for it is possible to compare by appropriate tests the rates of perception of the different Centres. They are also partly based upon the relation of time scales to states of consciousness, and partly upon certain cosmic relations which, as we shall see in a later chapter, determine the time structure of the solar system.

'The experimental methods, which will be discussed in the next lecture, show that the difference in speed of perception of the Instinctive Centre as compared with the succession of thoughts in the Intellectual Centre is in the ratio of some 30,000:1. The Instinctive and the Moving Centres work at the same speed, and therefore their processes appear to the Intellectual Centre as almost instantaneous; or, alternatively, to them the Intellectual Centre appears to be standing still.

'Experiences of this difference are not at all uncommon. In moments of danger, when consciousness is transferred to the Instinctive and Moving Centres for the needs of self-preservation, we say that 'Time appears to stand still,' that is to say, the Intellectual Centre appears to be arrested in mid-career, halfway through a thought. In such cases, the instinctive response is usually completed in the fraction of a second; consciousness then returns to the Intellectual Centre and the thoughts continue at their usual rate of movement. That time for the Instinctive

Centre is measured on an entirely different scale from that of the Intellectual Centre is well-known to psychologists. If this difference is not recognized, instinctive processes are almost inexplicable in the speed with which the most complicated operations are performed.

'Consider a man suffering from traumatic shock, resulting in a general breakdown of all his reflexes, in the disappearance of mental and emotional awareness, the cessation of co-ordinated movements, and even the power of instinctive reaction against the dangers which threaten his life. Now, let such a man receive an injection of an appropriate drug, and in one or two seconds, there is a complete transformation of the whole organism. If we attempt to enumerate the thousands of complex mechanisms which have been readjusted and set in motion, the complete reorganization of the instinctive economy and the release of energy for the Intellectual and Emotional Centres, we realize that we have witnessed what is truly a miracle.

'Without taking such an extreme example, we can see in so simple an action as the drinking of a glass of water by a man consumed with thirst, the almost instantaneous revival of bodily energy. We can attempt to calculate the number of signals which have been sent out to every part of the body, the elaborate mechanism whereby the blood adjusts itself to the sudden making good of the deficiency of body fluids, and the whole complicated process that takes place in a matter of seconds. We can also realize that it would have required a team of physicists and chemists, using a laboratory full of apparatus, to have reproduced in several hours, and even approximately at that, the work which the Instinctive Centre carried through in a few seconds. Equally striking examples can be found in the working of the Moving Centre.

'The Emotional Centre can have two different times. One corresponds to the work of the mechanical part and is the same as the time of the Instinctive and Moving Centres. The other time, which belongs properly to the Intellectual Part, is 30,000 times faster again, and is equal to the time of the Sex and Higher Emotional Centres. We can suppose a fourth time, belonging to the Higher Mental Centre, which is 30,000 times shorter still. However, it would be accurate to say that the Higher Mental Centre is timeless for it works under the laws of a world where there is no distinction between time and eternity.

'Whether the Higher Emotional Centre is reached through the slow ripening of mystical powers or is opened by some terrible experience, intended and deliberately created, or reached accidentally and involuntarily, in all the descriptions there is the same element of dying to be born again.

'Because so many descriptions are exaggerated and even morbid, most schools of modern psychology classify these experiences as hysterical or pathological. There is certainly something repellent in the self-inflicted sufferings of a Henry Suso or the ghostly nightmares of a Nicholas Flamel, but the obstacle which stands between us and the Higher Emotional Centre is neither mysterious nor pathological. It consists merely in the presence in us of negative emotions – of imagination, identification and self-love. As we saw in the working of Conscience, the antithesis of unbearable suffering and the radiance of positive emotion, both brought about by the same event – the awakening of the Higher Part of the Emotional Centre – so we shall find a more awful contrast in the approach to the Higher Emotional Centre for him who is free from the negative triad and for the man who is still under its sway.

'It is not the access to the Higher Centres which causes these apparently hysterical and pathological states, this darkness and this suffering, but the direct perception of negative emotions in their true significance.

'The Higher Emotional Centre, when reached by the normal and legitimate   processes of self-development, confers powers and experiences which are entirely positive. It is at one and the same time the seat and organ of the perfected individuality. It is the permanent 'I', for when consciousness joins it with the lower Centres, the whole being is unified. Everything that can be known and experienced, both inwardly and outwardly, by a perfected individual belongs to the Higher Emotional Centre and the Higher Emotional, when joined with the lower Centres, enables them to perceive reality beyond the here and now of their usual experience. Authentic clairvoyance and all supra-normal cognition belong to it.

'No practical work for the attainment of the Higher Emotional Centre can, without the danger of a catastrophe, be undertaken until a man knows his own weaknesses and has overcome in himself vanity and self-love. But when consciousness in the Higher Emotional Centre is actually attained, all the self-centred motives which arise in the lower Centres are made subservient to the objective motives beyond self or non-self.

'But nevertheless, despite the work of the Higher Emotional Centre within him, without help of enough men, able and ready to place themselves in such relations to him and to his aims, he is as helpless as a man with eyes in a country of blind people who cannot understand his language.

'These descriptions of the Higher Emotional Centre may seem dull and colourless when compared with the vivid accounts of supra-normal experiences which we find in mystical literature. If, however, we reflect upon the implications of these descriptions we shall see that in fact they go beyond what is usually regarded as mystical experience, for they refer not only to supra-normal *cognitions*, but also to super-human powers of *action*. It is unfortunate that the descriptions which we find in literature frequently suffer from the inability of the author to indicate clearly the exact nature of the miraculous. . . . .

'The greatest difficulty in our understanding of the Higher Intellectual Centre arises from the fact that it lies beyond individual existence. In our present state, we can only make the first halting steps towards experience beyond our individual selves. This is in the working of the Sex Centre. A great extension occurs in the ecstatic experiences which belong to the Higher Emotional Centre. In all this, the distinction between 'I' and 'not-I' remains, even though in the full working of the Higher Emotional Centre all self-centred separate motives have disappeared. But in the Higher Intellectual Centre the last distinction between any form of existence and all sense of separate individuality vanishes entirely. Later on, after we have completed our study of consciousness, we shall therefore return to the cognitions of the Higher Intellectual Centre. However for the moment it may help us to remember that there is only one way to the Higher Intellectual Centre. This begins with the purification and unification of the lower Centres and then leads to the attainment of consciousness in the Higher Emotional Centre.'

Chapter 12

MYSTICISM

When the study of the Emotional Centre began to expand and brought us at last to the Higher Centres, I was inevitably drawn sideways into a deep consideration of Mysticism, though like others before me I did not like the label and could not understand why the dictionary definition in its shortest form provided the rather strange term of 'spiritually allegorical'. I was now finding most of my reading matter in a small number of second-hand bookshops, while keeping an eagle eye out for the genuine reprints of classics which wartime publishers, very hard pressed for adequate paper supplies, could still manage to produce.

Here there was allegory enough. Ragwort and willow herb were already beginning to flourish on the bomb damaged sites near St Paul's Cathedral where the London booksellers' warehouses had stood earlier in the war, though their provincial offices could still produce a thin trickle of erudite works. Among these were transcriptions of such regular events as the Gifford Lectures on Natural Religion at St. Andrews and Edinburgh, sometimes important enough to be re-issued, revised, after a lapse of more than twenty years, and it was a piece of good fortune that introduced me to a re-issue of Dean Inge's lectures on 'The Philosophy of Plotinus' as well as to his thin wartime volume 'Mysticism In Religion'. In this he stoutly declared that "it is quite inadequate to treat Mysticism as a branch of psychology - which is really a Natural Science not concerned with ultimate truth. The psychological approach is now the most popular and is a part of the disintegrating relativism of modern thought, which, by ignoring it, really denies the faith which for all mystics is the sole justification for the choice which they have made".

Inge gave what must have been his first lecture on Christian Mysticism over a century ago, and believing that he had some influence in "turning religious people to the subject", he pointed out that in the past the word 'mysticism' had been used very loosely, and more often than not in a disparaging or even contemptuous manner, though the Germans had two words, *mystick* and *mysticismus*, by which they could distinguish between Mysticism as a genuine type of religion, and the perversion of it. While feeling it was a pity that we could not do the same, he now thought that the word was better understood than it had been half a century ago. And he quoted a number of definitions which he hoped clarified the issue, for we still had to recognise that there had been two schools of mystics - one which distrusted and rejected affirmations of ordinary every-day consciousness - and the other which only welcomed the visible as a partial manifestation of the spiritual.

Explaining how in the Third Century both Pagans and Christians were pessimistic with "humanity at its last gasp", Inge believed that political calamities actually liberated philosophy and religion by compelling man to attend exclusively to their own business.

'In the sphere of religion, the rivals were the Oriental mystery cults (now recognised by the Empire), and the Christian church. In philosophy, the Greek schools, now coalescing into what is called Neoplatonism, were winning an easy victory over the Gnostics, who represented a barbarised Platonism; but behind these controversies there was a deep cleavage - between those who wished to preserve the classical culture as a whole - and those who, at first indifferent to it, had been provoked to hostility. This was indeed a tragic conflict which need not have arisen . . . .

'There were faults on both sides, but by far the largest share of the blame rests with the stupid and obstinate policy of the Roman emperors, who after a series of sporadic and futile pogroms against the Christians (never politically dangerous), made a systematic attempt to extirpate the new faith at a time when it really was much too strong to be attacked.'

Writing 'Mysticism In Religion' more than fifty years ago - when modern scholars were just beginning to be interested in the thought of Plotinus - Inge was not alone in believing that he was by far the most important figure in that age of transition, and in contrasting Plotinus with Origen, his learned Christian contemporary, Inge managed to sift out three truths he had been anxious to establish:

1) the spiritual nature of reality (compared with the materialism of the Epicureans and Stoics);

2) the possibility of gaining a real (personal) knowledge of ultimate truth (compared with the Scepticism of the New Academy and the pragmatism of the eclectics); and

3) the unity, goodness and sacredness of the Universe (as against the Gnostics).

When I got to this point of Inge's disquisition I suddenly realized that I must retrace my steps immediately and read again both the Preface and the Introductory Syllabus to the third edition of his lectures, since in this way I should acquire much of the philosophy I really needed without a surfeit of ancient history.

And this at once produced a very important question: when, in fact, could I hope to run to earth the full text of 'The Enneads' which had been translated by Stephen MacKenna between 1905 and 1930. In the second part of Inge's Introduction, these had been described as 'Notes for the inner circle of his disciples', but now, nearly twenty years later, no wartime bookshop or academic library had found it possible to help me and so, for the moment, I would have to be content with an extended study of the Commentaries.

But in feeling that Inge brightened many dead corners of accepted theology I experienced once again the echo of bewilderment I had known in my early teens when I tasted the thinness of the religious fare which had come my way alongside my one providential mystical experience which, though battered and compressed so cruelly down the years, could still hold sway in an unequal contest.

And as examples multiplied, it seemed to me that I drew most from the one which was not actually connected with the religious life. I felt that I already understood that in the cloister the practice of prayer and meditation brought the soul to God. And I was, as it were, convinced that the history of 'saintliness' fully demonstrated this. What I needed to know more practically was the existence of a route whereby positive feelings could pierce reality, and I was interested in the events that brought this about and the routes that were different from the Christian way. It was beginning to be clear to me that the better states that I had known in adolescence were happy accidents, surplus energy which somehow made use of beliefs and thoughts that had been laid down instead of being wasted in the usual way by negative emotions. In adulthood one couldn't expect this agreeable state of affairs to continue, and my long experience of being controlled by thoughts that I neither liked nor sanctioned gave enormous point to my allegiance.

Sometimes, sitting alone in a city church at lunchtime, feeling weary as the war, and impatient with my lack of understanding, I would leap back to what seemed a new if partial optimism, betrayed by me again and again, always defeated, rising and falling, but never disappearing altogether. Then I would go over the recent lectures as best I could, turning the new memories round like a numbered page. I was impatient with the idea that the higher experiences of the Emotional Centre could not yet be reached, but I also saw the justice of this claim. And I was quite incapable of discussing with anyone what I had already glimpsed and where I hoped this might eventually lead.

What was discussable, and only too obvious, was my need to solve the inconsistencies in my mind, which produced a kind of almost observable chaos if emotional subjects had to be talked about. And it grieved me too that my self-sufficiency was like a second skin - quite unobservable while in action and only to be repented of afterwards.

It would have been easy just then to have concluded that I was merely impatient and that in time it would be a matter of *tout comprendre, tout pardonner.* But I did not assent to so many things that went on in my life, and I had already accepted that a great deal of energy had to be saved before my Emotional and Intellectual Centres would be sufficiently balanced to endow me with even a limited kind of freedom.

At the same time, I had not yet discovered how to look at the energy that sometimes ran over in a kind of radiant but all too brief joy which sprang from the sudden perception that something was owed for the incredible benefit of being alive at all. This was unconnected with the fact that I might easily not have lived as long as I had, or that I might soon, perhaps, die. It was actually a kind of recognition that all this energy could just as easily have gone into a rock or a tree, and was therefore a very definite feeling of gratitude for life itself, as well as for the moment that was passing and would soon be gone. One thing that was very clear about these brief experiences was that they did not lie in my ordinary memory, or in what I had privately called my *quid pro quo* self, and I rarely brought them to mind when they were not actually present, though immediately afterwards I would be filled with a great silent calm, and a feeling that the immediate problems of ordinary life suddenly had no relevance.

* * *

But Inge was by no means the only teacher who had risen from the past to instruct me in the heights and depths of mysticism. Before I had finished the first volume of his 'The Philosophy of Plotinus' and had more or less absorbed his preface to the third edition, with its reference to McKenna's translation of 'The Enneads', I was already reading 'The Varieties Of Religious Experience' by William James. And delving into the five hundred pages or so that James had devoted to his subject gave me one of those rare experiences that had all the hallmarks of another genuine turning point. Here I found, actually gathered altogether in the one volume, my reservations, my guilt, my sympathies, my acceptances and my certainties about the religious life I had felt obliged to leave behind.

Until this point there had been a loneliness in my mental position that had been extremely baffling. I did not doubt for one moment that in Gurdjieff's teaching I had found something immense that I badly needed, and I recognised this as an incredible opportunity. But side by side with my optimism and gratitude, there was an often recurring discomfort and disappointment when I stumbled towards questions that led up to actual experiences of a higher level of consciousness or hoped for a genuine change of being. It was impossible to put any doubt upon the theoretical basis of our teaching, but there seemed to be an enormous gap between the mode of our response and the promise of our possibilities.

It seemed to me that I should have heard of James before, but I had found out nothing about him until I read the introduction to the Everyman edition of his 'Selected Papers on Philosophy'. Here at the very beginning was James' description of his own teacher, Agassiz: "He was so commanding a presence, so curious and inquiring, so responsive and expansive, and so generous and reckless of himself and of his own, that everyone said of him 'Here is no musty savant but a man, a great man, a man on the heroic scale", and we are told that this is exactly the impression that James himself made upon his students and associates.

I wish I could summon up and communicate the feeling of delight which actually enveloped me as I read that first book by James. By now, of course, I was no stranger to 'The Gifford Lectures on Natural Religion', but I had never read anything half as lively as this account of talks given long ago, at the turn of the century. Nor had I thought that I should discover so much that had so far eluded me in the relationship between innate religious impulses and what I had begun to recognise as genuine, practical, psychology. And it was this particular field, that Dean Inge had questioned, but James, from his entirely different background, had much to say that seemed valid for me,

"I am neither a theologian, nor a scholar learned in the history of religions, nor an anthropologist" says James in his chapter 'Religion and Neurology',

"Psychology is the only branch of learning in which I am particularly versed. To the psychologist the religious propensities of man must be at least as interesting as any other of the facts pertaining to his mental constitution. It would seem, therefore, that as a psychologist, the natural thing for me would be to invite you to a descriptive survey of these religious propensities.

"If the inquiry be psychological, it is not religious impulses which must be its subjects, and I must confine myself to those more developed subjective phenomena recorded in literature produced by articulate and fully self-conscious men, in works of piety and autobiography . . . . .

"It follows from this that the documents that will most concern us will be those of the men who were most accomplished in the religious life and best able to give an intelligible account of their ideas and motives. These men, of course, are either comparatively modern writers or else such earlier ones as have become religious classics and the *documents humain* which we will find most instructive need not be sought for in the haunts of special erudition - they lie along the beaten highway . . . . .

"The question 'what are religious propensities?' and the question 'what is their philosophic significance?' are two entirely different orders of question from the logical point of view. In recent books on logic, distinction is made between two orders of inquiry concerning anything. First, what is the nature of it? How did it come about? What is it's constitution, origin, and history? And second, what is its importance, meaning or significance now that it is once here? The answer to one question is given in an existential judgement or proposition. The answer to the other is a proposition of value, what the Germans call *werthurtheil* a spiritual judgment or proposition. Neither judgment can be deduced immediately from the other. They proceed from diverse intellectual preoccupations and the mind combines them only by taking them first separately and then adding them together.

"Having discussed criticism of the Bible in the light of these different sorts of judgments and shown that existential facts are insufficient for determining their value, James goes on to say that there are many religious persons who do not yet make working use of the distinction and who may feel a little startled at the purely existential point of view from which in the following lecture phenomena of religious experience must be considered. When I handle them biologically and psychologically as if they were mere curious facts of individual history, some of you may think it is a degradation of so sublime a subject, and may even suspect me, until my purpose gets more fully expressed, of deliberately seeking to discredit the religious side of life. Such a result is of course absolutely alien to my intention; and since such prejudice on your part would seriously obstruct the due effect of much of what I have to relate, I will devote a few more words to the point.

"There can be no doubt that as a matter of fact, a religious life, exclusively pursued, does tend to make the person exceptional and eccentric. I speak now not of your ordinary religious believer, who follows the conventional observations of his country, whether it be Buddhist, Christian or Mohammedan, His religion has been made for him by others, communicated to him by tradition, determined to fixed forms by imitation, and retained by habit. It would profit us little to study this second-hand religious life. We must search rather for the original experiences which were the pattern setters to all this mass of suggested feeling and imitated conduct. These experiences we can only find in individuals for whom religions exist not as a dull habit, but as an acute fever. But such individuals are 'geniuses' in the religious line - and like many other geniuses have often shown symptoms of nervous instability. Even more perhaps than other kinds of genius, religious leaders have been subject to abnormal psychic visitations; invariably they have been creatures of exalted emotional sensibility.

"Often they have led a discordant inner life, and had melancholy during a part of their career. There can be no better example than is furnished by the person of George Fox. The Quaker religion which he founded is something which it is impossible to over-praise. In a day of shame, it was a religion of veracity rooted in spiritual inwardness, and a return to something more like the original gospel truth that men had ever known in England. So far as our Christian sects are today evolving into liberality they are simply reverting in essence to the position which Fox and the early Quakers so long assumed. No one can pretend for a moment that in point of spiritual sagacity and capacity, Fox's mind was unsound. Yet from the point of view of his nervous constitution, Fox was a psychopath or *detraque* of the deepest dye. His journal abounds in entries of this sort."

Having given the example of Fox's famous visit to Lichfield, where he cried out against the Christians martyred in the time of Emperor Diocletian, James then very carefully explains that the intellect is bound to class the experience as pathological, just as if they occurred to a non-religious man.

We cannot, of course, follow James fully as he describes how the intellect lays bare the causes from which a thing originates and gives the example of Spinoza analyzing man as if it were a question of lines, planes or solids, nor when he quotes doctors in their decision that the 'greater the genius, the greater the unsoundness'. No. The soundness of James' own intention is clear. If we are to examine religious experience with sincerity, we must stop working for validity in one thing by always comparing it with something else. And above all, we must not be led astray by what he calls the "darling dream of philosophic dogmatists" by seeking for "origins. . . . ." And in the end it has to come down to our empiricist criterion, "by their fruits ye shall know them", not by their roots. . . . .

If I had ever supposed that my peculiar mixture of chaotic thought and acute sensibility were in danger of being called psychopathic, I should have certainly been much comforted by everything that James had to say here, but the extreme activity of my ordinary daily life had somehow rescued me from this. At the same time, I was greatly cheered by the clarity of his exposition when it came to some reasonable kind of assessment of the ideal link between 'being' and 'doing', and the necessity of accepting certain states which appeared to arrive naturally. And James had much more to say about comparisons; he did not reach mysticism itself until he had discussed important byways: the appeal of a modern movement which he calls the Religion of Healthy-Mindedness; traumas of the divided self; and the actual usefulness (or otherwise) of Saintliness, because, like Inge, he finds the word 'mystical' unsatisfactory, and thoroughly disapproves its use in connection with modern versions of 'the occult', or with spiritualism. He goes into some detail to describe the feelings that distinguish mystical states from states of intellect, gathering together four basic criteria:

1. 'Ineffability - the handiest of the marks by which I classify a state of mind as mystical is negative. The subject of it immediately says that it defies expression, that no adequate report of its contents can be given in words. It follows from this that its quality must be directly experienced; it cannot be imparted or transferred to others. In this peculiarity mystical states are more like states of feeling than like states of intellect. No one can make clear to another who has never had a certain feeling, in what the quality or worth of it consists. One must have musical ears to know the value of a symphony; one must have been in love one's self to understand a lover's state of mind. Lacking the heart or ear, we cannot interpret the musician or the lover justly, and are even likely to consider him weak-minded or absurd. The mystic finds that most of us accord to his experiences an equally incompetent treatment.

2. 'Noetic quality - although so similar to states of feeling, mystical states seem to those who experience them to be also states of knowledge. They are states of insight into depth of truth unplumbed by the discursive

intellect. They are illuminations, revelations, full of significance and importance, all inarticulate though they remain; and as a rule they carry with them a curious sense of authority for after-time.

'These two characters will entitle any state to be called mystical, in the sense in which I use the word. Two other qualities are less sharply marked but are usually found. These are:-

3. 'Transiency. - mystical states cannot be sustained for long. Except in rare instances, half an hour, or at most an hour or two, seems to be the limit beyond which they fade into the light of commonality. Often, when faded, their quality can be imperfectly reproduced in memory; but when they recur it is recognized; and from one recurrence to another it is susceptible of continuous development in what is felt as inner richness and importance.

4. 'Passivity - Although the oncoming of mystical states may be facilitated by preliminary voluntary operations, as by fixing the attention, or going through certain bodily performances, or in other ways which manuals of mysticism prescribe; yet when the characteristic sort of consciousness has once set in, the mystic feels as if his own will were in abeyance, and indeed sometimes as if he were grasped and held by a superior power. This latter peculiarity connects mystical states with certain definite phenomena of secondary or alternative personality, such as prophetic speech, automatic writing, or the mediumistic trance. When these latter conditions are well pronounced, however, there may be no recollection whatever of the phenomenon, and it may have no significance for the subject's usual inner life, to which as it were, it makes a mere interruption. Mystical states, strictly so called, are never merely interruptive. Some memory of their content always remains, and a profound sense of their importance. They modify the inner life of the subject between times of their recurrence. Sharp divisions in this region are, however, difficult to make, and we find all sorts of gradations and mixtures.'

Though warning against any connection with what have been called the 'dreamy states' preceding epileptic fits, he believes that the edge of the mystical states such as those described by Charles Kingsley are not uncommon and, in order to reach some acceptable conclusions, first gives examples of feelings like Kingsley's, with no special religious significance,

'When I walk the fields, I am oppressed now and then with an innate feeling that everything I see has a meaning, if I could but understand it. And this feeling of being surrounded with truths which I cannot grasp amounts to indescribable awe sometimes . . . . Have you not felt that your real soul was imperceptible to your mental vision, except in a few hallowed moments?"

An extract from Amiel's Journal, 'In Time', continues this theme:

"Shall I ever again have any of those prodigious reveries which sometimes came to me in former days? One day, in youth, at sunrise, sitting in the ruins of the castle of Faucigny; and again in the mountains, under the noonday sun, above Lavit, lying at the foot of a tree and visited by three butterflies; once more at night upon the shingley shore of the Northern Ocean, my back upon the sand and my vision ranging through the Milky Way; such grand and spacious, immortal, cosmogenic reveries, when one reaches to the stars, when one owns the infinite! Moment divine, ecstatic hours; in which our thought flies from world to world, pierces the great enigma, breathes with a respiration broad, tranquil, and deep as the respiration of the ocean, serene and limitless as the blue firmament; . . . . . instants of irresistible intuition in which one feels one's self great as the universe, and calm as a god . . . . . What hours, what memories! The vestiges they leave behind are enough to fill us with belief and enthusiasm, as if they were visits of the Holy Ghost."

Then, after quoting Walt Whitman's famous passage "I believe in you, my Soul. ." as well as one or two others, he reminds us about Dr Bucke's experience of what he afterwards called 'Cosmic Consciousness'.

'I had spent the evening in a great city, with two friends, reading and discussing poetry and philosophy. We parted at midnight; I had a long drive in a hansom to my lodging. My mind, deeply under the influence of the ideas, images, and emotions called up by the reading and talk, was calm and peaceful. I was in a state of quiet, almost passive enjoyment, not actually thinking, but letting ideas, images, and emotions flow of themselves, as it were, through my mind. All at once, without warning of any kind, I found myself wrapped in a flame-coloured cloud. For an instant I thought of fire, an immense conflagration somewhere close by in that great city; the next I knew was that the fire was within myself. Directly afterward there came upon me a sense of exultation, of immense joyousness accompanied or immediately followed by an intellectual illumination impossible to describe. Among other things, I did not merely come to believe, but I saw that the universe is not composed of dead matter, but is, on the contrary, a living Presence; I became conscious in myself of eternal life. It was not a conviction that I would have eternal life, but a consciousness that I possessed eternal life then; I saw that all men are immortal; that the cosmic order is such that without any peradventure all things work together for the good of each and all; that the foundation principle of the world, of all the worlds, is what we call love, and that the happiness of each and all is in the long run absolutely certain. The vision last a few seconds and was gone; but the memory of it and the sense of the reality of what it taught has remained during the quarter of a century since it elapsed. I knew that what the vision showed was true. I had attained to a point of view from which I saw that it must be true. That view, that conviction, I may say that consciousness, has never, even during the periods of deepest depression, been lost."

Chapter 13

THE CRISIS IN HUMAN AFFAIRS

When Bennett asked me if I would like to do the transcription and editing of an entirely new series of lectures, I didn't hesitate. As someone else could take down the questions for me it was an ideal situation. I was housebound: being occupied with a son who had been born about eighteen months earlier, so that my sole contribution to 'Organised Work' would now only be a mid-week visit when I could wheel him in his pram to Coombe, cook the lunch for the resident group, and after a bowl of soup for both of us, take him home again.

I could easily start the transcripts in the afternoons, when instead of doing gardening I should be able to take my typewriter and a table into the orchard for well over an hour, where Tristram would scramble about very happily, though always in need of someone to look after him.

The lectures that Bennett had referred to were to celebrate the inauguration of the Institute for the Comparative Study of History, Philosophy and the Sciences. With the ending of the war the whole mode of Bennett's teaching had changed. Hitherto he had kept very strictly to what he had received from Ouspensky, though he had also shared some of his philosophical developments with older people. In future, the entire operation would be different.

Instead of Saturday afternoon lectures concerned with the central ideas of the System, there would be evening meetings on weekdays announcing some theme which would attract newcomers. The re-opening of Coombe Springs (which had unfortunately been closed to us because of the complexities of Bennett's career) would host seminars run by a resident group, as well as weekends of organised work. And there would also be discussion groups for newer, younger people who were somewhat different from the older Ouspensky pupils with their sophisticated disillusion.

'The Crisis In Human Affairs' was without doubt the most ambitious of all Bennett's serial lectures, and some of his most original philosophical ideas came to light in the first chapter of the book he eventually published. His portmanteau words, such as 'megalanthropism' - the tendency to overrate the importance of man and to exaggerate his powers and capacities - and the terms 'psycho-static' and 'psycho-kinetic' could be used over and over again in new combinations which cut away the need for endless discussion and repetition.

Thus the psycho-static view claimed that the *psyche*, or 'essential nature' of man, is unchangeable, and the solution of his problems can be sought only in some new relation to his environment, generally some new relation both to the community in which he lives and to his fellow men. The alternative or 'psycho-kinetic' view asserted the possibility of movement or transformation within man's psyche or essential nature. These two views lead us to think about adaptation to the circumstances of life in terms of either external or internal change.

But we must first decide what we meant by man's psyche or essential nature. His body, his mind, his physical or his mental powers were not at any given moment his psyche. We all knew that we are born with small and feeble bodies, which grow and mature, acquiring powers which were absent at birth. In the new born child the mental powers are not active, and do not begin to be active for several years. They usually mature and reach their greatest strength and flowering at a later stage than the body. Apart from our physical and mental powers, we have experience, knowledge of the world and capacity for making judgments. All these develop at different rates, and reach maturity at different times. Later they begin to diminish and withdraw, until inevitably, unless cut off by premature death, they come to old age and final dissolution. This cycle of birth, growth, maturity, decline, old age and death is a part of the essential human nature. It is something, moreover, that we share not only with other men, but with everything we see in the world around us. Everything that exists in time is under the law of this cycle. We are not entitled to isolate one fraction - the period of growth to maturity - and regard it as constituting a change in man's essential nature. It is just as much a part of our essential nature that after maturity is reached decline should set in. The 'psycho-kinetic' view of man refers to changes other than his capacity for maturing in the sense of development of his physical or mental powers, or even his capacity for judgment. The acceptance of these latter facts is common both to the psycho-static and the psycho-kinetic views.

"It was also very important not to confuse the psycho-kinetic view with 'evolution doctrines'. During the past one hundred years the doctrines of biological evolution had been very widely accepted, and man, in common with other beings living on the earth, was regarded as having evolved from lower, or at any rate simpler, forms, and so may be expected to evolve into higher or more complex forms. This process, if it could be rightly applied to man, involves a slow change in which the individual is passive, and it is because the individual is short-lived and feeble in relation to his environment that the mechanism of evolution or natural selection is presumed to act. At any given moment, however, the essential nature of man is regarded as stable, and the change, if any, is presumed to occur over long periods of time.

"It would, of course, be possible to regard the evolutionary sequence as providing a means of determining direction, so that we could find value in evolution from lower to higher, from simpler to more complex forms, and accept the evolutionary doctrine of value which was widely held in the last century. We could think, like Tennyson, of 'waxing and waning leaf', or of Nature saying, with George Meredith, to man, 'Live in your offspring as I live in mine.'. Such a view regards man as the passive element in a process which goes very slowly and almost in spite of him.

"There are also doctrines according to which evolution is either purposive, and even divinely directed, as proposed by some modern Christian apologists, or without purpose and proceeding by blind conflict, as suggested by dialectical materialism; but in all its forms the evolutionary doctrine regards man, the individual, as passive in relation to a great secular process, occurring over long periods of time, which at any given moment leaves his essential nature unchanged. Such doctrines as these belong to the psycho-static view.

"There is still one more point to be made clear about the distinction between the psycho-static and psycho-kinetic views. So far we have spoken only about human life as we know it, from birth through growth, maturity, and decline to old age and dissolution. Men in all conditions of life and over long periods of time have entertained and do entertain beliefs about survival after the death of the body. Survival doctrines are not necessarily psycho-kinetic. On the contrary, the survival beliefs of the great majority of mankind, both in the West, where they have been associated with reward and punishment, heaven and hell, and in the East, where they are connected with reincarnation doctrines of repeated lives, all are held in forms in which the presumed survival is a continuation of the same kind of experience as exists in life. The interpretation of this doctrine can vary between wide extremes, from the simple reappearance of the body, in some islands of the blest, complete with all its accustomed equipment, to resurrection and survival in an earthly paradise, or translation to some supraterrestrial or disembodied existence. The form does not matter. So long as experience 'beyond the grave' is conceived as analogous to the experience of life, the doctrines belong to the psycho-static view.

"The distinction between psycho-static and psycho-kinetic is not a distinction between religious and secular or non-religious conceptions. Religious doctrines can be, and many are, psycho-static. In notions of reward and punishment we make use of conceptions of right and wrong, pleasure and pain, which are based on our essential nature as it is, and in so far as we project these notions out of this life into another - thinking of rewards as somehow corresponding to what we should call pleasant and desirable things in life, and punishments corresponding to what we should call painful and undesirable experiences in this life - we assume a continuity or sameness of the essential nature of man, which necessarily brings the doctrine into the psycho-static group.

"Religious doctrines can be psycho-static in one of two ways. They can be expressed in language corresponding to our ordinary pragmatic language, making use of ideas derived from sense experience and thoughts. Their value system thus comes to be based upon human experience, and religion becomes, in effect, humanitarianism. The criteria of right and wrong are derived from what the religious dogmatist has come to know and understand of essential human nature and of the human psyche, through applying to their study the same methods that he would use for acquiring pragmatic knowledge. All such forms of religion must be psycho-static, because they start from human nature as it is and make no allowances for the possibility that it may change. Alternatively, we can have simple ritualistic religions, and the religions of good works, based on the notions of reward and punishment which we have already discussed or upon obligations towards God derived from our traditional or habitual conceptions of obligations towards a human father or tribal group, thought of in a way that implies a temporal sequence of experience, corresponding to the ordinary process of our sense perceptions and mental operations.

"In order to understand the power of psycho-kinetic religion, we must steep ourselves in the writings of a man like St Paul, for whom the very meaning of the religious life is the dying and being born again in Christ. The change in the essential nature of man which is symbolised in this death and rebirth takes place, not in another world, but 'here in this very life'. It is an eternal transformation and not a temporal process. Through it, a man becomes concretely what he has always been in potency. This is the root of the Psycho-kinetic Doctrine and without it any religious teaching remains on the psycho-static level.

"If we took the view, as we might well do, that all essentially religious doctrines must be psycho-kinetic, and demand a change in the essential nature of man, we should have to dismiss as secular much that passes for religion today. At the same time it is clear that the idea that man's essential nature must change occupies a central place in the origin of the great religions. The Christian religion is based on the doctrine that men must be born again, or die and rise with Christ. The conception of the 'twice-born' is the central teaching of Buddhism and all the great religions of India. It is in the subsequent development and expansion of religions that a progressive tendency towards psycho-static notions appears. The cause of this tendency can be fully understood only by seeing clearly what is meant by the psycho-kinetic doctrine of man."

Having set up this picture of man as a being who inevitably has to be accepted as belonging to either psycho-static or psycho-kinetic theories, with no possible rationalisation or amelioration, or comfortable adjustment of our long held personal views, Bennett's theme was infinitely simplified. Somehow the bottom dropped out of a take-it-or-leave-it psycho-static opinion, for although psycho-kinetic views might be much more difficult to accept at the outset, at least they left room for some kind of change. To become inwardly united and harmonious, to wake up, and acquire the power of choice would be a psycho-kinetic change and could not be open, accidentally, to a man who over-estimated his powers, and was content to muddle through and reap the doubtful fruits of his maladaptation. Put this way, it is easy to see why religion that has gone down a completely psycho-static path is unacceptable to serious people . . . . Bennett was obliged at this point to point out that since psycho-kinetic change meant alteration in the level of being, rather than the level of knowledge, and this was something that by its very nature could not be perceived externally, what is generally referred to as transcendental knowledge would be needed in order to describe the goal towards which we were striving. At this point, of course, our ordinary everyday experience failed us, concerned as it was with observable cause and effect and the inescapability of the Second Law of Thermodynamics, and our speculations would then have to be couched in symbols or in analogies which would not be universally acceptable.

And Bennett believed that the sense of contradiction in this problem brought us to the heart of all true religion which was concerned with a change in man's essential nature, quoting the question of Nicodemus 'How can a man be born when he is old?'. But despite the abstract questions which faced us we could sometimes take heart in our struggle to understand our real situation precisely from the very fluctuations in our state which at first glance seemed so undesirable, for sometimes we came upon moments of inner peace when we knew things differently.

Bennett then continued more slowly, "We are now confronted with the central problem of all religious and philosophical doctrines which attempt to deal with the possibility of changing man's essential nature. When, in the Gospels, we read 'Except a man be born again,' we ask with Nicodemus, 'how can a man be born when he is old?'. Whatever language men may use for describing psycho-kinetic doctrines, they always meet with the same difficulty. Similes are chosen perforce from our everyday pragmatic language; we can only fix on the meaning which those similes have for us, and do not see the meaning towards which they are trying to point, so we dispute and argue about the outward sign and miss the inward grace. If, then, there is no means of approaching the psycho-kinetic doctrine except by a mortal jump into the unknown, with nothing but blind faith to rely on, it appears that in order to discuss it we shall have to depart from our original principle of speaking only about facts. Nevertheless, I am going to try to convey to you in the next few lectures something about the transcendental aspect of the psycho-kinetic doctrine and hope, without asking you to make a leap into the unknown, to give you some idea of how man's essential nature can change.

"There are certain immediate indications which can show at least something of the character of the change which is possible in man's essential nature. These indications arise from the fact that man's nature is not stable and unvarying, but undergoes great fluctuations between extreme despondency and what is almost worse, a state of mere blind satisfaction with ourselves and our activities, or just complete immersion in activity when no thought of discrimination is present at all. Among all these fluctuations we sometimes come upon moments of inner peace, when we know things differently, and there are also moments of similar value but quite different character, when we know the excitement of participation in beauty, with knowledge, with understanding and with insight. Between these and our worst moments there is a whole gamut of experiences, duller, or more vivid, with less sense of existence and value, through which we find ourselves fluctuating incessantly.

"Together with these fluctuations we also find, if we care to verify it, that we have a limited power of choice, different from the imaginary power of choice which people ascribe to themselves without testing it or knowing what it means: to have a real power of choice, a real power of standing apart from ourselves and saying 'yes' or 'no' to our own activities. We can verify the existence in us of a real power to say yes and no, and because of these two things - the fluctuations of our state and the possession of a real limited power of choice - we can say that if we only knew how, we could strengthen the higher and better states and weaken or even banish the worse and lower states. A realisation of this kind is a concrete indication that it is possible to bring about a change which would in fact be a change in our essential nature.

Bennett then suggested, "Let us pause to look more closely at the expression, 'change in our essential nature'. There was a grave risk that it might be interpreted in too temporal, or too pragmatic a sense, associated with the acquisition of powers, knowledge, abilities and skills of various kinds; but these are not the changes to which he referred. The true meaning of the phrase was implicit in the Greek Mysteries, in which the inner life of man was taken to be analogous to the harvest. Man himself was conceived as a grain, which could die as a grain but be reborn as a plant, different from the grain. A bushel of wheat has two possible destinies - one, in which it is ground and made into flour and becomes bread, and another, in which it is sown in the ground, germinates and, gives a hundred grains for one that was sown. This idea was borrowed by St Paul in describing the resurrection, where he says, 'Thou fool, that which thou sowest is not quickened except it die . . . . .'; 'It is sown a natural body, it is raised a spiritual body'. These illustrations show that the change referred to is not a difference in the use to which a substance is put, but a transformation of the very substance itself. Many have sought to express the idea that man is not a complete, final being, but a being in whose own hands it lies to transform himself. This is a very hard notion to convey, but it is the essence of the psycho-kinetic doctrine. In order to understand it better, we must have a clear idea of the distinction between time and eternity and this will be the subject of the next lecture, as everything I want to say about the psycho-static and psycho-kinetic views can be conveyed adequately only if we have some idea of the nature of our existence in time and eternity, and how the two are necessary to each other[19]."

---

[19] Cf. Albert Schweitzer, *op. cit.*, p.99 "...He who has the true knowledge can be conscious of himself as at one and the same time in the transient world and the eternal world." Schweitzer rightly emphasises the importance of the eschatological basis of St. Paul's mysticism, but does not see that the coexistence of worlds on different levels must have been present to the apostle in a passage such as 2 Cor. xii. 2.

Christening of the third of the Phillpotts children, with
J.G.Bennett godfather (second from right)

Chapter 14

THE ROSE GARDEN

On a sultry afternoon in June 1948, some seven years since my first introduction to the Work, while minding my three month old daughter, I was summonsed urgently to hear the reading of a letter from Bennett about his visit to Madame Ouspensky in America. There was an urgency in the voice at the end of the line that despite the heat of the day and the unsuitability of the hour, made it easy for me to put my baby in her pram immediately and push my way out of the shady garden, up the hill and along the hot gravelled road, arriving at Coombe Springs in about half an hour.

Ouspensky had died about nine months ago in October 1947, having returned to England at the beginning of the previous year, a frail shadow of the infallible man who had left almost exactly six years before. Madame Ouspensky did not accompany him.

Within a month he had restarted his old type of long question and answer weekly meetings at Colet Gardens. Although, theoretically, all Bennett's people were out of touch with what was happening around Ouspensky, in reality this news spread to us by strange routes. There was no question that the interdiction held as firmly as ever, but the feeling of being cast out which we had first experienced had certainly disappeared.

From an onlooker's point of view, Bennett did not cease to behave impeccably for, despite all the problems that had descended on him, by continuing to talk about Ouspensky's teaching with open respect, ignoring his wounded feelings, he took the sting away from our isolated state. In 1945 it had certainly been overlooked in America that one or two of Ouspenky's older pupils who had been left behind in England had grown-up children (or friends of children) doing professional scientific work for Bennett's organisation. Under the Defence Regulation, none of these offspring were free to leave their jobs but had to stay in close contact with Bennett, whether they liked it or not. It was partly through this unlikely channel that various mixed items of news spread sideways in our direction, but it was not until very much later that we could piece it together to something resembling the truth.

The centre of gravity of what had been happening was entirely unexpected, for at one of the large and apparently popular meetings, Ouspensky had categorically repudiated the System. This electrifying information was quickly enough followed by an inevitable contradiction, but nevertheless, one or two large meetings followed. So what were his plans? Something like two months elapsed before he announced that he would not be settling down in England with what seemed to be a revivified organization, but would be returning to America, and there would be no more meetings.

It transpired that what he had hoped for were at least two hundred entirely new people, completely fresh and uncontaminated by the already set ideas of the original pupils who had kept his work alive at Lyne Place during the six years of war, and he was impatient with the uncertain efforts of people undoubtedly new, but already demonstrating a different mould.

It was perfectly true that for those who were not conversant with his mode of teaching, in genuinely wishing to know the real needs of any particular questioner, he did appear to repudiate quite sincerely all knowledge of a pre-existing System. He called for more sincerity and a rejection of both the 'System language' on which he had previously insisted, as well as the Work on which his many years of teaching had been based before the war.

But having announced his dissatisfaction and his imminent departure, still he stayed on, taking much smaller gatherings, for old pupils at Lyne Place, as well as one or two of the larger meetings which were resumed at Colet Gardens. And it was at Colet that there occurred a slight breakthrough because of his partial acceptance of a questioner who had asked about 'remembering'. Here at last was his preferred starting point − although in fact by now some of his intimates had come to accept that he really had quite genuinely 'abandoned the System' - for in answer to a question put at another meeting he had again replied firmly "There is no System.".

Others looked deeper. Behind the man, behind the meetings, what could still be hoped for from an Ouspensky who might not have very much longer to live? And what was it that prevented 'remembering' after almost a lifetime of so-called 'Work'? What personal difficulties acted as a barrier to remembering, and would go on acting in that way?

Of course, it was true that mere words, a too tight reliance on 'System language' alone, with its scientific theory and small-scale psychological engineering, would always stand in the way, and produce connecting blind alleys of useless and bewildering complexity.

Now, about a year later than all these stirring events, to Bennett's pupils the authentic questions and speculations that had been re-aroused had begun to appear rather academic and faraway, although the word 'repudiation' certainly had an unfortunate echo, and kept returning. Some people felt that if this word held any message at all, it could only be the work of older pre-war pupils which had been repudiated. Others believed that what was now being abandoned was the tight 'Ouspensky version' of Gurdjieff's ideas, and the notion began to gain ground too that at the eleventh hour Ouspensky had at last understood the constant betrayal always implicit in his own never-ending intellectualization. But whatever was true or false in all of this, although it considerably affected our attitude to the past, paled before the actual mundane problems of the present.

Things had moved fast since 1947 and deep practical questions about the exact nature of our future organisation, which should legitimately have occurred to us long before, were only just beginning to be voiced.

Some of the reasons for our communal silence and diffidence had been admirable. Clearly we had striven not to gossip sentimentally about the nature of any future changes that must be opening up, and also not to lie to ourselves about what we could or could not do - a useful effort. But on this occasion the old rule dating from Ouspensky's day, which frowned upon any discussion whatsoever that could be construed as some kind of direct criticism of a carefully worked out organisation made by group leaders or by older people who were trusted with the transmission of ideas, was being stretched too far.

And though, for historians, the timescale of what happened next might be important, the picture is extremely blurred. A few months after the death of Ouspenksy, Bennett had made a professional fact-finding tour of the coal mining enterprises in South Africa. And on his return home he had apparently written to advise Madame Ouspensky that he would soon be going to America in connection with coal research there, and as a result she had invited him to visit her in Mendham.

What he did not announce was that this correspondence was actually the outcome of a cable received from America, which had been dispatched previously by Madame Ouspensky's grandson Leonide Sevitsky. Some years before, when Bennett had been hard at work in his job for the coal industry, he had been enlisted to tutor Leonide – commonly known as Lonia, who was actually his godson – for his entry into Trinity College, Cambridge, a mammoth and all but impossible task, and succeeding where others had failed completely, was in that quarter regarded with both warm affection and gratitude - probably only very few of us were aware of the fact that Bennett, never overflowing with funds, had also footed the entire bill for Lonia's Cambridge career.

For some reason that was never fully explained, the exact contents and even the very existence of the cable itself was never referred to, although two people had actually seen it arrive. Inspired guesswork attributed this to the fact that the message imparted was highly confidential, and almost certainly contained important news about other erstwhile pupils of Ouspensky. Doubtless this cable had really emanated from Madame, and it had galvanised Bennett overnight. Gone were the various professional problems about the future; gone were the financial problems concerning the Institute; the new overriding preoccupation was how to get to America as soon as possible. Since all private journeys to the States in the first years after the war were still subject to long delays of one kind or another, time taken up with planning a genuine professional tour concerned with research and technology would be amply repaid and certainly enable him to arrive at Mendham very much earlier than he otherwise could have done.

Bennett had always spoken very appreciatively of Madame Ouspensky. He had become acquainted with the whole family on the island of Prinkipo in 1921, during his time in Constantinople, when he had first met both Ouspensky and Gurdjieff, and little by little his appreciation had developed into an admiration linked with affection, and was a kind of muted hero worship that never seemed to be overdone. When he was willing to talk about the past - after a Seminar, on a holiday evening or at a dinner with a few older people - he would tell us, now that Ouspensky was dead, relaxed stories about his special debt to her. It had surprised me a good deal, at first, to realize that in fact Ouspensky and Madame had actually operated more or less separately at Lyne Place, although to the outside world which revered Ouspensky as a writer, lecturer and quasi-philosopher or Teacher, he was regarded as the director of the whole organization.

The country house at Lyne was the home Ouspensky and his wife, as well as headquarters of the practical work. It had only been acquired in 1934. Before that all the practical work had been carried on experimentally at Gaddesden in Kent, on a much smaller scale, although the house itself was large, with grounds of about seven acres, and it was Madame who had set the entire practical work in motion, requiring a quality of response which the fainthearted could not always aspire to. It was to this period that Bennett really looked back so nostalgically. Despite her apparent role, Madame was very emphatic about her aims and, explaining the unflagging war she waged on the self-regarding impulses of those who met her face to face, she declared that she must not be regarded as a Teacher, she was only a 'nurse', and as such only equipped to look after a 'kindergarten'.

In a difficult period, just after the final Gurdjieff and Ouspensky break of 1924, Bennett had put her on record as having written a letter reaffirming completely her adherence to Gurdjieff as a Teacher, though in somewhat oblique terms, stating:

"All that I know is that he is my teacher and it is not right for me to judge him, nor is it necessary for me to understand him. No-one knows who is the real Georgy Ivanovitch for he keeps himself from all of us. It is useless for us to know him and I refuse to enter into any discussions about him."

This rather endearing candour about Bennett's need for Madame Ouspensky's help and advice came back to me as I neared my destination. Caroline, having been charmed by the motion and the quick pace was now fast asleep, her continual contentment being safely buttressed by her substantial two o'clock feed. Leaving the pram in a shady place, I went swiftly across the rose garden and, entering by the front door, I stopped to listen. Should I go on to the music room where there might be a temporary meeting? I decided against this and taking the stairs two at a time I made my way to the Bennetts' flat - the door of the drawing room was ajar, and needing to slacken my pace and relax a little as I walked along the short corridor, by a careful manoeuvre I could get a glimpse of one empty seat, quite close to the entrance.

As I sat down I looked straight ahead, and out of the corner of my eye I could just see Mrs Bennett looking in my direction. And after what seemed an exceedingly long silence she began to explain to us that her husband had expressed a wish that all the members who lived near

Coombe should share the news that he had sent to her about his visit to Madame Ouspensky.

When Bennett had arrived at Mendham, Madame Ouspensky had come straight to the point, ignoring the break and her husband's interdiction, as if he had remained in their circle for the past eight years, "What will you do", she asked "now that Mr Ouspensky is gone?".

In answer to this. Bennett explained that when he had given lectures in Paris the preceding winter on *'La Pratique du Psychocinetisme'* and its relationship with psychoanalysis, he had taken the opportunity to make extensive enquiries about Gurdjieff, though without success. If he was alive still, he was now unknown and untraceable. But perhaps he was not dead. It was true, after all, that he had gone mad. "Mad?", said Madame Ouspensky "he is not mad. He has never been mad. He is alive and working in Paris. Why do you not go to him?".

This reply had startled Bennett as much as it now startled us. Afterwards he called it 'shattering', and for me at this very moment of revelation it was certainly a shock that can hardly be described. Two thoughts took prominence . . . . . *'Alive and never, never mad'.* The originator of a way we had with so much difficulty maintained; the promulgator of what had been borrowed by Ouspensky; the enabler who had left just enough for people like me to hang on to, was alive and working in Paris. Had the occasion not been quite so solemn and the company so serious, I was so much stirred that I could easily have cried out. As it was, more or less stunned, I listened to the question which had been put to Bennett and was now to be passed to us,

"What would you do if a Higher Teacher came?".

The long pause which followed seemed to exclude thoughts. Was an answer expected? Clearly no answer was possible to this. I would do nothing. I could do nothing. A perception of my nescience seemed to enfold me, a positive judging that I had not known before of my complete emptiness and lack of significance and with this recognition a new certainty. Of course, Bennett would go to him, perhaps very soon, and maybe others would also go. For myself, now, it did not seem that

I actually ever needed to see him face to face. To meet him, for me, at that moment, would be far too much.

The mind tried to steady itself and failed. Instead of a reasoned acceptance of unusual opportunities, a recognition that I should surely by now be prepared to grasp the nettle, some passages from the Sermon on the Mount which I had learnt by heart during my last pregnancy swam into view, but nothing else lucid. No acceptance or rejection by the head came to the surface. I appeared to be permeated by a feeling of paralysis.

After a silence which seemed endless - no-one at all spoke - it began to be clear that no answer was actually expected, and at length an old friend began to read from St John's Gospel. My sense of yet another level of surprise now shifted the paralysis completely. It was rare for the New Testament to be part of an open discussion, and there was a vivid taste of real life, a coming to myself where nothing had been predicated by an ordinary level. And the meaning behind the word 'why', a lively feeling of questioning without the word itself, gave way to the familiar verses. These verses came slowly, clearly, but not loud, although accented in some way as if they were intended to be received specially by each one of us.

"My meat is to do the will of him that sent me, and to finish his work. Say not ye, there are yet four months and then cometh the harvest? Behold, I say unto you, lift up your eyes and look on the fields, for they are white already to harvest. And he that reapeth receiveth wages, and gathers fruit unto life eternal: that both he that soweth and he that reapeth may rejoice together. And therein is that saying true. One soweth and another reapeth. I sent you to reap that whereon ye bestowed no labour. Other men laboured and ye are entered into their labours . . . . ."

I let myself out of the front door. Then, as I walked fairly fast, skirting the top of the drive and arriving at the entrance to the rose garden, I was suddenly stopped in my tracks. Looking back, I can hear the scrunch of the gravel and see the faded green paint of the tall wicket gate. Across my path were the first rose beds and behind them the bright sky of late afternoon. Too many things happened at once for me to describe them accurately. My need to get to the pram at the other side of the garden had vanished completely, but was not replaced by any kind of questioning.

I just stood there, taking in the ever brightening sky, and the feeling of readiness, of actually waiting for some kind of communication, arrived with a perceptible jolt somewhere around the heart, expanding into a new, light perception of the present moment. Then a voice reached me, seeming to be above my head, quite near, but somehow also inside me, and yet at the same time coming from far, far, away. The gentleness and deep calm of this voice imparted a welcome state of reassurance and joyfulness combined with the recognition of truth. A feeling that I had never before experienced coursed through me, seeming to flow upward and outward, almost impossible to receive. And the certainty of being made aware of truth, so simple but so profound, surrounded me in waves. Now I was in the very heart of my most difficult problems. It was right not to have accepted Man as a mere unit in an evolutionary chain - but the potential heir to the very stuff of consciousness released in the Universe at the dawn of creation which now had to complete a circuit in me, and in others like me.

It was in this circuit of response that one would at last find freedom, and not only freedom. I who had long been suspicious of the word 'love', and for so long chary of its use, particularly in any philosophical connotation, was now forced, just as I was, with my difficulties a mere breath away - and without any preliminary or apparent justification - to make acquaintance with a great arc of feeling, and to assent once again to the difficult word 'God' which had been smothered by my deep inherited reserve, tasting the approach of a newness that now had courage, fulfillment and reassurance as a recognisable part.

I do not know how long I stood there, and it is not possible to communicate the true experience. I simply continued to receive reassurance and the answers to all my old and impossible questions, quite unconscious of my surroundings - of the house nearby, the baby a little further away, and the bright and rather unusual light outlining distant trees and illuminating that part of the rose garden where I stood. But at last, when a sense of wonder at this extension to my life had filled me to the brim, an encompassing solemnity suddenly descended, wrapping me completely like an enveloping garment, almost propelling me in the direction of my daughter, and I moved across the garden to the pram and pushed it slowly away.

* * *

Once home, I made tea, gave the baby to someone else to mind, and shut myself in my bedroom with St. John's Gospel which for the moment inexplicably demanded to be read. How was it, what was it, that had begun in me when I heard the gospel words after we had been informed that Mr. Gurdjieff was alive? I read from the beginning, and on and on as if my life depended on it, and as I read, in the silence and half-light of my room I could still experience a feeling of great joy, as if my torso were filled and my head empty but prepared for a new kind of recognition. Passages I had long known came alive and I left them with regret though this was tinged with a growing wonder and satisfaction. It was as if the encyclopaedic part of my mind with its love of words and comparisons was completely stilled, and the messages that I digested flowed like a river of soft colours and lodged in empty places. It was not until I was aware of the slight change in the light and the sound of footsteps and running water that I put the book aside. When I felt obliged to rejoin the family, one of the sayings of John Bunyan, which I had been fond of many years ago, leapt into prominence - 'And all the trumpets sounded for them on the other side . . . . .'

Later when my husband came home from the laboratory I told him without any preliminaries,

"Gurdjieff is alive. Madame Ouspensky has told Mr. Bennett that he has got to go to him in Paris."

"In Paris? Gurdjieff alive? And Madame Ouspensky actually telling him to go?"

George thought a little.

"And of course he will go, even after everything. But what a change! And now we shall see immense changes."

"Great changes have already begun", I said.

Silent questions, too immense to utter, reverberated in the space between us as an entirely different landscape of new possibilities blossomed before our eyes. Comment was superfluous, and the event so momentous that I did not go into any but the briefest details about my unexpected visit to Coombe. And I could not mention my own life-saving experience or the silence that had succeeded it.

When there were no meetings, my husband and I had always spent the evenings very quietly together, listening to music, and in this atmosphere my silence was appropriate and went unnoticed and I could not speak about it for a long time.

Next day it was still with me, and I awakened to a new world - I was not yet looking for analysis - a subdued happiness of an extraordinary kind filling every corner of my being. I was still silent, but without being withdrawn, fully aware that there was a new quality in me which was essentially different from anything that I usually called silence. My most potent impression was that I neither lacked nor looked for anything; suddenly I lived as I had wanted to live since my childhood. And when two new thoughts struck me - the first that day - I laughed aloud. Pushed to explain myself, I might have proffered the comfortable feelings that had inhabited me long ago, in my earliest home. I had long protested, inwardly, at the idea of a search for happiness - happiness always came as a by-product. In my case, it arrived with a certain level of busyness. It had nothing to do with success or approval, or a long-wished for attainment. In the latter case, actually, when fruition, often deferred, matured, there was too often a taste of dead sea fruit, a kind of nostalgic feeling and a deep cry of regret which arose from the heart - 'too late, too late . . . . .'.

But now, in this new world which I had actually glimpsed from my earliest days, there had entered an entirely new element, happily defying my old love of definitions. Like a stranger in a vast landscape, it was as if I was making acquaintance for the first time with completely new meanings, and the familiar gears in my head could not engage. But I was not to be hurried away from where I stood drinking it in, since the blind alleys which usually enticed me had all disappeared.

And it was still much too early for me to look for explanations and parallels in the 'language of the System'. In an extraordinary way I felt 'settled', recognising that the brilliance of yesterday's experience had indeed departed, but in its place I was being allowed an incorruptible taste of new life. This was utterly different from the splendour I had viewed in the distant sun, and had nothing to do with the kind of Arab poetry, which speaking of honey and roses, evoked images that had once made me impatient, being too close to hopeless and fruitless intoxication. Paramount among all my impressions was the certainty that for me, just now, new life involved having my feet firmly on the ground, and if honey and roses came into it at all, it was only by the way.

As the middle of a family of five I should have liked to experience the devotion that was mostly exhibited by a generation older than myself. But I had been educated differently, so differently that the undoubted pleasures of domesticity all needed to be learned. If I had asked for special, personal work in connection with unbalanced functions, I could not have found a more suitable field than the opportunities bestowed by motherhood. I had learned one very useful practical thing from Bennett when he explained that many techniques which were in fact looked after by the Moving Centre, had to be learned first of all by the intellect, 'First you have to learn how, and then practice.' But as far as I could see there was no recipe for bringing non-existent feelings to life, and this was a grey area in the splendid teaching about the balancing of the functions . . . . .

Chapter 15

TO PARIS

A very long time seemed to elapse between receiving Bennett's message and seeing him face to face. More letters from America arrived for his wife, making it quite plain that Bennett was now planning to turn entirely to Gurdjieff, believing that the expansion of the work at Coombe Springs was becoming too much for him. We knew that he had now visited Madame Ouspensky twice, had run the gauntlet of fanatical pupils intending to stick to Ouspensky, alive or dead, and that in between he had made an ambitious professional tour of American mining research stations and coal mines

Most of us felt that after such a momentous happening he would come rushing back. But obliged to complete some arduous research on American mines in order to finance his trip, he had set off again on complicated scientific travels, with scarcely any delay. He was, in any case, obliged to come back the slow way by sea, as travel by air was reserved during this early post-war period, and extremely difficult to book.

Before setting off on this six day crossing, he had sent an enigmatic letter to Mrs. Bennett declaring that he could not and would not go on at Coombe Springs alone for "Madame Quspensky says she never has and never will allow herself to be looked on as a teacher".

These statements received a rather mixed reception, but those of us who had been most deeply affected by Madame's revelation were comforted by a repetition of her question 'What would you do if a higher Teacher came?', and Bennett's own answer that one must put oneself unreservedly in his hands seemed to indicate that he would now be abandoning his long term plan for the establishment of a community overseas, something that had actually been maturing since the death of Ouspensky. But was it a series of happy accidents that helped him to change his mind even before he visited Madame Ouspensky? It was rather a complex situation . . . . .

* * *

When Bennett returned from his visit to Gurdjieff in Paris, my husband and I were at Coombe Springs for the Summer Seminar. It was the middle of August and some fifty or sixty people were gathered together in the garden to hear what he had to say. And he began by telling us that having now had an ample opportunity to think about our new situation, he believed that the time had come to talk about the historical background of the teaching which had been given to us by Mr Ouspensky.

Bennett had been introduced to Ouspensky by a Turkish neighbour when he was working as an intelligence officer at Constantinople soon after the war was over in the early nineteen twenties. He would have liked to have gone to Ouspensky's meetings but as at that time he didn't speak Russian, he had decided against it.

Then, going at a fairly smart pace, Bennett outlined the events which had led him to Gurdjieff - who was also in Constantinople - and his astonishment at finding Ouspensky at a demonstration of 'Temple Dances' given by pupils of Gurdjieff who had recently travelled with him from Tiflis, en route for Berlin[20], where he intended to make contact with Jacques-Dalcroze, the founder of Eurhythmics. But it

---

[20] This was in fact a dramatic presentation of the Movements which we had worked on for several years.

was not until some time after this that Bennett discovered that among Gurdjieff's pupils was a teacher of Eurhythmics and her husband, a well-known painter, who had been painting stage sets for the Opera House in Tiflis: these were Alexandre de Salzmann and his wife, Jeanne, and it was actually Madame de Salzmann who had recently made the arrangements in Paris connected with Bennett's visit to Gurdjieff . . . . .

And then Bennett continued more slowly: for some unknown reason Gurdjieff decided against settling in Germany and after making a visit to a Group in England which was working with Ouspensky, he returned to the Continent and settled in Paris, feeling that this would provide him with an ideal background for the teaching he had planned and the re-establishment of the Institute for the Harmonious Development of Man which he had started in the Caucasus. After a few months of doing practical work at an apartment in the rue Michel Ange - to prepare costumes for a new performance of 'The Struggle of the Magicians' - his secretary Olga de Hartmann[21] had discovered that the Chateau at Avon near Fontainbleau was for sale . . . . .

And here Bennett stopped completely. We had heard many accounts of life at the Prieuré and knew that Bennett - on the advice of Ouspensky - had stayed there for a month at the end of 1922. But for a number of different reasons he had never returned. And having sold the Prieuré in 1933, Gurdjieff had moved to Paris.

Then, ending with a brief description of the daily readings and meals at Gurdjieff's flat, Bennett told us that Madame de Salzmann was now a key figure in the organisation, and had overall responsibility for the Work in America as well as in Paris, with a particular interest in teaching Movements[22]. Furthermore, she now held a weekly Beginners Class at the famous Salle Pleyel.

The two things which remained with me were his reiteration about our continual need for self-remembering, and the fact that the great

---

[21] The wife of Thomas de Hartmann the composer who had written so much of the music for The Movements
[22] See Notebooks - Movements.

importance he attached to his recent meetings with Gurdjieff meant that our regular studies must now be completely changed. We would start right away - on this very afternoon - with some very long readings that he had brought back from Paris in the form of a typescript. But before that we should have a short interval and he could then enlarge a little on what he had just said about self-remembering. Most of us had already discovered that although it was thought that self-remembering was indispensable for man, we could only experience it by moments; but while he was in Paris he had been shown an exercise that completely transformed his understanding, and now he was certain that if we could work rightly, and become aware of the powers that were latent in our bodies, self-remembering would be possible for all of us . . . . .

Explaining to us that the reading he had mentioned would be taken from an extensive work which was described as 'Beelzebub's Tales To His Grandson, 'An Objectively Impartial Criticism of the Life of Man', he then went on to say that in the near future we should be having the opportunity of hearing further readings from the same series, which were identical to those which were read every day in Gurdjieff's flat. This was obviously the moment to tell us that when he returned to Paris in a few days' time - and every weekend thereafter - he would be able to take two or three members with him. And this opportunity had only arisen because in the month of August Gurdjieff's French pupils were absent. . . .

This astonishing piece of news produced a rather unusual question time: dead silence for one or two minutes, followed by five or six people saying *"Mr Bennett may I...?"* at the very same moment, and the laughter of all the rest of us.

Some complicated decisions were made, and it was perfectly clear to me that while George could join the small party which would leave for Paris in three weeks time, I would not be able to accompany him. But although something in me felt a kind of sadness, there was no disappointment - I had not expected to go. I was still responding to the news which had come to me two months ago 'Gurdjieff *alive* and working in Paris'. And I would go when my children were older. . . . .

Sitting under the hot sun of that August afternoon, marvelling at Bennett's nonchalance and still rather astounded at his positive news from Paris, the most potent thing I carried away with me from this first reading of 'Beelzebub's Tales' was the inscription on a marble tablet left behind by Ashiata Shiemash which had survived through successive civilizations in the ancient world.

Here was set out under the heading of 'Faith, Love And Hope' the typical interaction of the lower Centres in sleeping people like ourselves, as well as in people for whom Conscience had actually become more than a word. How clear it was that with the decay of religion neither Faith, nor Love, nor Hope could save us, linked as they were to our personal emotions and the impatience and greed of our flesh. Consciousness could be allied to these three to gain a positive result but for the moment our undeveloped Consciousness was unable to reach a high enough level. . . . .

As the reading began to unfold, I was plunged into the deepest speculation about the real meaning of the experience which had come to me in the rose garden. In the past we had frequently been warned not to theorise about Conscience, as our daily mechanical state of sleep was so far away from a real feeling experience that thinking about it would only drive us further into delusion. I had accepted this warning without reservation, because I could continually see the inevitable unreliability of my feelings about myself. What was different for me now was that I had begun to observe some momentary states which seemed to be true - I could almost call them pure - but these were so quickly modified by some strong strands in my nature that they were virtually invisible.

And what actually happened when my feeling state suddenly altered I could never really see: it was as if, in changing direction, energy was now pouring away of its own volition. And there was no observable link of any kind between the two states. So, although something voiceless had the feeling I shall not get caught this way again, it was always proved wrong.

I had tried to prepare for actually going to Paris in the near future by returning to Bennett's idea that what we all needed was a clear question, but as I considered this I inevitably found myself back in the garden on that day when I discovered that Gurdjieff was alive. Honesty had to come in at this point: while I admitted to myself that my incomprehensible feelings might well be a better ambassador than any well thought out questions, I had been obliged to put all thinking about an actual question away.

But what did I really need?

The changes in my inner life, which had been harvested little by little over the years, though small enough and quite invisible to outsiders had been all-important to me. The most serious one concerned a recognition that all my earnest so-called 'Work' was vitiated by dreams. In everyday life I seemed to be a middle-of-the-road performer, reasonably practical and reliable. Inside myself I dreamed of enjoying life against a more exciting backdrop - through expanding friendships, my (already sacrificed) work as a writer, and my imagined talent as both a designer of clothes and landscapes.

In between certain invaluable set exercises of attention - where I was more fully 'myself' - my energy had poured into this counterfeit existence. And although in my earliest years of attendance at lectures it was our work of observing the *formatory* apparatus which had inspired me, much more recently I had seen the killing nature of my continual inner generosity to myself.

For years I had seen that I lacked *Attention*, and this was all that separated me from self-remembering. And the question which had arisen from that had seemed practical. I deflected my mind by giving it mathematical calculations or scriptures to repeat, and these had calmed down my urge to find solutions for various traits that disturbed me.

To bring all these many facets of work together in the form of a clear question could never be a simple proposition for me.

Chapter 16

SIX RUE DES COLONELS RENARD

Five weeks passed.

I was hurrying to my Movements class when I met Bennett striding in the opposite direction. He stopped at once, and said without any preliminaries,

"Why not take Caroline to Paris on the Golden Arrow?"

Why not! I knew that the Golden Arrow was a modern version of the Flèche D'Or which ran between Paris and London before the war, and which I had always associated with film stars and bottomless bank balances. Most of our friends travelled by cross channel steamer, which necessitated having their cars swung aboard a cargo boat by crane. But we had already decided against this, and it was not at all easy to know how we could transport Caroline in her Carrycot, and the more we thought about the Golden Arrow the more we liked it. I had only just begun to wean her and decided to backtrack immediately, since sitting in a private drawing room compartment would make it possible for us to travel as soon as we liked. That we could not afford it was obvious, and trying to remember the name of the famous philosopher who always said 'I will think about it *tomorrow*' helped me to silence most of my objections.

It was an extraordinarily easy journey: everything went our way, even to the extent of the advanced booking of a suitable bedroom in a nearby hotel who could give us a *cabinet de toilette* (dressing room) in which Caroline could sleep, plus a decorative chambermaid, Giselle, with a Renoir fringe, who from time to time would lend an ear. And even Caroline's evening feed could be worked in conveniently with the rather late time of a reading in the flat which would take place before Gurdjieff's dinner - although having to leave her alone was a rather hard test for me - but obeying a rather impatient friend who insisted on accompanying us to the door of Number Six Rue Des Colonels Renard could not be avoided. . . . .

*   *   *

On very small stools sat a few people I had never seen before, plus one or two of Bennett's pupils. All at once, just as I had decided that we must somehow infiltrate into this settled scene and find seats for ourselves, I heard the steady flip-flop of slippers approaching the entrance hall outside the room, not exactly a shuffle, but definitely the step of someone no longer young, whose weight and movement produced a disturbance in the air, something like a very slight echo. I cannot say, now, that anything in me responded to these impressions. Various delaying tactics happened rather quickly: a young Frenchwoman opened the glass door and very seriously, as if weighing something up, looked around. There were various nervous movements on my right, and then, suddenly, there he was, slowly advancing across the narrow room and smiling at an elderly woman who had risen impulsively to her feet and, with hand outstretched, stepped forward across the space in front of the stools. Indulgently, he halted to receive her greeting, looking neither to the left nor the right, a mere twelve or fourteen inches away from me, and it was as if he had brought with him some other quite potent atmosphere.

What I felt then was beyond evaluation; there was no inner comment at all. Nothing : neither approval nor disapproval. I just stood there, quite free, as if suspended in a state of steady perception. Long afterwards, I remembered hearing an account of Mr Gurdjieff's teaching which exactly described this moment: 'You will experience something completely new, and must hope that in your struggles to understand you do not lose it too quickly.'

Standing, more or less immobile, strangely outside the scene that was being enacted barely a foot away, I was suddenly deeply re-connected with that unknown 'me' who had reacted so strongly to the original news of Gurdjieff's survival 'But he is *alive* and teaching in Paris'. This note, sounding once more across the intervening months, re-awakened what I had previously experienced. Blossoming again in a kind of deeply personal and secret confidence, an understanding which was much more than hope, and a kind of meekness and *readiness for anything* filled the places often reserved in everyday life for my restless analyses and constant self-justification – my endless comparisons, commitments, re-shufflings and deeply hidden belligerence.

As words and elementary thoughts began to filter through this ideal state, uppermost in my mind I found the taste of truth which recent visitors had brought back to England. This man bore no resemblance whatsoever to the kind of mountebank with piercing eyes who had been written off by some of the dilettante commentators from an earlier generation. Now, face to face, I took in the faded extensive bruising left by the recent motor accident on his honey-coloured skin, as well as the wide, warm smile which somehow masked his eyes. A maroon-coloured *fez*, worn at an unexpectedly carefree angle, completely obscured the shape of his head, and his air of deep relaxation and generosity was completed by loose clothes: a kind of grey smoking jacket cum dressing gown, also edged in maroon, over baggy old trousers surmounted by a white Russian blouse with an embroidered neckline.

Just as he began to move rather slowly but very deliberately away from his central stance, I realized that despite the extraordinarily positive feelings that inhabited me, and my strong sense of 'belonging', I had in fact been completely outside his field of vision, both literally and metaphorically. Now he wheeled around surprisingly lightly on his heavy body, making a small affectionate salute in the direction of an old friend of mine, and saying 'Who have we here?' before seating himself in a dark blue velvet tub chair near the entrance, and I suddenly found myself seated in the front row of the audience, much too big for my stool. Affecting a nonchalance I certainly did not feel as I wrestled with my excessively long legs, I then prepared myself inadequately for the reading, fully aware of Gurdjieff's eye upon me.

At first, my unexpected sense of having at last come into harbour after a long, rough and dangerous voyage deepened. But as I concentrated on what was being read I was aware of an unforeseen difficulty, a new incapacity somewhere in my head. In the days when I had been employed professionally as a reporter, I had very often been obliged to separate form from content in something that necessarily had to be recorded rapidly without questioning, and one had not to allow oneself at any moment to be carried away by a happy phrase. Instinctively, and at the risk of oversimplifying, I had been obliged to hang onto the verbs, and relied on a dogged persistence to carry me through. This aptitude now appeared to have deserted me completely and, despite what I had felt in England when I thought I was growing familiar with the intentionally complex style of writing, I followed the words but understood practically nothing. Quite new words, with syllables culled from other languages - and unusual idioms - I did try to hang on to, not noticing that it was these that principally led me astray, and it was almost as if some elementary function which I was accustomed to had been inconveniently switched off. Later I was able to diagnose this as either the result of fatigue, or the breakdown, through shock, of my customary mechanical emotions, for the new ideas aroused neither approval nor disapproval and no wishing or wanting. Had I been questioned just then, I should have replied that I wanted above all to hear the reading, and that I *must* listen, but in fact, just at this juncture nothing in me wanted to hear any more words at all, however much I was ordinarily addicted to them.

All this time I was sitting very erect on my small stool, but looking forward and down as if to examine minutely the oriental carpet a few feet away from me. Gurdjieff was on my right, not much more than four feet away at an angle of forty five degrees, more or less facing the reader who sat to my left at the side of the fireplace, at right angles to the wall, on an ordinary chair with a seat well above the rest of the audience, and I was extraordinarily aware of the simple relationship in space of just the three of us, who made a kind of slightly crooked and flattened isosceles triangle with me at the apex.

I could never remember afterwards what caused me suddenly to raise my head and look directly at Gurdjieff, not rather diffidently and 'politely' as I should have done elsewhere finding myself in the middle of new acquaintances, but without any reservations at all, and with an openness that ordinarily I should have felt contained an element of effrontery. As I looked my fill, it was as if I were saying with deep feeling 'So *now* I *am* here, *here* at last, *here*', connecting extraordinarily with a realization that without any words having passed between us, he was already well acquainted with me, and that in this realization – something quite new - I was touching a different level of consciousness, apparently endowed entirely by him.

This experience seemed to go on for a very long time, and if my usual kind of analysis was struggling to re-assert itself out of sight, it did not succeed. Words went away completely. I sat there, shifting my gaze forward. I listened. I was alive to my blood and my muscles and the movements in my thorax, until the sudden arising of an indescribable solemnity which, spreading throughout my torso, gathered together and multiplied warm feelings that swung back across my entire life to about the age of three. At this unexpected turn of events, I bent my head once more, quite overcome, suddenly tasting my naivety and ignorance and not knowing at all how to respond to this sudden intrusion of my awkward past into what seemed a joyfully free present. But I was not to be abandoned to my ordinary state without any resource at all. The solemnity, which had at first appeared to threaten everything, somehow blossomed in the need for me to turn away from my old self and embrace new ideas which absolutely could not be expressed in words but were apparently the fruit of a kind of deep trust that had a completely invisible and unsuspected root. The reading going on and on called me back, and it was as if something had ordained that at all costs I must now oblige myself to continue outwardly with an everyday level to which I was not actually attached, while entirely another part of me appeared to be recognizing that there was much more to the expansion of attention than I had ever guessed, and that even daily life might be lived against a background essentially different from that which could be captured and explained by the busy formatory apparatus.

Before such a challenge, I was inevitably more or less paralysed, and all that mattered was just to sit there, apparently calm, outwardly listening, though actually adrift from the kind of assent or criticism that usually accompanied any inrush of ideas to my greedy everyday mind, until little by little my awareness welcomed afresh the strange combination of solemnity and infant satisfaction. When we were eventually released from our stools so that we might proceed into the next room for dinner, I hung back a little, anxious for a real interval of silence by myself, hopefully free from the notice and even the welcome of friends.

Chapter 17

FIRST MEAL IN GURDJIEFF'S FLAT

When, at last, I found myself seated at the historic table, it seemed natural enough that the atmosphere evoked a long lost and almost forgotten response. What arose in me then to meet this unexpected event was a feeling of solemnity such as I had never known before. Here was something indubitably new set against a stilling of the mind which was paradoxically recognizable. No words or images arose to blur the first impression. No reaction appeared.

It interested me afterwards, that looking back rather sentimentally to my earliest meals in the flat, I always saw myself sitting opposite Gurdjieff, at the side of Madame de Salzmann, but if I brought my attention fully to the experience I actually remembered that on the very first occasion of all Madame was seated on the far left of my immediate neighbour, whose face I was not able to recall.

I had no sooner taken the seat that was indicated, tightly wedged between two strangers, both women, when the solemnity which enveloped me - still cutting out extraneous associations - turned into a kind of compelling awe. This feeling, deeper by far than solemnity, had the familiar flavour of my very early childhood, which had arrived first during the reading, but instead of a strong accent on bodily sensitivity, I now experienced the simple warmth of gratitude, which linking with something like patience connected me directly with Gurdjieff himself.

Once or twice, barely raising his head, Gurdjieff looked in my direction, while with his extraordinarily young and expressive hands he began to prepare some titbit for a pupil. And the awe, little by little increasing, as if the solemnity from which it sprang could no longer contain it, swirled back and forth within me, ebbing and flowing like a kind of expanding helix until revealed very suddenly as the earliest religious feeling I had ever known. This potent state, quite definite although unconnected with doctrine - a kind of certainty, both sophisticated and innocent - pushed back the boundary of words altogether and for the first time since I arrived I could look outwards instead of inwards, reminding myself that I was no longer locked in alone with my awkward past, but linked instead to an unusual consciousness of the present moment.

I had expected before I arrived at the flat to be landed at the table in some kind of really intensive testing ground. And I knew that as well as trying to understand long readings in the still unfamiliar language of 'Beelzebub' I would also be listening to conversations in French, Turkish and Russian. Because of all this I realized that my attention would need to be razor sharp. What I could not have expected, of course, was the arrival of a strangely invisible teaching which, revolving like a primitive plough, worked deep down within me to bring absolutely forgotten but essential things to light.

An air of expectancy in the room was now sparked off by apparently meaningless exchanges between Gurdjieff, now bareheaded and seated on a kind of short banquette-divan, and a woman at the table, as well as between Gurdjieff and a man addressed as 'Director', who was standing to his left - Russian flowing in one direction and French in the other.

Before we left England my husband had explained to me about the Director, and the complicated toasting ritual at every meal. This was part of an ancient survival called 'The Science of Idiotism'. The archaic meaning of the word 'Idiot' was unexpected, meaning man in his very simplest, original aspect - his 'private' self – and at the table, of course, we must all wish to aspire to it. Though clear to me that I did indeed wish for such simplicity, I did not know how to choose from a scale which

I could not pretend to recognize - and that we all must try earnestly was certainly inescapable, bravely accepting the risk of actually being very widely off the mark. In ordinary life I should certainly have found this taste of complete ignorance insupportable, but here it was simply a challenge. That I did not, falsely, choose the first or 'Ordinary Idiot' which to begin with seemed the easiest to understand, was certainly fortunate. I was very strongly tempted to do so, but luckily something made me delay, and I decided that I must first look and listen before choosing, and find out a little more if I possibly could.

But if I partly understood, and could even memorize the order in which the toasts were placed, this still couldn't help me at all with their intrinsic qualities. What, for instance, would approximate to a 'Super Idiot' or an 'Arch Idiot'? Luckily, my puzzlement and acceptance were about equal and later I was ready for some more or less accurate homespun descriptions. What defeated me cruelly, again and again, was the idea that the scale was both moving and static. Idiots progressed - and yet, I said to myself, if they were properly chosen to start with, they must surely, for the time being, have a kind of dynamic permanence. The 'Ordinary Idiot' was deceptive as actually it could represent a fully developed, regenerated man who, having struggled for self-knowledge, had traveled upwards through the entire Scale of Idiotism, and then returned to genuine innocence - the simplest definition of all when it actually came to being oneself.

* * *

The Director on this particular day was a man, an old and long established pupil; but on some other evening the role might just as likely have been taken by a young woman, quite fresh to the task. Although the people changed, the role was constant, the Director being responsible for the announcing of the toasts and the service of the guests. But he was actually not only a toastmaster. As a kind of honorary head waiter he also had to be continually aware of what Gurdjieff wanted, or would perhaps need later. Often he had an assistant known as the *Verseur*, who poured the drinks throughout the meal and therefore had to remember what had been chosen by each guest. The choice was between red and white vodka, although Armagnac or more rarely Calvados were sometimes given to very esteemed persons, the men consuming one third of a small glass and the women one sixth, at each toast.

All this serving of drinks had to be finished before the meal itself could rightfully commence, and if the room were destined to fill up completely there were many other delays. The table held about fifteen people and was wider near the door of the dining room - a sort of fat L-shape - composed of two pieces of furniture arranged at right angles in order to seat the very greatest number of guests that the room could hold. People stood behind those who were seated, balancing their plates in the air, as well as at the upright piano or chimney piece, and a card table was occasionally erected in the only empty corner to the left of the entrance, to accommodate a small overflow. Sometimes several courses of the meal were already stacked at each place on the table before the diners were seated and as the guests were taking their places, the remaining plates were being propelled by a human *chaîne* along a corridor which stretched from the dining room to the kitchen. This chain was composed of younger French pupils, plus a sprinkling of *habitués* from both England and America, and was set in motion by a call from the dining room.

As we all waited in this somewhat vibrant atmosphere for the last glass to be filled and the last standing diners to be served, I was suddenly richly rewarded with an extension of time, as if the seconds and minutes meted out to my world were indefinitely prolonged, consolidating an emerging experience of long buried feelings. I was there very simply, just watching, and too satisfied with watching even to recognize or record that this was exactly the state I had struggled and struggled for when, seven years ago, I had first heard about self-remembering and I had said repeatedly 'But why does it disappear so soon; why can't I do it?'.

How long the mysterious simplicity of this new moment of time could have lasted, I was not to discover, for we were suddenly called very loudly to attention,

'Attention, please. To the health of all Ordinary Idiots . . . . .'

Was it only the modulated voice of the Director that had made this extraordinary reverberating call? Aware that I must at last take part in the meal, and that my knowledge of ritual toasting was elementary, I now had to pay much closer attention to what went on around me. First I must listen carefully to the precise name of each toast, then memorize. When I had reached some kind of conclusion about the appropriate toast for myself, and after thinking of this for a day and a night, I must inform the Director of my choice.

In advance, described very simply by my husband, taking part in Gurdjieff's Science of Idiotism, though certainly unusual, had not sounded quite so testing an ordeal. But when I was actually confronted with it at the table, my first thoughts actually objected, finding it quite impossible.

But little by little I realized that there was a purity in the strange simplicity of the terms that had to be accepted (I genuinely had no associations) - one could really consent to be fully oneself as if no complexity had to be reckoned with or hastily rejected.

Until the moment when we all had our glasses full and even the last standing diner had been served, I had no proper thought of what I should eventually find myself eating, faith in the whole enterprise having apparently replaced the usual reservations of a nursing mother. Nor did I consciously regret the absence of the necessary glass of water. I was glad of the sudden lull in the proceedings and looked somewhat wonderingly at the stack of plates in front of me, but no-one at all was eating yet.

People from earlier visits, genuinely sympathetic that I could not accompany my husband in the summer 'because of the baby', had tended to overstress the importance of knowing what to do, and had tried to tell me what to expect at every stage so that I should not miss anything. I had generally managed to wriggle out of this assistance, realizing very deeply that what I should need above all would be my own unassisted first impressions, free of both words and expectations.

But now I was sufficiently prepared, anyway, for the first toast, though not exactly ready for the strength of the white vodka which had been recommended to me as the easiest of the drinks, and I was certainly thankful to have had that brief but concise account of the 'Science of Idiots' from my husband, as this basis of the whole toasting ritual became more and more complex as I strove vainly to bring it into focus. I knew already that I would have time during the first day to become acquainted with all the different toasts: I had only to listen carefully.

I steadied myself a little by eating the *salade* in its small bowl very slowly and carefully and endeavouring to decipher its contents - a sort of *salade provençale* but with an anonymous tang, and some unrecognizable isolated ingredients. I was not so sure of the succulent rissole which followed with a Persian-seeming vegetable, and after another toast, unguessable in its implications, I was thankful to be passed a whole spring onion and a long sprig of French Tarragon to somewhat neutralize the richness of the generous meat course. And now the importance of the baby's next meal began to be remembered, and even if I could not bring it quite into focus I was thankful not to be handed paprika delicacies or the bear meat generously proffered to my neighbour as a great delicacy.

I looked straight forward, affecting not to notice or be caught up in this dangerous kind of gift. George had warned me about an attractive looking piquant sauce in a little bottle that almost entirely removed the skin from the back of one's throat, causing near asphyxiation en route, but if such an offering came one's way it was impossible to refuse. What a simpleton I was at the table on that day, and on the days to follow. Not once was I offered anything to cause an infant extreme discomfort or diarrhoea. Gifts flowed to right and left, always missing me so easily and naturally and I actually did not understand until years had passed that Bennett would obviously have told Madame de Salzmann in advance that I was taking a baby which I was feeding myself. When this suddenly hit me after Gurdjieff had been long dead, I experienced that first visit once again, but so poignantly, in a kind of wonderment at the sight of the extended spoon and his withdrawn eyes, always missing me out. And out of sight too were the riches which his presence activated.

From time to time I stopped eating altogether as if to gather strength to finish the whole meal by degrees, as in this way I could summon just enough attention to follow more of the toasts. Had I been plunged there and then into the idea of the absolute necessity of being really and truly myself, and of aspiring to know my idiot completely without the foretaste I had met in the reading room, I think I would have been submerged forever. As the meal progressed it was as if ideas flew past me like birds wired to a complex figure in a science project, passing away and returning again, proving something to someone or other but certainly never to be caught or remembered by me. And it was only the deep feeling from my childhood, that still persisted, which kept me both outwardly calm and inwardly still.

Little by little, as I became used to sitting receptive in this pool of quiet, I could feel a clear wish rising to the surface of my consciousness, a gentle movement in the direction of truth which finally represented itself quite definitely as a real prayer - something I had hoped to regain years before, but with all my seeking had never found. This recognition so filled me to the brim, that I was obliged, half turning in the direction of Gurdjieff, to look upon him with a quite new gaze before inevitably looking down again, away from his presence. More came to me now, almost unbearably, than the simplicity of the prayer - but it was only the merest hint - as if the old feeling of religiousness could be tasted more fully, but what I had been given for the present was really more than enough.

Aware that I had been brought to the very brink of a conscious possibility in which there was a strange combination of both suffering and rejoicing, I then heard the toastmaster again, 'To the Health of all Hopeless Idiots'.

This was not dramatic in the way earlier events had been, but I recognised it as a direct answer to my questioning. Here was my idiot,

'This is what I must inevitably choose!' And I could not have known then, but this was the idiot that could always earn an extra comment. How inevitable had it been?

I certainly did not hear the toast for Compassionate Idiot, only discovering its existence later as if it had never been.

I sat there leaning very slightly forward, with my eyes down, as if still listening, and with a torso that seemed the most improbable part of me, dark and quiet and edged with my external shape, disguised in dark brown velvet corduroy, a little tight, which to a really perceptive eye might well have betrayed my nursing role. Now and again Gurdjieff would address someone near to me, or converse with Madame de Salzmann in Russian, and once he told a story that became my favourite of all the things he liked to tell,

'You look at me like cow at new-paint *porte*.', said he to an old friend of mine, who was staring relentlessly at him, apparently unperturbed, her dark eyes wide open, and the faintest smile almost breaking out beneath eloquent, rounded cheeks which quivered so very slightly that perhaps only I, who knew her well, would translate this as a deep need for reassurance and understanding.

This story had many versions. The cow was lost in the forest - and it also could have a calf that was lost in the forest - and when returning home in the evening, it was unable to find its home.

Here Gurdjieff would act out both calf and cow, bending his head back and from side to side, rolling his eyes, for how could the new-paint *porte* ever be recognised? On this occasion, the smile of my friend creased right across in open laughter. Others joined her, and I was now orientated so differently in myself that it did not occur to me at all that there might be two views about this spontaneous merriment. Six months earlier I would have regarded this untrammeled spontaneity rather differently and the question 'why laugh?' would certainly be visiting me again and again during the ensuing year.

Chapter 18

UNDERSTANDING

Caroline, always a good baby, settled in at once to a completely different routine. Happiness, shot through with tranquillity, brilliance and tension, and a kind of knowledge that real striving must sometime begin soon, sustained us. I was like someone who, having climbed up an immense mountain with all its hazards and promises, suddenly finds herself transported to the top by a celestial agency. Here the view was entirely different and the last few miles of terrain completely unknown. How had it happened? And, since I wasn't intended to live on the heights alone, could I descend and perhaps mount again?

Before the meal, waiting to hear the second reading from 'Beelzebub's Tales', I was still unaware that what, until now, I had looked upon as 'Work' was about to lose its significance. Sitting on my small stool, divorced once again from my stale daily thoughts, I was aware that Gurdjieff read my state across the crowded room, not once but a number of times, and as he did so unexpected sensations rose to the surface - in my arms and legs, my back, my solar plexus and my blood - and my thoughts and feelings were inspected and put on one side. And throughout this experience a kind of timelessness invaded me.

When it had been impressed on me, before I left England, that if I tried to clarify my most important question I should get all the help I needed, I had not believed it. I was very impatient, and I felt that in

Paris I should be looking for confirmation of the unconfirmable and knowledge of the unknowable. Besides these, the defects in my nature seemed rather trivial. Many years were to pass before I understood the real basis of Gurdjieff's help and the depth of his compassion that had patiently set me on a true path. Nothing could have been further away than asking for help. Help was in the very air we breathed. It was the quintessence of all good things that had happened throughout my life, gathered together and offered back. Two days passed like this, incredibly slowly, with the unforgiving minutes crammed down and spilling over. . . . .

One day, as we sat late for lunch, Bennett drew attention to me, staying well past the time for the midday feed.

'I have to feed my baby' I said.

'What? Baby is here?' said Gurdjieff, his voice rising at the end of the question, 'Two, three days and I not see? Please,' he beckoned with his head, 'baby my weakness. Bring tomorrow, lunch. When eat? First we will have Christmas tree'.

'The baby's only six months.' said Bennett.

'All babies like tree' said Gurdjieff. I arranged to bring her at two and departed. Next day when we arrived with Caroline we in fact went straight to Gurdjieff's little room to drink coffee. Feeling nervous, I sat opposite him with Caroline on my knee. In this confined space Gurdjieff seemed enormous. Caroline gazed and gazed, unsmiling but focussed, and clearly seeing something I couldn't see. After a very long time, Gurdjieff said 'Which is it, English or Irish?'.

My husband, George, said, a little too eagerly, 'You mean it is possible to tell already?'. Gurdjieff said nothing.

Then, presently, 'What she like?'

'She has two teeth', I replied, proud.

'Ah, she can eat', and he opened a box of Turkish delight.

'Chew it', he said. Anxious, as I saw the nuts - Caroline had never chewed before - I gave her a small piece, but now she chewed as if this were quite normal, eventually spitting the nut out.

'Clever baby.' said Gurdjieff, 'Better not that, better this', giving us a large tin of guava jelly. 'Give twice a day. Now she can go sleep.' As I lay her on the bed in Lisa's dark bedroom at the far end of the corridor I half expected a cry, but no. With a very wondering look in her eyes she lay there quietly and so I left her and went to the reading.

When I went to collect her afterwards, I met Madame de Salzmann in the corridor and she said to me 'It was very courageous of you to bring the baby.' But, feeling very emotional, I could not reply to this, and we just stood there silently and looked at each other.

We were to stay on half a day longer than everyone else and when we said goodbye he said: 'That baby, she my pupil. She understand everything, all *Beelzebub*. You not understand, but she understand'. Not recognising myself, I handed him the photograph of Caroline in her christening dress which he said he would keep, adding with great satisfaction, 'She my youngest pupil'.

So what was it I didn't understand?

I had started by answering silently 'You know what happened before I came here and what I have experienced in these few days; I understand something, but it is true that I do not understand the future' . . . . .

And I had not yet added this feeling about the future to the thoughts, which so often invaded me, on how long would it actually be before my Centres were better related and the self-knowledge which I thought I had acquired could be of use?

* * *

Caroline slept comfortably between us on the night ferry and as we sped onwards in the darkness I reflected on my latest question.

I had never doubted that I still took understanding on a perfectly ordinary level, inevitably referring new ideas to reference points that had somehow been already established in my head, and there was a part of me, quite strong, which simply looked upon this as a necessary kind of questioning. At the same time, I had also become completely convinced that work on oneself could lead to an absolutely different kind of understanding, for what one 'understood' in the ordinary way was *really* only 'knowledge' - the function of one centre. How feeling and sensation could ultimately be united with this perception, ensuring a balanced work of the three lower centres, remained a mystery.

A conversation with Bennett of two or three years before sometimes returned to me in this connection. I was deeply dissatisfied with my 'being', and readily acceded to the idea that I was asleep, and even welcomed this as a clarification of earlier problems. But I had not the feeling that my efforts rewarded me with an adequate approach to the level of consciousness I had glimpsed before I had begun seriously to try to bring attention to my ordinary working day. At the same time, it was not too much to claim that doing small tasks with attention had radically changed my entire life.

Where was I going wrong? What did I need? Why was there a very definite limit to the level of consciousness I could acquire?

Privately I was tired of hearing everyone say that they could not remember themselves. Bennett had been very patient with me, had abstained from pointing out my exaggerated expectations and my vanity, but had turned my attention very deliberately in a new direction. I must realize that whereas I now knew about and was inspired by the idea of recognising and acknowledging my mechanicalness, and the corresponding necessity for efforts in this direction, really, I did only *know* it. Despite my apparent success with daily tasks, the effect of all this lay only in the mind. It had to be felt much more deeply. When I could *feel* it, then I would understand.

At this point I had expostulated, quite unaware of the real delicacy with which Bennett was approaching my situation, but he, both gently and strongly, held his ground. Whereas I might be genuinely deeply concerned about my feeling of failure and lack of any real sense of direction, he personally was not disappointed in me. I had kept going with what I had seen as the primary effort to increase and expand my moments of consciousness and thereby lessen the heavy weight of my conditioning. Most of us, when we began to observe our inner atmosphere of demands, and the lies of negative emotions, had this longing for being that I was now expressing. I had to realize *now*, in a completely new way, that only the whole Work - the Movements, the practical activities, the recapitulation of the lectures and so on - could eventually give me what I felt I needed. He naturally did not put into words that I could not expect to work on myself alone, or ever get a positive result from tasks I might devise for myself, but I was very much left with that atmosphere, plus a strong feeling that one line consistently pursued (which in my case was a continual emphasis on the need for a change in consciousness) could by its very nature only be a beginning.

It was extremely interesting in that talk how Bennett had laid the basis of a more active form of work for me. I understood suddenly - you could say *practically* - that my desire and initiative were truly the active force in my daily life, but my stale ideas of long ago and my ways of 'going on' - i.e. my own psychological approach - were a strong passive or negative force, inevitably producing inertia and actual opposition. All this I already knew in theory.

Could I now recognise fully that it was the new knowledge I had been open to which produced a third force and strengthened the initiative I already possessed? This was indispensable. But only if I really *understood* as fully as possible would I be able to take advantage of the new situation, of all the different lines of work promoted by the Institute. And I must not merely take advantage haphazardly, or in a way that happened to suit me personally. I must work on these different lines simultaneously, and somehow become stretched in my endeavours beyond my usual habits, but well within my capacities. Such a stretching would not come about mechanically; I must look out for opportunities. Somehow my efforts must be multiplied, not merely extended in duration, which is what I had been looking for.

This talk with Bennett, which had hinged entirely on *understanding* had caused me to look much more deeply at what I had learned up to that moment, as well as at all the various opportunities that were already open to me.

The war was still on: to get to meetings and days of practical work one travelled backwards and forwards in the blackout, on buses and trains with heavily obscured windows very necessary for the protection of passengers in the high explosive raids. When the buses stopped in the heaviest raids, one must brave the shrapnel whistling down, or even the bombs themselves, throwing oneself flat on the ground, running into doorways or down into the areas of Victorian houses to wait for a lull in the bombardment before finding communal shelters in the Tube stations.

To all this, one had soon become perfectly adapted. What other purely external obstacles could I find? I went over the details of my life fairly scrupulously and was suddenly shocked to realize I was host to an incredible number of quite invisible fears. And part of this was even concerned with my work at Coombe, where I saw I had often greatly feared the intolerance of an older student who made the practical arrangements for kitchen work, but that my picture of myself had not at any point included this realization. Forcing myself to assent to what I actually witnessed at that moment had such a profound effect on me that I received a completely new and quite unsuspected impression of the value of practical work. If I had to learn to struggle on every possible kind of front before attaining self knowledge, I would have to stop wriggling away from unpleasant impressions of this kind.

Many more shocks, many more failures, and many more disappointments had filled the years between that conversation and the present moment, and they had certainly given me a kind of understanding that I could never have dreamed of in advance. My understanding of the three forces at work in my search waxed and waned. From some points of view the idea of 'Triads' became a private study which I could not leave alone, a sort of intriguing puzzle which I knew I could never solve but which activated everything most active in my intellect.

One was, at that time, completely accustomed to the fact that no literature of the Work existed; no rushing to Ouspensky to take a refresher course in the Law of Three was possible. What I had caught onto firmly at the first lecture I had attended had been strong and undeniable in its ability to convey that, such as I was, I could never hope to understand and apply the Law of Three unaided, and this impossibility was actually part of the operation of the Law which nothing in me could possibly ever defeat. And even with the very best aid available, perhaps I should still never understand. This dramatic statement had struck me so deeply that it somehow reinforced what natural abilities I had for listening and recording. Let me record, if only inside my head, and later there might be a possibility to go further. This one little merit of mine had seemed small enough in comparison with the ambitious notions included in my picture of myself, and if it did nothing else it had matured a mustard seed of reality in connection with triads - something there was no possibility of imagining about. Somehow or other I must just keep this as a distant aim for which, like the ant, I could and would put by material.

It was very appropriate for the whole subject of Triads to have come alive for me in Gurdjieff's flat. How had I ever supposed that what I would meet there could be understood in an ordinary way? What any of us could understand here and there were like scintillating points of light, now growing and now diminishing, and I was gratefully taking this bright experience back to my very unordinary ordinary life.

And so this crux which I carried homewards, this statement of Gurdjieff's that I understood nothing at all, and that my baby of six months understood everything, what in fact was it meant to arouse in me?

And what was it I didn't understand?

This is where I came back to again and again as the months lengthened. Autumn hardened into winter, not wanting to give way to spring, but April came eventually. We were still without books and the only help I could hope for was in my memory. In the flat there had been a good deal of talk about Intentional Suffering and Being Duty and I felt cautiously in this direction, decided on 'pushing myself' and took in hand a whole host of things I didn't like doing, aware that in my case this would at least do me no harm, even if it was only a weapon against laziness and self importance.

Our work had been changed. Now there were no more lectures with questions and answers. Instead we had regular readings of Gurdjieff's book 'All And Everything, An Impartial Criticism Of The Life Of Man' which Gurdjieff had always referred to succinctly as 'Beelzebub'. Useless to suppose that this would be a language that my memory could help me with. Like everyone else I struggled to understand. Relating to the efforts I had previously made was not merely difficult. It was impossible. As against this, I had been given a morning exercise and was beginning to have a new conception of how self-remembering might change. And the rose garden experience was still exerting its influence.

I was helping to organise some local public lectures for Bennett and as I called on strangers, distributed leaflets and delivered tickets was very much aware that the obvious concern behind their interest actually did not move me. This hardness of heart which I had at first re-glimpsed in the flat was an old enemy which had lain low for a considerable time. As a girl my life had been filled with good causes. All my pocket money would go on tramps and street musicians and my time was given away ruthlessly to the charitable cause of the moment. Now, face to face with people who expected something from me, I listened and squirmed inwardly, finding myself cold and unresponsive. But something new felt this inhumanity and almost cried out against it. I saw bleakly what a great way I should have to travel before my feelings could correspond with my pretence. Apparently there were very many kinds of so-called 'work' that I could attempt, but the acquisition of one simple, positive emotion seemed beyond me. Up to now I had scarcely glimpsed the implications of this, but now I began to meet it head on. Could Paris already have opened up this situation for me? Had I 'understood'? Despite my changed attitudes, was I irretrievably a pseudo-intellectual?

I wondered about this and went back at the Russian Easter-time.

Chapter 19

RUSSIAN EASTER

On my first visit, when toasts were drunk, I had chosen to be Hopeless Idiot and six months later to the day when toasts had been long and drawn out I was not prepared to be included in the conversation as Doubting Idiot.

'Guest here for the first time,' said Mr Gurdjieff 'see how she doubt, what she doubt?'

I must have looked as I felt, not willing to commit myself, but with strong feeling. Madame de Salzmann, who sat opposite Mr Gurdjieff at the side of the long table, had placed me next to her with the introduction *'Bennettski'*.

After the meal I said to Gurdjieff 'It's not the first time, Monsieur, you remember, I brought the Baby?'.

Gurdjieff replied very quickly 'Baby I remember,' but, very firmly, 'you I not remember'.

Saturday was the Russian Easter Eve and we were surrounded by dishes of hand-decorated Easter eggs painted variously in blue, red and yellow. These were handed around. Quite by coincidence, as a gift, I had brought fresh eggs from our own hens.

'Only twice a year I eat eggs,' said Mr Gurdjieff, looking at me as a special dish was set before him, 'but not possible to get eggs so fresh here'. I felt unreasonably pleased, and smiled like a small child, relaxing visibly.

The toasts got on again. We had reached Swaggering Idiot, and Gurdjieff, who had been concentrating on the toastmaster, very suddenly turned to me and said:

'You Swaggering Idiot, like turkey - turkey even swagger when no-one there'.

Seated at the table, as he was, and continuing, he then gave his wonderful imitation of a peacock with turkey stance, showing off his tail to all and sundry by swaying from side to side.

'Turkey cock think he a real peacock. Swaggering Idiot think he understand everything.'

Then Madame de Salzmann turned to me and asked 'You understand what he is saying?', and I replied 'Yes, perfectly', feeling somehow lighter and much more free. Gurdjieff, nodding his head, observed 'I like this idiot'.

After a long pause, during which time he looked at me pretty closely, he said, 'You excuse, Miss? I use you to prove a cosmological principle. You not offended with me and for this I give you *cadeau*'.

At that moment it seemed to me there was no-one else in the room - in fact the table was crowded. I bent to listen as he told me about the gift.

'You sensible.', he said, explaining that the gift was just half of something I needed and that I must get the other half later.

'You come back soon, you remember. Maybe one month. Maybe one year, maybe two. You persevere. You *never* give up. You not satisfied till you get other half'.

It was very quiet in the room.

Aware that the conversation had left me while I needed silence to accustom myself to the challenge of the *cadeau*, little by little I began to listen to Gurdjieff talking about Easter Mass at the Russian Cathedral.

He asked a question.

'Some of us would be going to the Rue Daru tomorrow? This feeling experience - such good thing . . . . .'

Although he was speaking more quietly than usual, and it was difficult to catch every word, there was something very deliberate in his short phrases, followed enigmatically by isolated words,

'Togetherness - Consciousness.'

And all at once one lifted finger in teaching pose and the single word - '*Douze*', followed by complete silence and attention only for eating.

I had heard that attending Mass at an Orthodox Church was likely to be unconventional. One arrived at the time most convenient to oneself and might leave before the service was over if it was necessary. But on Easter Day the Mass was very special and it could last for three hours.

Fearing I might be late, as I observed small parties of people hurrying ahead of me, I was also a little apprehensive, and slowed up as we reached the doorway, rather awestruck by what was approaching.

I was totally unprepared for the splendour that met me - whether the nave was lit more brilliantly for Easter, or the choir had been powerfully augmented, I couldn't really know. Never before had I heard antiphonal singing of this quality, and the sum total of these very rich impressions filled me with indescribable emotion.

I should have liked to move a little further forward, nearer the gleaming icons, but it wasn't to be. I stood transfixed, as if riveted to the spot only a few feet away from the entrance, and was gradually absorbed by the Russian families who surrounded me.

At lunch that day Gurdjieff included me in some cream and buns he was giving to the Calves - this was the name he had given to the young women who were daughters of his old and valued American pupils.

'You Calf?' he asked. I shook my head doubtfully, aware that I was nearly twice the age of some of the Calves, but not fully sure of all the implications.

'Oh, you bring Calf' said Mr Gurdjieff, 'you already cow. You ask someone explain who is cow'.

Six months before I had heard his story about the cow and had seen his marvellous imitation of a cow with great rolling eyes and vacant stare, as it looked at the 'new paint' *porte*, thinking it was lost. This time the story was directed at me.

'You look at me like cow at new paint *porte* - you look sometimes good, but

this evil for me. After, I am drained. You all vampires.' He waved his marvellously expressive hand, looking around.

'I very tired.' Then he paused, looking down before he looked at me again, and after a little while adding,

'First day, roses, roses. Second day, half and half. Third day, thorns, thorns'. Explaining this rather painstakingly and then leaning back a little and repeating with expression, 'Today, roses, roses . . . . . .'.

After a short silence, during which I felt with fair accuracy the exact anomaly of my position, he began to speak again. He needed people who could be useful for his aim, such as those who could help him with the publication of 'Beelzebub', and at this meal were some of his longest established pupils. In comparison with the present position my aim in coming back to Paris seemed out of all proportion and I determined not to tire him further by trying to speak to him.

* * *

Monday evening, twenty fifth of April, was French night, but with good luck I was again at the table. I was now beginning to think that I would see if Madame de Salzmann could help me over the question of whether I should have more children and what to do about my need for the Work if I did so; I had completely abandoned the idea of trying to see Gurdjieff.

Well through the meal he passed me one of his special dishes, which he had peppered and salted, etc., with his special 'hi you' air and a smile. He asked me if I liked it. I was tongue-tied and could only manage a diffident thank you, feeling unusually solemn. Then as I went out of the room I almost collided with him. Vera, the widow of

René Daumal, was standing by the door. Saying something to her in Russian he asked me how I felt, but I shook my head slightly, unable to frame any reasonable reply, though Vera observed 'Very good, if she has partaken of your emanations, Monsieur'. I then watched him walk slowly away down the corridor. A friend with whom I was leaving the flat had some business with Madame de Salzmann and as I waited for her at one side of the small hall Gurdjieff came back again.

'Good mother' he said to me, 'good cow, gives milk and cream to calf'.

'And it's a beautiful calf, Monsieur' replied my friend, joining in. But suddenly, Madame de Salzmann had somehow encircled her and all at once they were gone.

'Come, drink coffee' said Mr Gurdjieff.

I remember how enormous he seemed as he led the way, and often, afterwards, I questioned this, for it was an impression I had again and again, though when in the previous autumn on the very first day, I had found myself standing next to him, unaffected, as it were, by his atmosphere, I had discovered he was actually shorter than me. Now, quite unprepared for the interview which for weeks I had anticipated, I was full of trepidation. Where to start? How to find in myself a true moment, a spark, or a seed that could grow?

All at once, I found myself asking about the necessity of having another child and explaining rather unnecessarily about how I had planned a family of three children - but how best could this be achieved in my present circumstances? . . . . . . With three very young children, I would not be able to do so much for the Work. He answered at once, very clearly, from the physical standpoint.

'Not always possible - not always come together right.'

I considered this and then tried again, 'But from the point of view of the Work, practical work? . . . . . . lectures, time, another child ? . . . . . .', the unfinished sentence did not so much hang in the air between us as call forth a completely unlooked for response.

'Not necessary now do Bennett stuff.'

'But - while I am in England?'

Gurdjieff dismissed Bennett in uncomplimentary terms, raising his chin. I considered this. All at once I had a very clear, open feeling, my timidity having quite disappeared. 'He works.', I said.

Gurdjieff dismissed this, too, with a wave of the hand, 'Necessary only come to *me* here'.

I relaxed further, but was pulled up short as he leaned forward a little.

'Now you understand what I tell'. He was very emphatic. 'You have children. *You* finish now. You make a task, sacrifice for children. What you would like eat yourself, give children. Be good mother. If you rich I would not say this, but something different. But children cost much . . . . . . '.

Quite free now, I began to reply, 'But I must do good work now in order to be a good mother, a good example'. Gurdjieff, however, interrupted me quickly and started by repeating himself.

'You must make a task. Be mother. You die - you sacrifice for children. You do this *exact* and Work will come into life. You never do this before. Necessary *learn* sacrifice'.

* * *

When I was able to visit the flat for more than a bare weekend, I spent most of my daylight hours making copies from some of the chapters in 'Beelzebub's Tales To His Grandson' which were needed for group meetings in England. After the late Easter, the spring weather was exceptionally hot and sunny and I rather enjoyed the contrast to my cool hotel bedroom with its French windows open and the noisy world outside.

From time to time, some other guest would appear to help me check the typescript and an unusual silent bond would soon develop between us, broken only occasionally by our sudden laughter at one or other of my more unusual or stupid typing errors.

We were expected to be at the flat by midday for readings which would last one or two hours. Sometimes these were taken from

'Beelzebub's Tales' - the First Series of Gurdjieff's writings - but now and again we would be given the Second Series 'Meetings With Remarkable Men'. There seemed to be no set period for the length of the readings, which more often than not would actually depend on the time when lunch would be ready.

One day, when we had been waiting rather a long time for a reader, one of the Calves from America put a typescript from 'Meetings With Remarkable Men' in my hands, telling me that today I should read page so and so. . . . . Feeling that I would have been grateful for a little more time so that I could consider what was in store for me, I slowly left my stool and settled myself in the reader's chair, little realizing that fate had actually caught me by the ankle.

Quite unaware of the steady flip-flop of slippers which announced that Gurdjieff was approaching the salon, I took a breath and began to read the intentionally overdramatic paragraph describing the river Amu Darya:

"The mountain peaks are gilded by the rays of the still hidden sun. . . . ." but, I had barely got as far as this before I sensed that Gurdjieff was standing in the doorway and looking at me. Externally I scarcely paused, but I felt that I was blushing and would have done almost anything to have been able to stop reading. Horribly aware that I had been smugly pleased by the sound of my own voice, I then went through an agony of self-denunciation and almost came to a dead stop; but I pulled myself together and managed to read on, slightly slower than before, and obviously embarrassed. Could I have relaxed more? Being aware of a tension in my solar plexus which now threatened to cancel all my efforts of self-observation, I was suddenly prompted to glance in Gurdjieff's direction. He was no longer there.

But the silent teaching I had just been given left an unforgettable legacy. I only had to think of sitting in the salon for regular readings to see that my everyday functioning was now being sharpened to such a degree that the hidden complexities of work on myself were very much nearer the surface.

And even the salon itself was a challenge.

But I had visited the flat a good many times before I could take this in, and when I had first seen the Enneagram decorating the wall beyond Gurdjieff's chair, the clash of contradictions arising from the fact that it was placed on its side and outlined in red sequins on a black velvet background, somehow made it more approachable. I was not entirely ignorant; some years before I had studied it with a special reading group, but although I grasped it as a diagram of perpetual movement, my real understanding was practically non-existent. And every time I looked at it I wondered . . . . .

After the meals were over, we would return to the salon for coffee, and Gurdjieff would give us some music. Sitting in his tub chair, with his piano accordion on his knees, one hand worked the bellows while the other produced haunting melodies sustained with minor chords and intervals. This was not like listening to other kinds of music - the sensations in my chest were almost alarming and my head swam.

But the music was a fitting end to my Work days in Paris. I had typed 'Beelzebub' in the morning, and one or two hours after the reading and the lunch were over I had attended a movements class at the Salle Pleyel, and in the evening there would be another reading followed by dinner.

During all this time there had been talk of a trip - 'tomorrow we go Cannes' - and the Calves were in a flurry of activity. Having come for the summer in order to study the Movements, which later they would teach in America, when any trips were promulgated they were the first guests to be invited. A kind of subtle protocol existed, rather difficult to untangle as it was not connected with any one set of rules. Longstanding 'near' people might be excluded just as easily as the chance monthly visitors, and the uncertainty had a crisp edge to it. Those of us who had been instructed to 'return one month' could find it a little puzzling if they presented themselves when everything was boiling up for an immanent departure, while cars were being hired, cancelled or even bought, money borrowed and telegrams despatched. And it was all too clear that baffling decisions might have to be made at very short notice. But on this occasion the trip did not depart until my time in Paris had already begun to draw to a close, and at last the party left for Cannes. The Calves were ready to go long before Gurdjieff; he sat in the hall without his jacket and was helped on with his boots. He shook me by the hand and said:

'*Diable* will help you - *Ange* too busy - will not listen; he makes so' and waving his arms above his head he gave his inimitable representation of an angel praising God.

There seemed to be only one other person who was not going on the trip, and this was Lord Pentland - an Ouspensky person who had just come from the States. We went downstairs together to see Gurdjieff off. He gave us a handful of sweets, got into the car, and was gone.

'It was good about the eggs, wasn't it?' said Lord Pentland to me.

Chapter 20

GURDJIEFF SCOLDS

From time to time during those first few months, a nagging thought would occasionally present itself, 'What, then, had become of the System?' The fact that we were still calling it the System showed the depth of our intellectual addiction. But for some of us there was something that went deeper. That System had brought us here in the first place and could not be jettisoned overnight. My situation was rather like that of a person who had just learned one foreign language rather painstakingly over a long time and then finds himself suddenly called upon to converse in an entirely different one. I was willing to leave aside the words which jostled for prominence. But what was happening? Where did it fit in? Where were the rules of this particular piece of grammar?

A merit of this state of affairs was the deep assent which arose from some level previously unglimpsed, and occasionally a more united approach silenced the self that looked for labels. Something so right was taking place. And everything that one was 'going through' had sooner or later to fit in somewhere in the majestic arena of Gurdjieff's presence. Sometimes, privately, I struggled with what I knew of the teaching on Essence and Personality, which I had discovered to be deceptively simple, embodied in the introductory lectures I had originally attended. One had been born an essence; not pure, as some ancient philosophers had thought, but real, oneself, a bundle of inherited characteristics combined and original in the form of a new creation, vital, if limited. Personality had formed only little by little, implanted, as it were, by our parents, nurses, teachers and friends, and as often as not heartily welcomed, until, as the sincerest form of flattery, it grew out of all proportion.

At first glance, one felt that 'simple' uneducated, uncultured people, living in natural conditions, and more themselves, had a greater possibility of eventually acquiring consciousness, and it was troubling to be told that this was not in fact the case. If our personality was not sufficiently developed, we lacked experience, knowledge and information, and with such a lack there was nothing on which we could base our hope of waking up, or our notion that it was necessary to struggle with 'ourselves' in order to 'be'.

At that stage I accepted this part of the teaching without believing all the details, and I don't remember ever hearing anyone mention that we actually needed the friction of our shallow personalities, and that we should go on needing it. At the same time, that Essence was the only part of us that could grow was fairly obvious. Personality changed with one's company, one's job, or the time of day, though in some people set patterns developed into almost dangerous artificial compulsions. Artificiality was a key word for me just then, for I was often being pushed by circumstances towards a completely artificial and insincere reaction. This helped me a little, if only a little, to accept most of the theory behind the teaching about Essence and Personality, but on more than one occasion I found courage actually to voice the feeling that simple people were not necessarily worse off than a man whose 'good', if changing, personality could help him in his search for truth.

From time to time I wrestled with the conviction that an essential piece of the teaching was missing at just this point. Why, or in fact how, was it that the growth of personality drove essence underground?

In beginning to rear my own children this seemed to pose a desperate dilemma. Searching for myself was one thing, guiding an infant consciousness was quite another. And looking around at the great educational experiments, 'free expression' schools with the devil in constant attendance finding work for idle hands, did nothing to reassure me. Now, faced with quite new experiences, the need to re-assess was healthy though somehow out of focus. Pushed into a corner, I might have been tempted to declare 'But those old teaching methods can't matter for the time being.' What did matter were the weekly and sometimes daily readings of 'All & Everything', where some familiar truths in a new guise had already been recognized. Listening to the difficult text, anxious to miss nothing, one was revisited by the paradoxes, and it was almost as if I had a kind of genuine conscience constantly pointing in a direction that could not possibly be followed.

*　*　*

I had gone back to Paris round about the middle of August and George came with me. Gurdjieff remembered me this time, he greeted me with:

'You here?'

I said 'Yes'.

Then the next day, 'You not forget what I tell you?',

I said 'No'.

I had wanted to ask Gurdjieff about various unexpected results that had come from the exercise he had given me. Before I arrived there, I was in an extraordinary state. Had I been pushed for a description, I should have said that I was not asleep in the ordinary way, but there was a kind of apprehension. A sort of 'what can happen next' which, if I looked at it fairly, had been exacerbated by various things explained and over-explained by Bennett. At the time I was not perceptive enough to regret this. It did not occur to me at all that I could, in fact, lose my way, and feeling that I was in Gurdjieff's hands endowed everything with a kind of inevitability which was reassuring. Was this passivity unexpected? Could my manifestations have been different? Puzzling about it afterwards produced no light and the conviction that

I was being prised out of a pattern that I had perhaps been landed in by mistake was very little help.

It started simply enough. I was sitting next to Madame de Salzmann and opposite Gurdjieff when he began to warn me about being alone in Paris, 'dangerous place'. He laboured this somewhat, while I, confused, thought 'he must know I've worked in London, what is this all about?' After that he switched to Bennett before rounding on me in apparently one of the kinds of fury that I had seen others provoking in the past. The difference in this case (if in fact it was a difference) was that the sound and the fury were actually falling short of the target. It was as if a heavily armoured battleship had decided to make war on a trawler and was purposely sending all its torpedoes short, trusting that the noise of battle would draw other enemies into play. As I listened to this furious onslaught, I assented willingly enough to the centre of gravity of the attack. I was a nonentity and nonentitiness was not becoming. Nor did it actually affect me to hear Bennett blamed for all this. Since I was a *Bennettski* etc., etc., such failure was his responsibility. Though this was perhaps fair enough, it was not the get-out for me that an onlooker might have appreciated. I was simply gripped from first to last by the conviction that the reason for the onslaught must be sought elsewhere. Nevertheless, the idea of inevitable nonentitiness (if no work was present) affected me. I had something new to look at. The states I had known and the positive anticipation of 'help' did not alter the fact that by myself I was nothing. I, who to a certain extent had basked in the rose garden experience and in the being of 'real mother', together with all the new possibilities that had seemed to flow from my last visit, was now face to face with an essential unworthiness that had never before been honestly examined.

But as we exited from the room I was not surprised when Bennett said to me, 'Don't upset yourself unduly, that was all intended for me, you know'.

'I see, that explains it', I said, not upset, though certainly seriously questioning. In fact, there and then, nothing at all had been explained. A stick had been thrown in a pond that later caused many ripples, and the shock that started small, grew. Attitudes changed, buffers collapsed. I was beginning to look at my essential 'lopsidedness' instead of at the things that had so long disturbed my self-satisfaction. Paradoxes appeared at every step. Was a search for happiness always egoistic? Suddenly, the need for Gurdjieff to help me as only he could do took on a new dimension. Once again, Bennett had been elbowed out of the way in his role of adviser, and I needed an entirely new assessment of where I was going and what I could hope for.

But I was not so sure. I had often before felt that Gurdjieff had received my thoughts and feelings direct without any verbal exchange. This time it was as if something in me was being refused and accepted at the same time. Perhaps for the first time ever, I glimpsed that different levels of perception in fact belonged to different parts of my being. I did not at all see that this was the ground that would have to be reached for me to stop saying 'I' in the old way. I was still very naïve in my understanding of what Gurdjieff had given me, and why. My arena, if 'I's' had lined up behind the rose garden experience in a way that had stopped me saying 'if only', but my understanding about the need for balancing the functions was elementary in the extreme.

During the last few months I had heard a great deal about suffering and sacrifice. What Gurdjieff had told me about the need to sacrifice for children had put the organized work in an entirely new light. I was sure I understood this, perhaps too sure, but I had gone over and over what I remembered of the 'old ideas' taught by Ouspensky and at this place they seemed to hold water.

I could still remember the emotion that arose in me when years previously I had heard that Gurdjieff had said one must be ready to sacrifice one's freedom - but one always, consciously or unconsciously, struggled for how one imagined freedom to be - and this spurious freedom prevented one from tasting real freedom. What one had to be prepared for was to be willing to sacrifice the illusion. If one were successful in this sacrifice, everything that was real in one's desires and sympathies would return, together with a feeling of unity and Will. But to get to this point a man must obey inwardly as well as outwardly.

I went to see Madame de Salzmann before lunch. She said I was too *émotionée* and apt to blur my task. I must be quiet and work. I was not strong enough, and it was no good to go from one slavery to another: 'You must be free', she said.

I had been pondering not long before this on how true it was that one had to stand on one's head to see life rightly. But I had stepped aside into trying to 'understand' in a perfectly ordinary way and I was already unstuck, trusting feelings that were unreliable instead of relying on silence - a struggle with words and a struggle with meanings.

At one point I had understood that those whom Gurdjieff had referred to in the past few days as 'Initiate Person' realized their own nothingness, and that I had been wrong when I felt that various high emotional experiences meant that I had tasted enough of what was meant by nothingness. It was true that I had tasted it anyway, but my understanding was too shallow. Looking at it afresh, in the light of the scolding, I found myself appallingly shallow. The inevitability of this was very hard. At the same time I was right to remember that Gurdjieff had promised me various things. Strictly speaking, I had not failed in my task, but I needed to recognize where my possibilities lay.

When I said goodbye to Gurdjieff he questioned me.

'You *have* to go? But I have the habit to see you . . . . .' and suddenly my emotion overcame me, 'Mr Gurdjieff' I said 'I cannot bear it.' My cheeks trembled.

'I not know you so sensitive . . . . .' and rising from his chair and going back into the dining room, he fetched a very small phial of white pills and told me to take them twice a day saying, 'Come back one month.' And he indicated that I should kiss his forehead, while he kissed my cheek,

'Do task for me, *chaque jour*. . . . .'.

Chapter 21

FRAGMENTS

I noticed how interested Gurdjieff was to learn people's names, which he often used for puns and many unlikely kinds of joke, involving those who were new at the table in a quite unexpected sort of way. People I had always thought were 'shy' would suddenly open up and smile and be there, appearing in an utterly different light, very endearing. At such a time all one's feeling flowed to Gurdjieff and, without any justification at all, I suddenly felt that I experienced what it meant to be one of his 'near' people. At the time there was no point in analysis: total commitment carried one's whole life along, and for the time being this was an incredible state, a position of great possibility; anything might happen, and all would be good. It was only afterwards that I remembered this was self-remembering without the label, with all the hallmarks of two-way consciousness. The external scene, the exchange, the other people glowed; vibrations could be measured. Internally, it was as if one rested, potent, aware, and able for anything.

And there was always a surprise just around the corner. One day, when he asked my name, I was not at all prepared for his comment 'Six Dorothys have already'. I was *de trop* before I started.

This startled me out of all proportion to the proposition. Not only were there six already - and there might even be eleven - they were all very old pupils, 'important for his work'. Then again, it might be fewer? In any case, it was made perfectly clear that I could not be numbered with them. It was a very odd experience; you could say my heart sank. I had, apparently, a very 'expensive' name. Then, all at once, this discussion stopped and I had the impression that after all I had passed some kind of invisible exam and I was allowed round the other side of the turnstile. Relief flooded in. Inwardly something was calling out 'What does my name matter, I'm here, it's me. Perhaps I'm not a 'Gift of God', but I'm me, I'm all I've got and I'm here.' Something didn't mind being at the bottom of the list despite the many glimpsed tensions that I wouldn't be facing just yet.

I was to hear the idea of 'expensive' many times in the future. Gurdjieff's own saint, George, was also 'very expensive', and my husband George, needed comment here,

'He very young - he need three zeros - good task for him *hein?*.'

And as he was leaving the table Gurdjieff drew my attention to him, and at that moment he certainly did look just about nine years old - but zeros were an awkward field for research. As well as apparently meaning money, they could occasionally mean Centres. And Gurdjieff, in a moustache-twirling mood, was enjoying himself.

* * *

There came an evening, after a hot September day, when I arrived at the flat to find a family occasion in progress. Twelve new white wooden stools helped to crowd the already full reading room and all was unusual festivity and bustle. It was French night and there were twenty five people waiting for a reading. I was crammed against my left-hand neighbour with my chin, Duchess-fashion, on the shoulder of the woman in front. Impossible in this position to move away from a cloying scent that deadened the atmosphere. But after a little, the top light was turned off and an electric fan put on. This improved matters considerably.

What we were waiting for was the reading of Chapter XVII from the manuscript of Ouspensky's 'Fragments of an Unknown Teaching', which had been given to Gurdjieff when he had visited Madame Ouspensky in January. Up to now I had missed all the readings from 'Fragments', although I had heard a lot about them and my anticipation naturally reminded me of a conversation I had overheard on my previous visit between Gurdjieff and Lord Pentland.

Just after a meal in the dining room, when most of the guests had already gone into the Salon for the music, Gurdjieff was standing in the place where usually the Director sat, and talking to Pentland across the table. Holding Ouspensky's book in both hands, chest high, and almost tenderly, as though he valued it greatly, he was smiling warmly at Pentland as he said, very appreciatively:

'That fool Ouspensky, if he not leave me, he not had died . . He tell exact what I say . . '

Pentland did not quite smile in return, but stared rather hard and quizzically.

The strangeness of the moment stayed with me. And despite the fact that Lord Pentland would soon become Gurdjieff's 'Principal Representative in America', the aloofness of an Ouspensky pupil occasionally clung to him. This was hardly surprising. Gurdjieff clearly enjoyed joking at the expense of the Ouspensky pupils whom we saw frequently at the table. They were 'Candidates for a lunatic asylum' . . . . . 'All spoiled'. Bennett, who after all was originally an Ouspensky pupil, but had been cast off publicly when he continued to teach the System after Ouspensky had fled to America, could not resist the temptation to ask about *his* pupils. We too were apparently 'lunatic' but not 'spoiled'.

One guessed at the challenge behind all these statements, as well as the truths. But most of the people arriving at the table were at some time or other described as 'too dirty' and 'too spoiled'. Those whom one sensed as the self-promoted elect were equally 'spoiled'.

Listening to the ideas that we had been brought up on with the French, who had never heard them in this form, one marvelled afresh at the magnificent scale of the 'System' ideas. In this particular chapter Gurdjieff discussed Schools. Man could not hope to keep watch on the whole of himself. He could do a lot without the proper intensity or he would even do nothing, while thinking he was doing something. He spared himself, being afraid of doing anything unpleasant. Proper observation showed that one tried to accomplish tasks in the easiest way and became self-indulgent very quickly, trying to accomplish the task in the easiest way possible. Only School methods and School organization could bring man to super-efforts.

Being asked what super-efforts actually were, Gurdjieff had described the situation of a man who had been walking all day in bad weather. In the evening, after walking twenty five miles, he finds the house warm and pleasant, with supper waiting, but instead of sitting down to enjoy all this, he decides to walk another two miles along the road and then return home. Here the efforts were clearly different. In the first case it was simply an effort to get home, it did not count. In the second case the man must decide to go on walking in the rain and cold. This kind of effort became all the more difficult if it was required by a teacher who might at any moment ask for a fresh start when 'I' had decided that efforts for the day were over.

This reading, which I had never heard in its present form, began to affect me powerfully, for by now I had already discovered for myself that 'School' was necessary because such as I was, I could not work alone for any length of time: efforts first diminished and then disappeared.

The reasons for this, said Gurdjieff, lay very deep in our nature. Leaving aside the lies and insincerity that were a great obstacle for everyone, we were then actually faced by what he called 'the division of centres'. In man as we know him, a certain kind of thought was connected with a definite work of the Emotional or Moving Centres, and certain emotions evoked habitual thoughts or habitual movements. One thing could not exist without another. A man deciding to think in a new way still feels in the old way. Imagine that he dislikes 'R', this immediately arouses old thoughts and he forgets his decision to think in a new way; he begins to smoke a cigarette and thinks in the old way without noticing it. You must realize that a man can never break this connection by himself. Another man's will is necessary. He can do nothing himself. In life everything is arranged far too comfortably. In a school a man finds himself among other people who are not of his choosing and with whom it is very hard to live and work, particularly in unaccustomed conditions. The tension that is connected between him and the others is indispensable because it gradually chips away his sharp angles.

Various questions that Gurdjieff had dealt with then led to the objections that going towards another stage of being certainly required a wave of emotion but did not in itself change and repair moving habits that demanded special and lengthy work, which actually could only be learned in a School. This was summed up by the thought that 'No miracles are possible in a machine'.

And going on to explain about the paramount necessity for relaxation, Gurdjieff also demonstrated relaxing exercises and explained about sensation . . . . . All this had already become the centre of efforts I was now making in daily life, and my listening sharpened. I recognized as new truths for me certain of the subjects discussed. Previous to the last summer, these had been acceptable theories. But now some of them were actually facts. It was exciting to follow Ouspensky's experiences and recognize some of them, but the end of the chapter became almost intolerable to listen to. This account of the break in Ouspensky's 'confidence' must have been painful to more than one of us. Here, at last, in black and white, as it were, was the solution to the Ouspensky mystery - the explanation of all those peculiar stories I had heard about Gurdjieff when I first arrived at lectures - for the final separation between teacher and pupil led back precisely to this point and was nothing to do with the later 'accident' or Ouspensky's own explanation that Gurdjieff had 'gone mad'.

In Essentuki, after a period of intensive work which demonstrated the existence of various advanced experiences, and proved beyond doubt that Gurdjieff was as good as his word, that his work was soundly based, and that he genuinely knew what he was talking about, Ouspensky had changed direction. And he had changed direction because he failed to see that Gurdjieff's explanation about 'Man' included Ouspensky himself. Ouspensky already imagined that he was different from ordinary men, and that he understood on a different level, and that, above all, he was entitled not only to criticize Gurdjieff and make objections, but also that he could talk about separating Gurdjieff from his ideas, accepting the teaching without accepting the teacher. At this time Ouspensky, who had actually been attending Gurdjieff's groups for only a few years, had indeed acquired 'knowledge differing from ordinary knowledge' but had persisted in assessing situations from his ordinary intelligence and had apparently forgotten completely the dangerous existence of his Imaginary 'I', that plexus of motives in each one of us that actually acts from deeply ingrained egoism, owing to one's picture of oneself.

To the observer, removed from the scene by precisely thirty years, it was perfectly clear that Ouspensky had by no means undergone 'the long corresponding preparation' that Gurdjieff considered necessary. Later, when one acquired his book and studied it over weeks and months, one found that there was not even a pretence of taking in hand the kind of self-observation that Gurdjieff required as a basis to all 'rightly conducted work'. Ouspensky's own intellectual acceptance was always enough for him, though, oddly enough, he later appeared to require very much more from his own followers.

But the opening words of that fatal chapter actually give little away: 'I always have a very strange feeling when I remember this period'. Ouspensky's betrayal, if that is not too strong a word, is that he presumed to have assimilated things that he had only just been introduced to, and the 'very strange feeling' that returned when he thought of it again was a chance offered by a deeper level in himself, the repeated opportunity to choose, to reject the conclusions of the savant in favour of the confession of a pupil, and the realization of his own nothingness. This, he was not prepared for. He always 'understood' and could justify easily the things that took him away from Gurdjieff, especially when he was needed for something. Poor Ouspensky: did he at other times, also, observe that his professional expertise as a star newspaper reporter had perhaps hardened a part of him which should have kept pace with his undoubted intelligence?

As the years passed, after our visits to the flat I was often able to take the 'story of Ouspensky' as a much-needed object lesson. What a temptation it was to know just enough to be able to work alone and to crave the so-called freedom that went with it, and when we returned to study the lack of balance in the centres, here was the very best example ready to hand, and the 'wrong working of centres' which we were all too easily tempted to pass over, was a necessary field for observation and study. 'Better states' were all very well.

Sitting in the half-darkened room and listening to this critical period of the past was a vivid preparation for one of my most unusual evenings in the flat, where the combination of Gurdjieff's 'ordinary life' and the ritual toasting introduced a vivid realization of how little one knew or guessed about human relationships.

If there was one hallmark of this whole visit it was that I was now freely admitting to understanding very little of what was going on. Basic aims were clear enough, and the way along which I had travelled was acceptable. But now I was in new territory, almost frighteningly unknown. Gurdjieff had asked me to come back, but I was not genuinely clear about a new aim. Working for and with the children had filled my life, as he said it should do, but since the July visit I was experiencing an upsurge of feelings which were almost uncontrollable.

*   *   *

After the reading in the salon, the formalities of French night were resumed rather slowly. And I was by no means the only person who, having unwound my legs from an impossible tangle, discovered a solid phalanx of bodies between my stool and the dining room. But some of my neighbours with longer experience did a kind of nose-dive into the middle and escaped along the corridor to the kitchen, where they joined the 'chaîne' that was forming to take part in the serving, while others simply stood behind guests at the dining table.

As there were very few *Bennettski* in the room I was lucky enough to have a seat just by the *Verseur*, so I could see everything, though hearing the talk which Gurdjieff had with his guests was strangely difficult and I very soon found my attention pushed in another direction.

Above the piano, high in the corner, opposite Gurdjieff, hung an icon depicting the Virgin and Child. This was a diminutive Persian rug, 'Very unusual, very handsome, fine work, costing many millions of francs', and bought from the Shah of Persia. (But was this really the *Old* Shah and not the present one?). The Shah had been forced to sell because he needed the money . . . . . this all seemed so unlikely that it immediately sent my thoughts dashing away[23], but again I dragged them back to hear Gurdjieff saying:

'Everyone love, everyone reverence God's Mother. But where she come from? Where she go to? Nobody knows. Beelzebub might tell'.

Hoping for more, I studied the unusual icon, but lost the thread of the whole conversation when Gurdjieff added, 'if you kill a mouse you might find a dead elephant on your hands' - yet another reference to the necessity to understand what you were about if you started to change things, but that didn't occur to me until I was piecing together the scribbled notes that I made before falling asleep many hours later that night.

*   *   *

On the next day, towards the end of dinner, I dropped a handkerchief on the floor and had to stretch a foot to retrieve it. Meeting some soft, moveable objects, I glanced under the table and was astonished to see

---

[23] Thinking this was only another parable, but wanting to find out more about a Shah of Persia who would actually buy a Christian hanging, I did a little research when I got back to England. The despot Mohammed Ali who ruled from 1907, succeeding his father, had in fact found his treasury empty, and instructed his Vizier (suitably called Nasir ud Din) to overthrow the constitution and raise a loan, but unfortunately the Vizier was assassinated while he was raising it . . . . .

many different sorts of food – some rissoles, always a delicious part of the meal, rolls, and so on. More than once I had coveted my neighbours' rolls in the near past as a welcome bolster to the rich fare, but on this particular visit I had not been honoured with one. Generally these were handed ceremoniously to the Calves, or to some special guests, by Gurdjieff himself. As his hand stretched ritually across the table, a strong feeling reinforced my sense of presence, and inevitably from the past arose those other words 'Eat this, in remembrance of me'.

From the first gift of a roll, all food had taken on a new meaning, a new seriousness - life purchased with life. Seeing the rolls and the rissoles, remembering the generous hand and the words, I experienced a very deep shock. As never before, I laboured to eat every morsel on my plate, and though impeded by emotion, I sat on to finish after my neighbours to right and left had gone into the adjoining room. We had been sitting late.

Suddenly I realized that only Gurdjieff and I were left, and that someone stood in the doorway making very impatient signs for me to rise and follow her. I looked at my plate and then at him, and his eyes swept across the littered table of neglected meats, his chin jerking, his eyes sympathetic. He smiled at me.

'Honourable guest finishes food.' he said, dismissing with that now familiar wave of the hand the person in the doorway.

Chapter 22

THE NEW CHATEAU

At first when I heard several 'sideways on' references to a 'new Château' I did not believe any of them at all. For some time I had been in danger of catching the disease rampant on all sides of supposing that Gurdjieff never spoke in anything but allegory. Indeed there were times when it really seemed like that, but I was beginning to be aware, too, that he was indulging in a great game, giving with one hand and taking with the other. How easily and quickly could we be lulled into deep sleep and imagination about everything he said! For me, it was still safest just to record accurately, if I possibly could, and think about it later, but there again I too often lost the drift and got carried away by my constant need to say 'yes' and my inborn hatred of saying 'no', though this was nothing like as strong as it had been before I met Gurdjieff's ideas. And the game was both conscious and constructive, with the reward for a good try which was sometimes out of all proportion to the effort. But in connection with the Château the game was played in both directions.

At first he had talked of leasing an enormous property, the *Château des Voisins* at Rambouillet, but in a few weeks all this was changed and he was now thinking of buying *La Grande Paroisse*, an old station hotel near the Seine, which he intended to give to his

Sister.

I arrived in Paris one day when there was a lot of talk about this new Château. It sounded very much like 'The Pilgrim's Progress', with a house on a hill - a place where people could both live and work - and a double path paved with mosaic. And remembering the talk about the roses and drains in which Russell Page had taken an active part on the night of the family party, I had to struggle rather hard to separate fact from allegory. But here, at least, I was wrong, though perhaps it was right about the three houses which were described as the three states of the soul. And the idea of a small Château where Gurdjieff might rest, and 'only his nearest would come', spread a kind of glow.

Just before my October visit, there had already been one trip to the new Château, and there was to be another, for lunch, on Saturday. This time it was taken for granted, from the start, that I was to go, and this seemed all of a piece with the entire visit.

When, after the Movement Class, as Gurdjieff was sitting alone at the back of the hall in the Salle Pleyel I had taken the opportunity to say to him, 'A month ago, Monsieur, you promised to see me, *next* time', he had looked up at me, saying:

'Not now, not today Miss, today I must make for Jorganna'. (That is how he pronounced Giovanna, who had gone back to America).

'She very ill in America, she need . . . . .' He moved into a slightly different position and looked down and then up again, almost with a sigh.

And then registering my disappointed state, he continued 'I tired', and the word seemed long and drawn out, reverberating in the still room. And looking at him afresh, I saw that he looked grey and weary beyond belief, and a great bound of feeling surged through me, lifting me out of my selfish preoccupation, though my consciousness was only half-changed. It was as if I were suspended well beyond and above self-pity, almost in the state which I had mistakenly called indifference when I had experienced it so painfully in the spring before Gurdjieff began to rescue me. But was it indifference?

There was something extraordinarily soothing in being allowed from within not to react. Later I could see that this was what people

224

called 'rising above it', which was a state rarely expected of themselves but always a demand on others, and I felt that this 'rising' was nothing that belonged to me. I had done nothing. I had just stood looking at Gurdjieff and sharing the moment with him. Nor did I even need to escape from the sadness that filled me. Tinged with remorse, it was not something to struggle with. I had frequently wondered at Gurdjieff's use of the word 'honourable'. This state was 'honourable' only if it was maintained without reference to myself. Up to now, in Paris, in spite of my furious navigating, my balancing of opposing interests, and my struggle for a kind of hygienic purity, everything beyond isolated moments of effort that meant very little had been given to me. I had somehow wrestled with philosophical ideas that were far above my head, frequently forcing myself into a mould that was not mine and stretching and straining to extend genuine moments of self-remembering by even bludgeoning my sight and hearing. Today there was a gap which seemed different.

I knew that I should not have the heart to approach Gurdjieff again, though in a few days time I would be back in England. For his sake one must hope that his plans for the autumn would hold, and that he would soon be well enough to travel to America in about two weeks time.

For the moment I chose to forget this, and somehow, anyhow, live in the present moment - *Now*. Despite the discomfort - thorns, thorns, uppermost, almost without fear - not running away or looking for something easier.

Two immense Renaults were hired for the lunch party and this time there was none of the procrastination and dallying which attended the start of the longer trips. It was off and away by around eleven o'clock in bright autumn sunshine. Our car, driven by Bennett, with two *Ouspenski* and two *Bennettski* as passengers, tried valiantly to keep up with Gurdjieff who certainly gave every appearance of doing his best to drop us, so that even in the centre of Paris we lost our way several times before hitting the road for Fontainebleau. Here the impression of summer was intensified. Though there were piles of manure along the grassy verge of the road, and the trees were laden with apples, no leaves had yet fallen. Our car was not entirely happy, it smoked and made faint rattling noises, but we kept well ahead of the other Renault, sometimes losing it altogether. However, it was able to catch up with us in villages, where the gendarmes waved their arms, blew whistles and pleaded desperately with us to proceed *doucement.* At last, as we neared Fontainebleau, we caught up with Gurdjieff outside a garage, the roof of his Citroën piled high with boxes of food. One of his near people was beside him and in the back sat Madame de Salzmann and Gabo.

Soon we were dashing after him at speed, driving carefully through Fontainebleau itself and then suddenly out onto a winding forest road, twisting and turning as we went, until after going a little uphill the road actually petered out in a cart track. On one side of this track were enormous boulders, like the rocks in a Leonardo landscape, partly covered by moss and ivy, cool green and inviting, but suddenly growing narrow and coming to an end in an ordinary field.

While some of us were speculating on the obvious necessity of a break, a drink, a cigarette, and a stroll, Bennett was rapidly drawing the Renault aside onto stones and leaves at the edge of the forest, making room for Gurdjieff to turn about and lead the way straight back.

Returning to Fontainebleau again, we were obliged to ask our direction, and en route we passed iron gates, a flash of white and some trees, the original *Château-Prieuré -* and though I turned quickly to take it in, I was too late.

We had already heard that the new Château, known to us now as *La Grande Paroisse,* was in fact the *Hôtel de la Gare* in a village of that name. But where was it?

Briefly we were on the road to Sens, before crossing the Seine - or was it the Loing? Then, after running along a country road, next to a railway, for several miles, we suddenly found we had arrived, and before we knew where we were had mounted a flight of steps along with one or two French pupils who had appeared from nowhere, apparently having travelled by train, for the Sens branch line from Paris still ran.

Having feared an anticlimax, it was a relief to find a compact, three-storey squarish house, with shutters at the windows and a central entrance. Partly screened by chestnut trees, it was nicely placed in a rather original position on a terrace, high above the railway, from which it was approached by wide steps. There, sure enough, was the hill, and the view of the river confirmed the 'Pilgrim's Progress' connections. Whoever had gardened here recently had struggled with *causse*-like conditions, too sharp a drainage on too steep a slope, and had not won. Small cankerous fruit trees, neglected shrubs backed by outhouses and flowers which had probably sown themselves flanked a pleasant path running invitingly away from the building, but leading nowhere.

Though magnetised by the house, and speculating on what we should be doing, some of us joined forces with passengers from the other Renault, gazing across the landscape in the hot autumn sunshine as we walked along the grassy path, and wondered about the flat river-countryside lying beneath us, with the Seine and Yonne nearby and the Loing flowing away to the south.

Inside it was cool. In the kitchen, on our right, behind a closed door (was this the original bar?) lunch was already being prepared silently, swiftly, and in a self-sufficient way by French pupils, and instead of offering help, which we had meant to do, we backed quickly away.

On the right, in the dining room, seating was being discussed. The shutters were half-open showing faded green walls of pre-war distemper, a pleasant shade, above spartan scrubbed boards. Here, to one side, not far from a small fire, sat Gurdjieff with his legs on another chair, having arrived while we were immersed in the landscape. In this unaccustomed pose, still clad in his overcoat with the astrakhan collar, and obviously needing rest, he looked incredibly frail, much smaller than usual, and completely unconnected with what was going on.

Remembering so clearly our recent conversation, and the new strange sadness which, combined with acceptance, blotted out all lesser emotions, it was as if suddenly I saw myself reflected in a mirror and recognised that if now I could be granted the very talk I had been promised, nothing whatsoever would really be altered. At this I was pulled up short, and many contradictory thoughts contributed to a sudden paralysis.

Should I retreat? Should I help with the tables? I stood there for what seemed an interminable moment before turning away to join in the discussion. And as I looked back at him felt that for the present moment anyway, we were all equally excluded. But there was an immense tug in the feelings to see him laid so low, and the rising of an absolutely unaccustomed tenderness that threatened to swamp all my intelligence, until what seemed to be a chance flash of understanding suddenly highlighted the scene. Here was certainly no *abdication de la royauté*. Once again I had simply been caught out by appearances, and a second instinctive turning of the head in his direction discovered, in a light from the eyes, the multiplied beneficence that rarely shone so brightly and could be at its most obvious at a lucky moment of farewell, when after a particularly hard run of luck at the table, so very little had been either understood or retained. And the prospect of departure having softened the noisy mind, and for the time being wiped away all ambition, one sat on one's heels, at the door of the Salon, or even, somehow quite naturally, knelt by the low armchair where he always was to be found at the end of the day, and received a simple, gentle salutation, one global look, but enough to open the rusty flood gates and send one's inadequate craft swiftly back to the contradictions of life in an altogether new mixture of daring and hope.

When the table discussion evaporated and I began looking about me and wondering what to do, one of the French pupils who had come on the train from Paris rescued me and said I should take a chair which was more or less opposite the place where Gurdjieff would be sitting. But when the meal actually started and the first of the toasts was called I was more than a little *distraite* because the acoustics seemed to swallow the voice of the toastmaster, and instead of making the useless effort of listening to something that couldn't be heard, I tried to prepare for my own toast by calling to mind the various earliest visits before I knew the deep significance of the whole toasting ritual, and Gurdjieff's frequent use of the word 'honourable' in more than one connotation.

We made a very quick departure directly lunch was over, and as we were getting away before everyone else Madame de Salzmann came with us, so that she could get back early to take a Group before Movements. But what with excessive speed, engine noises and smoke we soon broke down completely. As it had been necessary to get three in the front of the car and I had been wreathed in an impossible way around the gear lever, I was thankful for the break, lying down without ceremony at the back of the grass verge in order to try and relax. Here I was apparently 'in the way' of other passengers who were walking nervously up and down, but I stuck it out and soon felt better, and when Madame stood over me, relaxed and laughing, I saw that I had at least provided some comic relief. It was some little time before we were on our way again in a new car, with Madame obviously destined to miss her Group altogether, and several of us uncomfortably aware that one of us should have remembered to warn her that our vehicle was not reliable. But this was rather a familiar situation to those of us who were *Bennettski* for, somehow or other, we frequently found ourselves responding to a kind of adaptability which plunged us into misadventure.

After all this the evening seemed to be blurred. But perhaps it was only blurred in contrast to the clarity of the earlier part of the day. Although I felt in myself a kind of insensibility from a deep tiredness which made further efforts impossible, I was awakened more or less by the mention of Lise being Doctor of Vibrations, ' Unique, the only one. But she not a musician', and this led almost inevitably to a mention of *Hadji Asvatz Troov*, shifting my fragile attention onto my inevitable ignorance of most of 'Beelzebub's Tales', so once again, trying to relate myself to the intricate subject of vibrations, I lost the whole thing. But I still recalled the talk about the mosaic path which was to be made at the new Château to depict the Enneagram, and received the same impression but with a new truth I hadn't tasted before - a kind of recognition that the gaps in my understanding were inevitable and even right, but I must learn not to get hung up on them.

Waking up, little by little, to this big subject and experiencing my own stupidity, I had time to wonder whether all of us were not justifiably tired, although I never felt that tiredness could ever be justified in that ambiance. Once, on my last visit, very late at night, I had yawned and Gurdjieff had roared at me, 'Never make such here!', then, leaning over, and looking more intently he had said:

'But I see, have not the habit. Afterwards, necessary rest, go horizontal, take precaution, restore', and this kindness that had followed so quickly on correction had brought in its train an unguessed-at legacy of wisdom when dealing with the planetary body.

This time, quite clearly, whether we were tired or not, it was perfectly clear that Gurdjieff was experiencing very great fatigue. For two days he had been on a very simple diet of dry rusks soaked in milk, cream and yoghurt, and with only one glass of alcohol. Often nowadays he ate practically nothing, for the food he so carefully prepared was all passed to others.

But still he joked, 'Why God make louse and tiger?'

* * *

In the next two weeks there was very little news from Paris, although I did hear that Gurdjieff's journey to America had now been postponed and at the very earliest could only take place during the first half of November. This meant that I should be able to fit in one more visit before his long winter absence. Usually I arranged the date of any visits in advance with Bennett, but this time I had not done so because he was very much occupied with the preparation of a series of lectures for new people 'Gurdjieff - The Making Of A New World' and there was no longer a pre-arranged time in his day when he could give attention to practical things which fell outside his present commitments. I was therefore completely unprepared when he told me that because of Gurdjieff's health all regular visits to the flat had been discontinued for the time being, although he had just been informed by Madame de Salzmann that he was still expected to go for the coming weekend.

We stared at each other - equally discomforted - and after a few questions from me I went lamely away. But hoping for the best and still uninformed, we were certainly not prepared for the telephone message from Coombe Springs which we received a week later - Mr Gurdjieff had just died in the American Hospital - and we and other pupils should go to Paris as soon as possible. Mr and Mrs Bennett had already left by air, and from today onwards there would be a Service at the hospital chapel every afternoon at 3.30.

Despite various practical hazards, and much to our surprise, we were able to get a flight to Le Bourget more or less immediately (our previous visits had all been by train and boat). So we hoped that we should be in time for the Service, though up to now we did not understand the implications. We arrived early enough to get one of the very few places inside the chapel. I had not formed any impressions in advance about our visit. Mr Gurdjieff was lying in state, clad in a brown tweed suit which was partly covered in some diaphanous material. And Madame de Salzmann had a place on the left near his head, and on the right immediately opposite her I took the seat which was vacant. And the great shock of seeing him without his warm and uplifting presence suddenly reduced me to tears which I was unable to stop, although my proximity to Madame de Salzmann gave me a kind of strength which gradually calmed me. We stayed more than an hour in the chapel but left when the Service was over so that other pupils who had arrived from England and America, and were waiting outside, could take part in the vigil.

When it became clear to us that the funeral could not take place before the third of November we had to make a difficult decision: we could both go once more to the vigil, George would then return to England and I would stay in Paris to attend the Requiem Mass at the Russian Cathedral before going to Avon for Gurdjieff's burial. At some point during the next two days after George had gone, Bennett asked me to help him look after one or two people who had come from Germany and America for the funeral, and I went out to lunch with them, and then in the evening joined the Bennetts and several other people for dinner.

On the day of the funeral those of us who had no cars were taken to the Russian Cathedral in several autobuses, and when we arrived there I followed the people in my bus - most of whom were Ouspensky's pupils - through the side entrance to the back of the building, and I suddenly found myself at the side of the coffin, which was heaped high with flowers, and close to Gurdjieff's family, his 'near people' and Madame de Salzmann. And this produced a most profound reaction - the vast congregation, the singing, the golden icons just a few feet away, and the candle I was holding in my hands all joined together to lift my state and award me with the gift of silence . . . . .

After the Mass was finished it took nearly an hour for everyone to pass the coffin and then we returned to our buses to wait for the afternoon journey to the cemetery at Avon, not far from the Prieuré at Fontainebleau. Walking in the *cortège* down the long path in the middle of the cemetery to the place where he was to be buried, little by little the silence left me, but in its place came a welcome memory of the invisible *cadeau*. In front of me and behind me were people I did not know, all equally affected by the piercing, icy wind, and when we reached the grave where his wife and mother were buried we stood in a circle to await the *enterrement*. Then a bowlful of earth was handed to us by a niece of Gurdjieff, and each one of us then took a handful and dropped it onto his coffin.

And when we got back to Paris in the evening I went to a meeting at Madame de Salzmann's flat, to hear her talk to the senior French Group and I was one of the very few English pupils who had been invited. She spoke about the future, stressing the fact that, 'When a teacher like Mr Gurdjieff goes, he cannot be replaced. Those who remain cannot create the same conditions. We have only one hope - to make something together - what no *one* of us could do, perhaps a Group can. We no longer have a teacher, but we have the possibility of a Group. Let us must make this our chief aim for the future.'

Funeral of George Ivanovich Gurdjieff, November 1949

And was it an accident that she looked fixedly in my direction? Although she was clearly addressing everyone in the room, she spoke very personally to me.

'You have all been given a task of special work. Work at it until you feel you have everything that can possibly be got from it. Then there are the Movements[24] - he left you the Movements, work on these as well.'

*　*　*

A few months later I was asked to write an Obituary for Mr Gurdjieff by an esoteric quarterly, and I ended this by asking a question 'Was he the genius who Albert Schweitzer sought in his 'Quest Of The Historical Jesus'?

"What the ultimate goal towards which we are moving will be, what this something is which shall bring new life and new regulative principles to coming centuries, we do not know. We can only dimly divine that it will be the great work of some mighty original genius, whose truth and rightness will be proved by the fact that we, working at our poor half thing, will oppose him might and main - we who imagine we long for nothing more eagerly than a genius powerful enough to open up with authority a new path for the world, seeing that we cannot succeed in moving it forward along the track which we have so laboriously prepared."

---

[24] See p.iv of Notebooks & Reviews

Chapter 23

THE BLACK DOG

For many years, my most poignant memory of Gurdjieff had nothing to do with his ideas, with the personal help he gave me, or the teaching that took place in his crowded dining room, twice daily during the last year of his life. This memory returned to me quite often. I would see him advancing slowly down Avenue Carnot, clad in a long black overcoat and black astrakhan cap, in his left hand a small bag of groceries and in his right hand a stick. At his heels was a black dog. He looked straight ahead, leaning back a little to compensate for the hill. The seriousness of his demeanour caught the attention, and his bag of groceries aroused speculation.

This simple picture never failed to evoke others directly connected with food and eating, and for me these were a strong source of calm and a statement of basic aims. Food was to be transformed, energy was to be transformed, and from the understanding of these two processes man's consciousness, function and will could also be transformed.

That this was not a simple proposition did nothing to mar the memory and the feelings that it evoked. Here was no mere bringing up to date of forgotten religious ideals, or the substitution of an active emotional stimulus for a passive automatic reaction. Very much more than this was being demanded, and this demand could bring a pause between the helter skelter of my life and the possibility of real responsibility.

One day, about fifteen years after the event, I was watching this unusually satisfying memory when something new burst out of me. Involuntarily, I spoke aloud, 'But the dog was dead, long dead, it certainly wasn't there in Avenue Carnot'. I was aghast. Knowing that there had once been a very devoted dog, had some quirk in my feelings helped the memory along? Surely, not this kind of memory about that particular person?

I ran through it again, willing myself to concentrate on the man and not to see a dog, but the dog came on, close at heel, quite oblivious of his death. From being aghast I became meditative. What had I actually seen on that cold winter's day so long ago?

I did not for one moment think in terms of a phantom. But why did it seem to matter so much, and what could be changed anyway if it had *simply* been a coincidence? Of course, it was a coincidence. A neighbour's dog, perhaps, investing in the past and interested in the string bag?

I paused, almost shivering, as the memory went cold. The dog, so alive, so much there, unquestionably real was certainly not invented. But it was also not the animal that had raised a ready response, producing benevolent feelings where they were out of place. I looked at him once more: black, four-footed, a perfectly ordinary animal without any influence at all, and suddenly relaxed, beginning to see the odd crucial mystery for what it was . . . . . I had quite simply not wanted to lose the comfort that the memory bestowed, and this recognition, deeper than thought, struck at my very roots.

It had been oddly easy, rather long ago, to begin to contradict my heterogeneous thoughts about myself, and to question my motives and even the happier images which life had laid down in me. Questioning the actual working of my memory at the very moment when I recalled the past was clearly a new thing.

In a world of constantly shifting inner relationships where my thinking out, and my thinking about, my speculations and my verbalised self-centred fears had been shown up as uncomfortably reliable, my memory, at first acquaintance a capricious friend, and by no means always there when wanted, had more often than not an actual reliability that was out of step with the rest of me.

While my so-called mind, the over-valued guardian of my daily life, was endlessly rearranging its conclusions, working overtime to appear well-informed or intelligent and beyond the usual reaches of ordinariness, my memory was plainly different; little by little, through the years of self-questioning and self-doubt, it had begun to emerge very simply in an almost placid and dependable role. It remembered or it did not remember. It did not insist. It did not embroider. It simply stood for itself and even went so far as to help me earn my living; if any reasoning or disapproval began to be connected with it, then I knew that it was not what I always referred to as *my* memory, something intrinsically mine, but a usurper.

What was I looking at now, while the black dog seemed so vividly present? Was it my thoughts or my feelings that had made this important to me? Plainly, I didn't know. I had been naïve in assuming that this innocent animal had travelled down the years completely unaffected by the lowest part of my mind. I could hazard a guess at what must have happened, but somewhere in me there must be a connecting link, which by now I really should have observed.

Gurdjieff's exact but paradoxical teaching on doubt had come across to me very painfully indeed when at one luncheon in his flat he had instructed us to doubt everything. To 'doubt' and not to accept 'ever'. And not even to accept what he taught when he taught. This was the difficult part.

I could hear once again the way he lingered on the word, with the diphthong long drawn out, making two syllables and endowing the sound almost with a life of its own, and when he had leaned forward a little, almost with violence, throwing this idea in my direction, I had cried out too hastily 'No, no!', nothing in me consenting even to look at the role of doubting. It was for me rather early days at his table, about my tenth visit in that last eventful year of his life, so that I was still trying to equate the daily teaching with the great volume of his ideas that had been laid down in me over the last seven years or so.

Knowing full well that some of these ideas had swept all before them, how could he extol the virtues of doubt? It seemed quite certain that the one thing he really wanted there and then was for his already cherished teaching to be set aside. For further reflection? And if so for how long? What was to be the basis for such a doubt?

At the table, where the brilliance of the present moment was like a furnace which annealed - more than it consumed - one could take away a piece of gold that would be difficult to fit in with the rest of one's experience, but I could not see sufficiently clearly the utility or even the possibility of questioning every new tool that might be handed to me.

Looking back at the great web of intertwined meanings, I could understand how my awkward strengths of perseverance and determination had got in the way, blinding me again and again. But now, suddenly, there was a moment of relief with quite a new taste, and I could look upon what appeared to be a valid direction, without any props or finely meshed explanations endowed by my ever ready and over-enthusiastic mind.

Up to now, my struggles with the mechanism of elementary thoughts had been aimed at deliberately rejecting the clearly unacceptable, and certain attractively simple techniques had bestowed on me the illusion that I was getting somewhere. Many times in the last decade, I had supposed that the freedom for which I had been striving was only just out of reach and would be there for the asking if only I could redouble my efforts. Now I had to ask myself a new question: How many more black dogs remained to be rooted out from the unrecognised certainties in my mind?

This question, though daunting, was liberating, for here was an entirely new way of looking at a very old problem, and one which had in fact originally eased my way into the difficult teaching of Gurdjieff, bringing me quickly to alien signposts which pointed to an entirely new sense of self, soon, and the promise of a different kind of consciousness, later.

EPILOGUE

For years I had been squeezed between the 'yes' and the 'no' in my mind, crying out for mercy as I sought for compromise attitudes that had no mirror in experience, but as a result of 'working' I suddenly recognised something new, just around the corner, half out of sight.

One of the most difficult things Gurdjieff had brought me to, which was ultimately more useful than anything else, was the necessary capacity to *doubt*. He had, as it were, placed his hand firmly in the middle of my back and pushed me from behind into the searchlight of a tremendous enquiry. I had looked for adequate answers to partial questions, and instead I found myself facing an abyss. I leaned over, I shouted, and a voice came back from the other side. It was not another voice that came back, it was my own.

Trying to reconcile the irreconcilable, to reject and compress the parts that would not fit into my idea of an ideal life, I nearly lost what life I had. But he had turned me around. Pulling the string of my awkward perseverance sharply, and to the limit, he had then walked away for ever, secure in the certainty that I would indeed never give up until I had inherited at least an echo of his truth, of his impeccable inner life, and a fragment - infinitely small - of his unquenchable courage and daring.

Dorothy Kathleen Phillpotts, aged 92, shortly
before her death on 24th April 2008

NOTEBOOKS & REVIEWS

(an appendix)

Notebooks:
    Origins
    Movements
    Behaviourism

Reviews:
    'The Enneads' by Plotinus, translated
        by Stephen MacKenna
    'Man & Time' by J.B. Priestley
    'Icons & The Mystical origins of
        Christianity' by Richard Temple

ORIGINS

As the years went by, I would speculate about the origin of the ideas I had received, and wonder and wonder again what lay behind the demand of 'know thyself' which had come from pre-Socratic systems and schools. What were the 'ancient systems and schools' hinted at? My knowledge of Greece stopped short of Plotinus – the heir of both Plato and Aristotle.

I had discovered that the name Babylon[25] meant 'Gate of the Gods' and, as I thought of this afresh, I experienced once more the strange impression I had received when suddenly, quite unexpectedly, I was faced with the Ishtar Gate. A natural interest in history had sparked off a long study of Herodotus while I was still at school, pointing me in the direction of Egypt. But it was a visit to Berlin, just as I entered adult life, immediately prior to the war, that had filled me with what seemed to be a real need to know more about Babylon. I had walked up and down beneath the reconstructed walls of Nebuchadnezzar's palace in the Pergamon Museum, trying my best to plumb the depths of the glazed brick animals of the Ishtar gate and unable to drag myself away. But in the end, I was left with more of a mystery than before and a sadness perpetually revived by passages about Nineveh in the Old Testament.

Although the famous hanging gardens of Babylon, ascribed to the legendary Queen Semiramis, were late by Assyrian standards (823 –

---

[25] Mentioned so frequently in *Beelzebub's Tales to his Grandson* and often referred to at Gurdjieff's table.

810 B.C.), Nebuchadnezzar, regarded as the great builder of Babylon, was even later (605 – 562 B.C.). Faced with the ancient world, my ignorance hit me – but, was history more important than philosophy and psychology?

* * *

Up until the fifties, the only written references that one could find even obliquely connected with what Ouspensky - writing openly about Gurdjieff's ideas - later referred to as an 'Unknown Teaching', were in his weighty 'New Model of the Universe'. The book was full of excitement, but in parts it was also disturbing, and with its excessive reportage and extreme dogmatism it too often seemed to contradict the reason for its existence. At the beginning, as Ouspensky unfolds the inadequacy of logical thinking and the need for a recognition that human thought could work on different levels, one feels an immediate sympathy and a desire to learn. But this is somewhat diminished by his claim that it is useless to read the book at all without some conception of the meaning of two ideas – 'esotericism' and 'the psychological method'. I had never liked the associations that the word 'esotericism' aroused in me, but Ouspensky's explanation – 'The idea of esotericism is chiefly the idea of higher mind' – though not strictly accurate, did give it a new slant, and the additional idea which I had already considered – that Gurdjieff's teaching was in fact 'esoteric Christianity' – put an entirely different complexion on the whole subject.

Why had I always found esotericism such an objectionable word? It was something to do with being deflected instead of attracted by the possibility of secret practices only open to initiates, and somewhere in my mind it was also connected with the wilder ideas of magic and the Theosophical Society.

But learning from Ouspensky in this book meant far more than being introduced in a roundabout way to the 'psychological method'. The book, dipped into, rejected and returned to again and again, little by little did me a strange service; for, in mirroring my own dilemma about the end point of all logical thinking, it slowly displayed modes of reflection and types of argument that I hadn't even suspected belonged to me, as well as to Ouspensky and every other serious writer who had ever pinned his faith on the desirability of logical exposition. We were all in it together. Sometimes quite by accident - and not so very frequently in those early days - my own longstanding fondness for sweeping statements, and my discomfort at the feeling of helplessness that these evoked, would suddenly come into view until some absolutely unseen element stopped the flow. This would be exactly similar to my experiments with self-remembering. I would be stopped in my tracks completely, not knowing where to look or how to proceed. What stopped me I still couldn't even begin to see, but now and again it seemed that I had unwillingly arrived at a genuine question, something of my own, and the rhetoric, all borrowed, embarrassed a tiny, almost invisible movement in the direction of truth. Had I been a little more observant in my search for self knowledge, I might have seen that these experiences stemmed from a common root – I suddenly went silent and I could not have picked up the argument again had my life depended on it.

It was perhaps fortunate that I didn't want to talk about this to anyone, for the experience, reasonably often repeated, had a boomerang quality with a long term beneficial effect which might have been interfered with.

This sort of discovery about myself, gave substance to the idea that the 'psychological method' referred to by Ouspensky must inevitably present paradoxes across the whole spectrum of life. I was not comforted by this conclusion, and although I rather badly wanted to study more and more 'psychological' ideas, I did not wish to become too familiar with his 'New Model . . .'. For me there was something very competitive and even dangerous in being too well informed about the highly speculative streams of knowledge which Ouspensky had gathered together. And it was as if my essential dilemma had even found a new channel in which to operate, a new way of deceiving *me*

. . . . .

MOVEMENTS, SACRED DANCES &
RITUAL EXERCISES
of G. I. GURDJIEFF

The movements, sacred dances and ritual exercises of Gurdjieff have seldom been presented to the public, but they were performed in London at the Fortune Theatre, Drury Lane on two days in the middle of May 1952. Previous public performances were given more than twenty seven years earlier, at the Champs-Elysées Theatre in Paris in 1923 and at the Carnegie Hall in New York in 1924. A very useful Introduction to a practical study of the Movements may be found in the official programme of the performances which took place in the Fortune Theatre:

"They are in no sense a spectacle, in the ordinary sense of the word. The genuine 'choreographic' quality of the performance, although of unusual interest, is not an end in itself. There is something in them that must be understood and a deeper meaning that must be discovered.

"This meaning, which one suspects but cannot immediately grasp, can be approached only in relation to the teaching to which they belong, a teaching based on a definite method for the inner change of man by means of the parallel development of all his faculties. Thus the Movements of Gurdjieff express, in their own language, the knowledge which is the very heart of his teaching. Each gesture, each position, is like a word of this language, and for every gesture and posture there is a definite inner attitude to which it corresponds.

"In Gurdjieff's teaching, such Movements are used as one of the ways of educating the student's inner force and of developing their attention, their capacity for thought and feeling, and so on. These Movements, which have been combined together in a special way requiring profound knowledge, enable the student to attain a fuller expression of these capacities.

"Such ritual exercises, as well as sacred dances, have always been one of the vital subjects taught in esoteric schools of ancient times. These dances had a twofold aim: they served for acquiring a harmonious state of being and at the same time they expressed a certain form of knowledge.

"The Dance had then a significance quite other than that which we of today are accustomed to give it. The ancient dance was a branch of art, and art in those early times served the purposes of higher knowledge and of religion. In those days, those who devoted themselves to the study of any special subject expressed their wisdom in works of art, and particularly in dances, just as we, today, give out our knowledge through books. Thus the ancient sacred dance is not only a medium for an aesthetic experience but also, as it were, a book containing knowledge. Yet it is a book which not everyone may read who wants - which not everyone can read who wishes.

"Some of the exercises being performed are derived from the art of the ancient East expressed in ritual gymnastics, sacred dances and religious ceremonies still preserved in temples of Turkestan, Tibet, Afghanisitan, Kafiristan and Chitral.

"During many years of investigation in these Eastern countries, Mr Gurdjieff became convinced that such dances have not lost the deep significance - religious, mystic and scientific - which belonged to them in far off ages, and he devoted much of the last twenty five years of his life to revealing their principles and laws through a series of new Movement-Exercises."

*   *   *

After Gurdjieff died, at the end of October 1949, one of the most immediate concerns of Madame de Salzmann lay in the realm of the Movements.

During the previous summer, accompanied by three young Movements teachers from Paris, Madame travelled to England - she had already paid two visits to Colet Gardens where Ouspensky had once held his meetings - and by the early autumn there were two Movements Classes held each evening in the studio, one afternoon class, and regular readings which were sometimes accompanied by Gurdjieff's music.

Although I could not join my husband at the classes held in the evenings, because of family obligations, I was glad to be able to go in the afternoons and not miss the opportunity of learning more of the Movements known as the 'Thirty Nine', which had been devised by Gurdjieff at the very end of his life. When the performance at the Fortune Theatre was planned[26], Madame de Salzmann brought together pupils chosen from England, France and America, and my husband was one of the people chosen from the class at Colet Gardens . . . . .

---

[26] The majority of the English pupils in this performance subsequently went to Paris to appear with the French in the first of Madame de Salzmann's films - the DANSES SACRÉES.

BEHAVIOURISM

In his hard-hitting book 'The Ghost In The Machine', written in 1967 and dedicated to the Fellows and staff at the Centre of Advanced Study in the Behaviourial Sciences, Arthur Koestler goes one step further than Dr Kenneth Walker.

By the time he died in 1983, at the age of 78, Koestler was widely recognized as a rebel. Born in Budapest in 1905 and educated at Vienna University, he worked as a foreign correspondent in the Middle East, Berlin and Paris. Joining the Communist Party in 1932 he travelled to the USSR and was subsequently imprisoned by General Franco. But in 1938 he left the Party, and arriving in England in 1940 wrote a string of popular books about revolution and politics, including "Darkness At Noon" - 1940, "Arrival And Departure" - 1943, and "Thieves In The Night" - 1946. His first book to be written in English was "Scum Of The Earth" - 1941.

As might be expected, Koestler was forthright in condemning Watsonian Behaviourism, which had become the dominant school, first in American academic psychology and subsequently in Europe, and having done away with the concept of the mind had put in its place the conditioned reflex chain. Naturally enough the consequences were disastrous, not only for experimental psychology but also in clinical psychiatry, social science, philosophy, ethics and the graduate student's outlook on life. And Watson had now become one of the most influential figures of the twentieth century.

Classing himself as a cynical onlooker Koestler now asked what was left for psychologists to study - the short answer is rats - and odd as it may sound, this was in fact an unavoidable consequence of the Behaviourists' definition of the scientific method.

Professor Skinner of Harvard University had proclaimed the same views in even more extreme forms . . . . . For Watsonian Behaviourism was unfortunately not a historical curiosity, but the foundations on which more sophisticated and influential neo-Behaviourist systems were being built, as rats and pigeons could, under appropriately designed experimental conditions, be made to behave as if they were conditioned reflex automata.

And Koestler's observations also assumed importance where the problem of free will is involved, declaring that once a scientist loses a sense of mystery he can be an excellent technician, but he ceases to be a *savant*.

Louis Pasteur has summed this up:

"I see everywhere in the world the inevitable expression of the concept of Infinity. The idea of God is nothing more than one form of the idea of Infinity . . . . . The Greeks understood the mysterious power of the hidden side of things. They bequeathed to us one of the most beautiful words in our language — the word enthusiasm - *entheos* — 'the God within'. The grandeur of human actions is measured by the inspiration from which they spring. Happy is he who bears a God within and who obeys it. The ideals of art, of science, are lighted by reflection from the Infinite."

But all is not lost. Some twenty years after Koestler's study - in July 1979 - the British Psychological Society hosted a five-day conference in Cardiff in the form of an extended symposium on the 'Models of Man'. This was addressed by no fewer than twenty principal speakers and the number of participants was limited to one hundred. One does not need to be a specialist to learn a great deal from the four hundred page volume that was published, and the twenty page bibliography presents us with over a dozen titles from an old friend like H. J. Eynsenck (who died a few years ago). And perhaps Koestler would have been soothed a little by some of the speakers.

In his long introduction to an analysis on Behaviourism, subtitled "Images Of Man In Contemporary Behaviourism", D. E. Blackman of University College, Cardiff tries to meet criticisms of current behavioural thought, and the accusation that it cannot handle the complexities of normal human behaviour in any but the most forced and impoverished way. And a speech by Professor G. Thines, of the *Centre de Psychologie Expérimentale et Comparée* at Louvain, made the point that the day has passed when one is either a Behaviourist or not, saying it is only very recently - remember that he was actually speaking in 1979 - that the important points of Behaviourism were being recognised: "There have, until now, been misunderstandings concerning conflicts between ethnological and behaviouristic approaches. But in fact, there is no true radicalism on either side . . . . . ."

REVIEW:

THE PHILOSOPHY OF PLOTINUS
'THE ENNEADS'
translated by Stephen MacKenna

Stephen MacKenna was a translator of great distinction and originality. Born in 1871, one of a large family brought up in very straitened circumstances, by the age of thirty five he had made a name for himself as a special correspondent of the 'New York World' as well as being their European representative and head of the Paris office. Prior to that time he had already published an English version of the 'Imitatio Christi' and had also begun a translation of Marcus Aurelius which was actually never finished, but in 1905 while working in Russia he was able to buy Creuzer's Oxford text of Plotinus in St Petersburg, and in Moscow he also obtained the Didot edition.

Soon after that he resigned his lucrative Paris appointment and settled again in Dublin, having confided to his private journal in 1906 that to translate and interpret Plotinus was 'really worth a life' - for he deeply believed that the translating of a great work of literature or philosophy was a sacred responsibility.

Professor E.R.Dodds, writing the foreword to MacKenna's second edition of 'The Enneads' claimed that this work must have ranked as one of the very few great translations produced in our time. In fact MacKenna soon discovered that he could not effectively serve two masters - Plotinus and daily journalism - and 'from 1919 onwards the adventurous generosity of Sir Ernest Debenham had made it possible for him to choose Plotinus'

Nevertheless in the years that followed MacKenna struggled not only with increasing poverty, continuous ill health, and deep intellectual discouragement - when the final volume appeared in 1930 he was a worn out man - he had judged the undertaking worth a life, and the price had been paid.'

*   *   *

The first edition of MacKenna's translation of The Enneads was published in 1917 by the Medici Society, and the second in 1930. More than twenty years after that a new revised edition was published in 1951 by Faber & Faber, and it was this volume that I was at last able to procure. After a long preface and introduction to this second edition, the body of the work starts off with a commentary by Porphyry - the chief pupil of Plotinus - written in the third century, and it then begins with the First Tractate 'The Animate and the Man'.

"Pleasure and distress, fear and courage, desire and affection, where have these affections their seat? Clearly, either in the Soul alone or in the Soul as employing the body."

Reading this I paused. In the original question-and-answer meetings I had gained the impression that all questions about the soul were obscure, and from one point of view we had no soul at present. I reflected a little and read on.

"And what applies to the affections also applies to whatever acts, physical or mental, sprang from them.

"We have, therefore, to examine discursive-reason and the ordinary mental action upon objects of sense, and inquire whether these have the one seat with the affections and experiences, or perhaps sometimes the one seat, sometimes the other.

"And we must consider also our acts of Intellection, their mode and their seat.

"And this very examining principle, which investigates and decides these matters, must be brought to life.

"Firstly, what is the seat of Sense-Perception? This is the obvious beginning . . . "

And here I was pulled up completely by a further reference to the Soul. Now I must try to lay aside everything I had ever heard or thought independently and really try to understand something new. And thinking over the most recent meetings I had attended I could in fact begin to understand that the work on which we were engaged aimed to by-pass a fundamental error which had arisen in Christian doctrine, probably from the end of the Third Century.

At that time Christianity had taken over the Greek idea of the dualism of spirit and matter, dividing man into the two opposing parts - a mortal physical body and an immortal spiritual soul. In the teaching that Mr Gurdjieff had initiated what was underlined were the real needs and possibilities of the physical body, not the negation of it. But I had not understood all the references.

It was not at all difficult to see that the physical body of ordinary man needed a kind of all-round development that everyday life did not provide. But the unfortunate duality in Greek teachings had sullied the clear prerogative of a religion originally based on man's purest feelings about himself.

But nevertheless, these pure feelings did sometimes activate a half-buried truth which was struggling to free itself from unnatural limitations, although I was clearly not yet in a position to draw any conclusions at all about the seat of my own sense perceptions or the quality of my affections.

At one of the early lectures I had heard an extended explanation about a simple diagram which on first acquaintance I had taken at face value. Meant to help illustrate the claim that one could not discuss man at all profitably in simple literary or scientific terms, the essential basic differences between one man and another were depicted

254

in a diagram by an arrangement of small square boxes running horizontally and vertically. And to help us differentiate clearly between men of different levels, these boxes were numbered. Those running horizontally were labelled Man Numbers One, Two, Three and Four. And the vertical boxes travelling upwards from Man Number Four, if considered together, made a reverse L-shaped diagram illustrating Man Numbers Five, Six and Seven. Having already accepted the idea of my own inevitable mechanicalness and the possibility of acquiring self-knowledge only after a very long period of self-observation, I could see that it was clearly going to be an advantage later on to be able to question myself quite minutely, and sometimes attain a more sophisticated understanding of mankind as a whole.

Recalling our detailed work on the lower Centres, we saw that people we might call Man Number One lived by their instincts and sensations, and their knowledge was based on imitation, or was composed of what was learned, at least partially, by heart. Man Number Two, Emotional Man, was on exactly the same level as far as his 'being' was concerned, but his knowledge, however much hidden, was always connected with something that affected him emotionally - with what he 'liked'. And although Man Number Three was someone whose thinking centre predominated, in fact he was on exactly the same level as the other two, with his rationality limited to subjective logical theorizing and his need to solve everything by labelling.

Now I was already getting the feeling that I, and all the people I was ever likely to meet, were described very precisely by the horizontal boxes in the diagram. But at the end of the horizontal boxes, before they became vertical, Man Number Four represented someone who had not been born 'ready made'. Starting out as Number One, Two or Three, he could only become Four if he made efforts of a very definite character. He could not develop accidentally as a result of ordinary influences of bringing-up or of education. He had a permanent centre of gravity which consisted in his valuation of the work of a school. And if he was able to work in a School for many years he would then become Man Number Five - the man who has reached Unity - and his knowledge would be indivisible, and much nearer to objective knowledge than the knowledge of Man Number Four. And whereas the knowledge of Man Number Six is the most complete knowledge which is possible for Man, the knowledge of Man Number Seven is eternal, and can never be lost.

So having reaffirmed the necessity to think of man in seven categories I was now much better prepared to follow the MacKenna dialectic, "What art is there, what discipline to bring us there where we must go?" Being postulated "that assuredly Sense-Perception, Discursive Reasoning and all our ordinary mentation are foreign to the Soul: for Sensation is a receiving - whether of an Ideal Form or of a bodily affection - and reasoning and all ordinary mental action deal with sensation" . . . . .

REVIEW:

'MAN & TIME'
by J.B.Priestley

I was to meet St Augustine again in an unusual quarter - J.B.Priestley's personal essay on 'Man & Time', a full length, lifelong study published in 1964. Here he explains that "Any full examination of the nature of Time must be deeply subjective, belonging to one man's inner world of thoughts, feelings, intuitive ideas . . . . . . and vague impressions".

In his chapter on 'Time, History & Eternity' Priestley points out that when Augustine comes to consider Time itself he asked a question and followed it by an answer that is famous, 'What then is Time? If no-one asks me, I know; if I want to explain it to someone, I do not know'. He then explains that Augustine's conclusions were the result of a series of brilliant compromises, "Augustine rejected Aristotle's bracketing of Time and Motion . . . . . Time was to be found in the soul and the mind." He then discusses measuring a given period of silence against a given period of sound, but this "involves a constant passage from the future to the past . . . . . . the past increases in proportion as the future diminishes, until the future is entirely absorbed and the whole becomes past".

The mind, however, has three functions "expectation - for the future - attention - for the present - memory - for the past".

And Priestley stresses that there is an important difference between Augustine's view and that of the first six persons we could stop in the street.   Having gone inward to discover Time, he believed that by going further inward still he would discover the true Eternity "the timeless realm of God".

And Augustine then discusses the "Eternal Light" and "Eternal Wisdom which abide over all, and seems to return to Jesus of Nazareth". . . . .   But Priestley now concludes that the mischief has been done, "By exchanging myth and symbol for history and fact, by making Time real in terms of expectation, attention and memory", Christianity had condemned itself to being an outward rather that an inward religion. "It had to work on the wrong level. History began to contain it - Time changed it - it sealed off springs of awe and wonder and joy across the desert of history".

Long after Augustine had died - in our age - we are told that Christianity has not failed, it has simply not been tried. But it must be held partly, if not chiefly, responsible for a climate in which it cannot be tried.

Priestley's outstanding contribution to the study of Time contains not only a full length study of J.W.Dunne and 'Serialism', but also a ten page section on what he has called 'Esoteric School', a long complimentary essay on the teaching of Gurdjieff (with whom he was never connected); a disquisition on Ouspensky and Eternal Recurrence, and a substantive review of both 'The Crisis In Human Affairs' and 'The Dramatic Universe' by J.G.Bennett.

His bird's eye view is particularly interesting. He starts off philosophically describing how the elaborate system of thought, behaviour and psychological development, taught by Gurdjieff and Ouspensky, was often called by them *the Work*. Priestley was clearly intrigued about the fact that although since the early nineteen twenties groups dedicated to studying the Work came into existence in Paris and London, in other European capitals - and in New York and Mexico City and various places in South America. He had on his bookshelves at least twenty full length studies, but there was nothing parallel to the

Work in the public domain. And although the only groups he knew about were in England, if their numbers were not very impressive, their quality was, and this was certainly not a movement supported by rich foolish women, for the benefit of charlatanism . . . . . Perhaps some rather dim people did drift in and out of the groups occasionally, but here Priestley gives the names of two of Gurdjieff's most famous pupils, now dead - A.R.Orage, once considered to be one of the most brilliant editors in England, and Dr Maurice Nicoll, a pupil of Jung and then a distinguished Harley Street specialist - who were anything but dim, and in order to study this movement, nobody would have to do any intellectual slumming.

And I much appreciate his point about a sense of fairness - he was never a member of any one of these groups himself, had not set eyes on Gurdjieff or Ouspensky and had only a limited acquaintance with their chief successors in the Work. He also particularly approved of the fact that the Work was far removed from the soft and sentimental doctrines of Higher Thought, Theosophy and so on, being hard, very demanding, and grimly unsentimental in its insistence that man must make unwearied efforts to free himself from a waking sleep and become fully conscious, building up a central commanding 'I' in place of a score of contradictory 'I's', and believing that in the end, through unremitting effort, he can create in himself an indestructible soul. (readers interested in esoteric Christianity should look at Dr Nicoll's books 'The New Man' and 'The Mark' - in which he re-interprets the Gospels).

Priestley then brings us to Ouspensky who had a special way of looking at psychology. Explaining how he had met Gurdjieff in Moscow in 1915 when Gurdjieff had gone to there to teach, "was soon under the spell of that powerful and enigmatic personality", accepting the authority of Gurdjieff's teaching without question, and becoming its leading exponent. But eventually he made a distinction between Gurdjieff the man and Gurdjieff the teacher, and by the time the famous Institute at Fontainbleau was opened in 1922, "having already separated from Gurdjieff , he was working in London with his own groups . . . . .".

After this forthright introduction Priestley is then at pains to give us the extraordinarily full background which can be discovered in 'Tertium Organum', published in 1922 - Ouspensky's first published book to be translated into English - and though this has been frequently reprinted he thinks it is much inferior to Ouspensky's second book, 'A New Model of the Universe', where in his prefatory note the claim is made that this book was begun and practically completed before 1914. But the chapters are dated, and what is the all-important chapter - 'Eternal Recurrence' - is dated 1912-1929, and by 1929 Ouspensky had not only accepted Gurdjieff's system, now being indeed its chief exponent, but had more or less broken with his old master. So whether this is pure Ouspensky, brought up-to-date from 1912, or Ouspensky fortified by the brandy of Gurdjieff, Priestley does not know. What he does know is that no examination of the Time problem can afford to let this chapter on 'Eternal Recurrence' go unnoticed.

Like Dr Nicoll, J.G.Bennett was one of the earliest students of Gurdjieff's system, and later, taught it to his own groups. But whereas Nicoll had a medical and psychological training, Mr Bennett was a mathematician and had been a director of industrial research. With two mathematical collaborators, he had produced a Royal Society paper on 'Unified Field Theory in a curvature-free five-dimensional manifold', Priestley tells that he possesses this but can only stare at as if he were an Eskimo. Not long after the war Bennett published two books for the general reader - 'The Crisis in Human Affairs' (a book which I both transcribed and edited in 1947) and 'What Are We Living For?' (which I actually sub-edited in Paris in 1949 in the last year of Gurdjieff's life).

After these two books Bennett also published the first two volumes of 'The Dramatic Universe', in an attempt to bring 'all scientific knowledge within the scope of one comprehensive theory of existence'. These books are close, hard reading, which Priestley undertook in search of Bennett's conclusion about Time. Bennett's contribution to

'Systematics' on Time are then abstracted. In replying to the question 'What is Time?', Bennett begins:

"There is no simple answer. Our experience of temporality is complex and it varies from one situation to another. The variations are so important that we should not speak of time in the singular, but distinguish different times and different kinds of time."

And he explains at some length that time is three-dimensional and how six-dimensional geometry describes both the movements of bodies and also the properties of matter. This raises the question whether the three kinds of Time apply to other situations such as those of function, consciousness and human free-will. In answer to this we must see what the three kinds of Time mean in terms of experience. And he follows this by enlarging on the three names he has adopted for the different kinds of Time.

"Firstly, *TIME*. We experience events as successive. This gives rise to the sense of 'before and after'.

"Secondly, *ETERNITY*. We are aware of persistence. Without persistence there could be no change. Pure potential is eternal and imperishable.

"And thirdly, *HYPARXIS*. A third degree of freedom is needed to pass from one line of time to another."

Bennett's last word certainly gives us food for thought - the three kinds of time are strictly quantitative - we can travel in eternity in our consciousness. We can move in hyparxis by an act of will.

And Priestley thinks that Bennett would not have reached these valuable conclusions if he had not been so long acquainted with the Work. Yet he was not merely giving us Ouspensky with a different terminology - he made full use on the way to these conclusions of his own knowledge and expertise, and summing this up for the last time Priestley asks a question,

"What did the old Master of the Work, Gurdjieff, say about Time when it was not masquerading as the Merciless Heropass?".

He referred to Time as the 'unique subjective'. And then Priestley concludes that our experience on any level seems to be conditioned by something we have to bring to it ourselves, something not in us, and that something always begins to look like Time -

"So perhaps Gurdjieff was right . . . . .".

REVIEW:

'ICONS & THE MYSTICAL ORIGINS OF CHRISTIANITY'
by Richard Temple

In reviewing the second edition of this book, originally published in 1990, it is stimulating to find a colour reproduction of the 15ᵗʰ Century 'Christ Pantocrator' on the cover. Both editions of the book carry black and white versions and a careful examination of the Pantocrator icon deepens our appreciation of Temple's approach, while his step by step explanations on many esoteric questions bring us to a quite new understanding. It is a great pity that we are obliged to cut short his descriptions of the Iconostatis, but of course it is inevitable . . . . .

"The iconostasis is the screen that separates the nave from the sanctuary in Orthodox churches. On it are tiers of icons that present, in visual form, all the theology of the Church; the sacred history and personages of the past existing eternally in the present. The total impression of the icons gives the spectator a sense of himself as though standing before the whole cosmos whose laws and energies are personified by the saints, personages and events of the Old and New Testaments and of the Church.

"The development of the iconostasis is a Russian phenomenon of the fifteenth century which, in earlier periods, had consisted of only one or two rows of icons. Full-size icon screens in Greece did not appear until the sixteenth century when the form was imported from Russia. In its full height it consists of five tiers of icons ranging from floor to ceiling; each tier stretching across the entire width of the church.

"The upper row shows images of Old Testament patriarchs and prophets; all of them face in towards the icon of the Mother of God with Christ Emmanuel at her breast, the 'Virgin of the Sign' and the result of the prophecies of the Old Testament. The Prophets row was not added to the iconostasis until the fifteenth century and was thus the last to come into existence. The figures of the prophets are otherwise rarely found outside the pages of illuminated manuscripts. In psalters and lectionaries they were presented in the full-face tradition of portrait images and did not need to be shown looking sideways as they did after the fourteenth century when they appeared on the iconostasis. The figures in the upper rows of the icon screen, therefore, belong to the portrait type of icon except that the axis of the body and the direction of the gaze have been turned so that the icon's place in the row, and the subject's relation to the central image of the Mother of God, are taken into account.

"The next group of icons constitutes what on the iconostasis is called the Festival row. The Feasts or 'holy days' illustrate a series of events - mostly taken from the life of Christ and the life of the Mother of God - that fall periodically within the liturgical calendar. Apart from twelve major feasts there are numerous minor feasts, several of which find their place on the iconostasis. The number of screens is partly dictated by the width of the screen and the number of spaces available. Beyond that, the choice of the subjects, which seem arbitrary at first glance, contains hidden meanings, both in the variety of subject matter and in the order in which the images are placed on the screen.

"The sequence of the festival scenes begins with events from the life of the Mother of God and it ends with the Dormition. This has a certain historical correctness since the birth and death of the Virgin precede and succeed the birth and death of Christ. But another idea emerges here when we see that the earthly life of Christ is contained in, or takes place within, the life of the Virgin.

"The form and content of the icons in which 'events' in the Virgin's life are depicted are such that their higher meaning will elude us if we take them only on the literal or historical level. We shall see that the deepest meaning of the icons of the *Theotokos* (Bringer of God) transcends the physical aspects of her being and is purely spiritual. At the same time we need to understand that transcendence is a process, a passage or journey towards spirit that begins at the lower level of matter. According to tradition, the Mother of God is associated with the earth and matter. It is at this level, in the ground of humanity, that the life of the spirit is planted as a seed, takes root and grows upwards.

And in completing our study of the Mother of God we are helped by Temple's explanation about the Annunciation.

"The iconography of the Annunciation returns us to the language of symbolic imagery where the Archangel, who as we know from Dionysius the Areopagite is a cosmic power one degree higher than angels, appears at a stage in the Virgin's inner life where she can receive the message that God himself will appear at the earthly level through her. The Virgin thus fulfils her role for which her humanity is intended; she has perfected herself to the degree where she has become the channel for the descent of divine energy."

"Below the festivals tier is the group of icons constituting the Deesis row. These icons, whose monumentality and power are visually so striking to visitors to old Russian churches, were not found on icon screens before the end of the fourteenth century and are part of the revival of that period. Hitherto figures on the Deesis icons were represented head and shoulders only. The word Deesis means prayer, and in the central group, which shows us the composition in its original form, we see the Virgin and St John the Baptist meditating on behalf of humanity at the throne of Christ. In its extended form, as we see here, archangels, apostles, saints and hierarchs of the Church are included.

"The central image is that of Christ Pantocrator, we see him majestically seated on a throne surrounded by apocalyptic animals, cherubim and seraphim and various geometric forms constituting a mandorla or aureole of glory.

"Beneath the Deesis row are the Royal doors, so called because the King of Glory, in the form of the sacraments, passes through them. On the doors are the four Evangelists surmounted by the Annunciation. The doors are the gateway into the divine world, symbolised by the sanctuary before which the iconostasis is situated. And it is an energy of the divine world, personified as Man, that the archangel announces to Mary and which the Evangelists announce to humanity.

"On either side of the Royal Doors are icons commemorating the saint or festival to which the church is dedicated and other subjects associated with local tradition.

"The fully developed iconostasis unites, in a visual form comprehensible to all levels, the divine world and the human. It places us on the threshold of the mysteries within ourselves. It is a visual recitation of all reality and, like the *legomena* and *deiknymena* of the ancient Mysteries, is capable of initiating us into the way of universal truth."

BIBLIOGRAPHY

GEORGE IVANOVITCH GURDJIEFF
Beelzebub's Tales to His Grandson, Routledge and Kegan Paul, 1950
Meetings With Remarkable Men, Routledge and Kegan Paul, 1963
Life is Real Only Then, When 'I Am', Triangle
    Editions, New York, 1975
Views From The Real World, Routledge and Kegan Paul, 1973

P. D. OUSPENSKY
A New Model of the Universe, Kegan, Paul, Trench, Trogner, 1933
In Search of the Miraculous: Fragments of an Unknown
    Teaching, Routledge and Kegan Paul, 1950
Tertium Organum, Routledge and Kegan Paul, 1949
The Fourth Way, Routledge and Kegan Paul, 1957

RELIGION AND PHILOSOPHY
The Bible of the World, Kegan Paul, Trench, Trobner, 1940
The Missal compiled from *The Missal Romanum*,
    Regina Press, New York, 1951
The Book of Common Prayer
St Augustine, *Confessions*, Everyman/Dent, London, 1917
Wills, Garry, *St Augustine*, Penguin, 1999
A Manual of Eastern Orthodox Prayers, S.P.C.K., 1945
The Philokalia, compiled by St Nikodimos
    and St Makarious (4th century –
15th century), Faber and Faber, 1984

Brill, E.J., *The Nag Hammadi Library in English*, 1977

Temple, Richard

Icons and the Mystical Origins of Christianity, Luzac
    Oriental Limited, 1990, 2nd edition; Element

Early Christian and Byzantine Art, Element, 1990

Icons: A Sacred Art, Element, 1989

de Beausobre, Julia, *Russian Letters of Direction Starets*
    Macarius (1834 – 1860), Dacre Press, 1944

Browne, Sir Thomas, *Religio Medici*, Macmillan and Co., 1892

Caulfield, S.F.A., *The Voice of the Fathers*,
    S.C.Brown, Langham and Co., 1905

Teilhard de Chardin, Pierre

Hymn of the Universe, Collins, 1965

Le Milieu Divin, Collins, 1967

James, William

Selected Papers on Philosophy, J.M.Dent and Son Ltd., 1917

The Varieties of Religious Experience, Longmans, Green and Co., 1903

Prestige, G.L., *Fathers and Heretics*, S.P.C.K., 1948

Neill, Stephen, *Anglicanism*, (for Cranmer,
    1525), Pelican Books, 1958

EGYPT

Schwaller de Lubicz, R.A.

The Temple in Man, Inner Traditions, Rochester, Vermont, USA, 1977

The Temple of Man (illustrated 9 x 12 inches), Inner Traditions,
    Rochester, Vermont,   USA, 1998

Symbol and the Symbolic, Inner Traditions,
    Rochester, Vermont, USA, 1981

BUDDHISM

Humphreys, Christmas, *Buddhism*, Penguin, 1951

Lati Rinpochay and Hopkins, Jeffrey, *Death,*
    Intermediate State and Rebirth, Rider, 1979

HINDUISM
Shri Purohit Swami, *The Geeta*, Faber and Faber, 1935
Swami Prabhavananda and Isherwood, Christopher,
    Bhagavad–Gita: The Song of God, Mentor, 1944
Reymond, Lizelle, *To Live Within*, George Allen and Unwin, 1972

ISLAM
Maulana Muhammad Ali, *The Holy Qur'an*, Pakistan, 1963
Mahmud Shabistari, *The Secret Garden*, Octagon, 1969
Jalalu'ddin Rumi, *The Mathnawi of Jalau'ddin Rumi*, (6
    volumes in 3 books), Cambridge, 1926, 1930, 1934
Jali, *The Way of Transformation*
Arberry, A.J., *Muslims, Saints and Mystics*,
    Routledge and Kegan Paul, 1966

JUDAISM
Crusemann, Frank, *The Torah*, T. and T. Clark, 1996

TAOISM
The Simple Way of Lao Tsze, Shrine of Wisdom, 1924
Waley, Arthur, *The Way And Its Power*, George Allen and Unwin, 1934

MYSTICS AND MYSTICISM
Buber, Martin, *I and Thou*, trans. Ronald
    Gregor Smith, T. and T. Clark,
Edinburgh, 1958
Bucke, Richard Maurice, *Cosmic Consciousness*,
    Dutton, New York, 1959
Inge, The Very Rev. W. R. (D.D.)
The Philosophy of Plotinus, Longman Green, 1941
Mysticism in Religion, Hutchinson's University Library, London
Hilton, Walter, *The Scale of Perfection*, (14th
    century), Watkins, London, 1948

Law, William, *A Serious Call to a Devout and Holy Life*, Everyman, 1728

Pascal, Blaise

Pensees, (1670), Collection de Flambeau, 1950

Reasons of the Heart, William B. Erdman, Grand Rapids, Cambridge, USA, 1997

Plotinus, *The Enneads*, (trans. Stephen MacKenna), Faber and Faber, 1917 – 1930

Unknown authors, *The Cloud of Unknowing*, (14th century), Burns Oats, 1943

Theologica Germanica, (from 1516), Macmillan, 1937

Underhill, Evelyn

Practical Mysticism, J.M.Dent and Sons, London, 1914

Mysticism, Methuen and Co., London, 1942

Von Hugel, Baron Friedrich, *Mystical Element of Religion (as studied in St Catherine of Genoa)*, J.M.Dent, 1923

Van Ruysbroeck, Blessed Jan, *Seven Steps of the Ladder of Spiritual Love*,

Dacre Press, 1941

TIME

Dunne, J.W., *An Experiment With Time*, Black, London,1927

Priestley, J.B., *Man and Time*, Aldus Books, 1964

ART

Clayton, Peter, *Great Figures of Mythology*, Magna Books, 1990

Dury, Carel J., *Art of the Ancient Near & Middle East*, Harry N. Abrams,

New York,1969

Roat, Michael, *Cultural Atlas of Mesopotamia & the Near East, Facts on File*, Equinox, New York, Oxford, 1990

BACKGROUND MATERIAL

Bennett, J.G.

The Crisis in Human Affairs, Hodder & Stoughton, 1948

What Are We Living For?, Hodder & Stoughton, 1948

The Dramatic Universe, (3 volumes) Hodder
    & Stoughton, 1951,1957,1966

A Spiritual Psychology, Hodder & Stoughton, 1964

Witness, Hodder & Stoughton, 1962

Gurdjieff, Making a New World, Turnstone, 1973

Chapman, Anthony, *Models of Man,* The British
    Psychological Society, 1981

Koestler, Arthur, *The Ghost In The Machine,* Pan Books, 1967

Walker, Kenneth

Diagnosis of Man, Jonathan Cape, London, 1942

The Circle of Life, Jonathan Cape, London, 1942

Venture With Ideas, Jonathan Cape, London, 1942

A Study of Gurdjieff's Teaching, Jonathan Cape, London, 1942

Made in the USA